THE OXFORD INTERNATIONAL RELATIONS IN SOUTH ASIA SERIES

SERIES EDITORS

Sumit Ganguly and E. Sridharan

After a long period of relative isolation during the Cold War years, contemporary South Asia has grown immensely in its significance in the global political and economic order. This ascendancy has two key dimensions. First, the emergence of India as a potential economic and political power that follows its acquisition of nuclear weapons and its fitful embrace of economic liberalization. Second, the persistent instability along India's borders continues to undermine any attempts at achieving political harmony in the region: fellow nuclear-armed state Pakistan is beset with chronic domestic political upheavals; Afghanistan is paralysed and trapped with internecine warfare and weak political institutions; Sri Lanka is confronted by an uncertain future with a disenchanted Tamil minority; Nepal is caught in a vortex of political and legal uncertainty as it forges a new constitution; and Bangladesh is overwhelmed by a tumultuous political climate.

India's rising position as an important player in global economic and political affairs warrants extra-regional and international attention. The rapidly evolving strategic role and importance of South Asia in the world demands focused analyses of foreign and security policies within and towards the region. The present series addresses these concerns. It consists of original, theoretically grounded, empirically rich, timely, and topical volumes oriented towards contemporary and future developments in one of the most populous and diverse corners of the world.

Sumit Ganguly is Professor of Political Science and Rabindranath Tagore Chair in Indian Cultures and Civilizations, Indiana University, Bloomington, USA.

E. Sridharan is Academic Director, University of Pennsylvania Institute for the Advanced Study of India, New Delhi.

THE OXFORD INTERNATIONAL RELATIONS IN SOUTH ASIA SERIES

Asymmetrical Threat Perceptions in India–China Relations

Tien-sze Fang

OXFORD
UNIVERSITY PRESS

Oxford University Press is a department of the University of Oxford. It furthers the University's objective of excellence in research, scholarship, and education by publishing worldwide. Oxford is a registered trademark of Oxford University Press in the UK and in certain other countries

Published in India by
Oxford University Press
YMCA Library Building, 1 Jai Singh Road, New Delhi 110 001, India

First Edition published in 2014

ISBN-13: 978-0-19-809595-8
ISBN-10: 0-19-809595-3

Typeset in Adobe Jenson Pro 10.5/13
by The Graphics Solution, New Delhi 110 092
Printed in India by Sapra Brothers, New Delhi 110 092

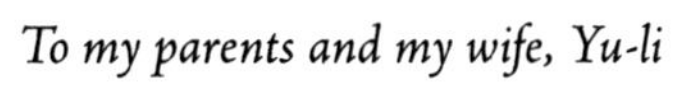

To my parents and my wife, Yu-li

Contents

Preface

The rise of China and India is undoubtedly a major feature of contemporary global politics. The interactions between the two rising Asian powers will not only exert a profound and far-reaching influence over Asian security, but is also seen as a decisive factor reshaping the international order. However, compared to their significance, Sino-Indian relations do not attract appropriate attention. People still lack due and comprehensive understandings of the complex and complicated relationship between the two neighbouring giants.

To shed light on these important issues, this book draws on evidence from interactions between China and India over the past few years to make an empirical case for the existence and impact of asymmetrical perceptions of threat between the two countries. The major issues of China–India relations, including the nuclear issue, the boundary problem, the Tibet issue, regional competition and cooperation, and China–India relations in the global context, are examined.

The first aim of the book is to provide a new perspective for understanding China–India relations by highlighting the asymmetry of the threat perceptions between China and India. The book observes the main interactions between the two countries: India tends to be deeply apprehensive of threats from China, while China appears comparatively unconcerned about threats from India.

The second contention in this book is that Sino-Indian relations are constrained by the asymmetry between their threat perceptions. The asymmetry in perceptions of threat will result in a dilemma for India. India will try to reduce the sense of insecurity by adopting some counter-measures, such as developing nuclear weapons. However, India is also very cautious and avoids angering China. On the contrary, China will be in favour of the *status quo*, and feels no urgent need to sort out the boundary disputes. The Chinese side has ignored the asymmetry and is in no mood to share India's expectations and concerns.

Thus, this book concludes that this asymmetry has made it difficult for China and India to forge a shared knowledge and to set a common agenda around which their expectations could converge. India will be on a perennial quest for changes in Sino-Indian relations, such as a final resolution of the border issue and securing a more credible nuclear deterrent against China. The asymmetry in threat perceptions has been a destabilizing factor in China–India relations.

Acknowledgements

This book is the result of a decade that I have devoted to research regarding the relationship between India and China.

Foremost, I would like to express my sincere gratitude to my supervisor, Professor Christopher Hughes at the London School of Economics and Political Science, for his significant and helpful guidance and support of my PhD study and research. Without his guidance and inspiration this book could not have been completed.

I worked in India for six years as a Taiwanese diplomat and had very good interactions with Indian academics. I would like to thank Professor Alka Acharya, Professor B.R. Deepak, Professor Sabree Mitra, and Professor Srikanth Kondapalli of Jawaharlal Nehru University (JNU), New Delhi, Dr Jagannath Panda of the Institute for Defence Studies and Analyses (IDSA) , Dr Jabin T. Jacob of the Institute of Chinese Studies, Dr Rajeswari Pillai Rajagopalan of the Observer Research Foundation (ORF), and Professor Madhu Bhalla of the University of Delhi, for numerous discussions on related topics that helped me improve my knowledge in the area. Needless to say, the author takes full responsibility for the views expressed in this publication and for any errors of omission or misinterpretation.

I extend gratitude also to Professor Lih. J. Chen, Professor Da Hsuan Feng, Professor Wei-Chung Wang, and Professor Hsiao-Chin Hsieh of National Tsing Hua University, for personal encouragement and academic insights. With their support, I have wholeheartedly enjoyed the challenges of academic life as a teacher-cum-researcher.

In addition, I extend sincere thanks to all the people who directly or indirectly helped me while I worked at the Taipei Cultural and Economic Center in Delhi (the *de facto* Taiwanese Embassy in India). I would also like to thank Ms Solvig Topping for proofreading my draft manuscript.

Last, but not the least, I convey my deepest gratitude to my family for their love and support. In particular, I am indebted to my late father, who shares my suffering and happiness in heaven. Without the support of my family members, this book would simply have been impossible.

Abbreviations

ARF	ASEAN Regional Forum
ASEAN	Association of South East Asian Nations
BIMSTEC	Bangladesh, India, Myanmar, Sri Lanka, Thailand Economic Cooperation
BJP	Bharatiya Janata Party
BRICS	Brazil, Russia, India, China, and South Africa
CBM	confidence-building measures
CECA	Comprehensive Economic Cooperation Agreement
CENTO	Central Treaty Organization
CEPA	Comprehensive Economic Partnership Agreement
CIA	Central Intelligence Agency
CICA	Conference on Interaction and Confidence-Building Measures in Asia
CTBT	Comprehensive Test Ban Treaty
DF	Dongfeng
FBIS	Foreign Broadcast Information Service
FDI	foreign direct investment
FMCT	Fissile Material Cutoff Treaty
FTA	Free Trade Agreement
IAEA	International Atomic Energy Agency
IAS	Indian Administrative Service
ICBM	intercontinental ballistic missile
ICT	Information and Communications Technology
IGMDP	Integrated Guided Missile Development Programme
IRBM	intermediate range ballistic missile
ITBP	Indo-Tibetan Border Police
JWG	Joint Working Group
LAC	Line of Actual Control
LOC	Line of Control

MGC	Mekong-Ganga Cooperation
MoU	Memorandum of Understanding
MRBM	medium range ballistic missile
MTCR	Missile Technology Control Regime
NATO	North Atlantic Treaty Organization
NDA	National Democratic Alliance
NPT	Treaty on the Non-Proliferation of Nuclear Weapons
NSG	Nuclear Suppliers Group
NSSP	Next Steps in Strategic Partnership
NWS	Nuclear-Weapon State
ODA	Official Development Assistance
PLA	People's Liberation Army
PMC	Post Ministerial Conference
PRC	People's Republic of China
PTI	Press Trust of India
SAARC	South Asian Association for Regional Cooperation
SCIO	State Council Information Office
SCO	Shanghai Cooperation Organization
SEATO	Southeast Asia Treaty Organization
SLBM	submarine-launched ballistic missile
SRBM	short-range ballistic missile
SSM	surface-to-surface missile
TAR	Tibet Autonomous Region
TMD	Theatre Missile Defence
WMD	weapons of mass destruction
WTO	World Trade Organization

Chinese Language Newspapers and Journals

Renmin Ribao	People's Daily
Pingguo Ribao	Apple Daily
Renmin Wan	People's Website
Huanqiu Shibao	Global Times
Zhongguo Dalu Yanjiu	Mainland China Studies
Nanya Yanjiu Jika	South Asian Studies Quarterly
Nanya Yanjiu	South Asian Studies
Wenti Yu Yanjiu	Issues and Studies
Xiandai Guoji Guanxi	Contemporary International Relations

Zhanglue Anquan Yanxi	Strategic and Security Analysis
Zhongguo Shibao	China Times
Zhanlue Yu Guanli	Strategy and Management
Ya Fei Zongheng	Asia and Africa Review
Dangdai Yatai	Contemporary Asia-Pacific Studies
Guangming Ribao	Guanming Daily
Guoji Xianqu Daobao	International Herald Leader
Guoji Guancha	International Review
Shujie Jingji Yu Zhengzhi	World Economics and Politics
Guoji Wenti Yanjiu	Journal of International Studies
Guoji Luntan	International Forum
Guoji Zhengzhi Yanjiu	Studies of International Politics
Nanyang Wenti Yanjiu	Southeast Asian Affairs

Introduction

Understanding the Instability of India–China Relations

ON 11 MAY 1998, the Government of India shocked the world by conducting three rounds of nuclear tests in the Pokhran desert in its northwestern Rajasthan state. The new National Democratic Alliance (NDA) government, led by the Bharatiya Janata Party (BJP), had been elected to office barely two months earlier. Two days after the nuclear tests, *The New York Times* published a letter from Indian Prime Minister A.B. Vajpayee to US President Bill Clinton. Aiming to explain the rationale of the nuclear tests, Vajpayee said,

> We have an overt nuclear weapon state on our borders, a state which committed armed aggression against India in 1962. Although our relations with that country have improved in the last decade or so, an atmosphere of distrust persists mainly due to the unresolved border problem. To add to the distrust that country has materially helped another neighbour of ours to become a covert nuclear weapons state. At the hands of this bitter neighbour we have suffered three aggressions in the last 50 years.[1]

Since the late 1980s, China and India have sought to reduce the tensions along the frontier and expanded trade and cultural exchanges. However, following Vajpayee's statement, China not only demanded that India should roll back its nuclear weapon programme, but also boycotted the decade-long bilateral dialogue for solving the border dispute.

The nuclear tests episode once again exposed the fragility of Sino-Indian relations. India was the first non-communist state to establish diplomatic relations with the People's Republic of China. The slogan *Hindi Chini bhai bhai* (Indians and Chinese are brothers) was trumpeted by Beijing and New Delhi in the mid-1950s. However, Sino-Indian relations soon deteriorated after 1959 when the Dalai Lama fled to India and the Sino-Indian border dispute surfaced, culminating in a brief but significant war along the disputed frontier. The border dispute remains unresolved, albeit diplomatic relations at ambassador level were restored in 1976.

The normalization of relations gained new momentum when Indian Prime Minister Rajiv Gandhi visited Beijing in 1988, the first visit by an Indian head of government since Jawaharlal Nehru's visit in 1954, and was reciprocated by Chinese Premier Zhou Enlai's visit to India in 1960. Since then, high-level exchange visits had increased and the cooperation in various fields had been expanded. Following the Pokhran II nuclear tests in 1998, Sino-Indian relations went into a deep chill again. Two sides then took strides towards reconciliation. However, their bilateral relations went into a 'tailspin' again (Jha 2010: viii).

Recurrent tensions seem to be a significant feature of Sino-Indian relations. Therefore, the central question that will guide this book is: Why are China and India not able to develop long-term stable and friendly relations?

Threat Perception in International Studies

Most studies about Sino-Indian relations emphasize the boundary dispute or the border war, but the conclusions of various writers are irreconcilable with those of others. Some blame China's ambition to expand its territory as the cause of the deterioration of China–India relations. Others blame India for misconduct or failure in foreign policymaking.

Moreover, most of these studies are based on historical accounts or are from the perspective of 'mainstream' international relations theory, namely neo-realism and neo-liberalism. The underlying premise is that, just like other states, China and India are driven to secure the support of other powers to maximize their interests in a condition of anarchy. Treating national interests as exogenously determined, the realists often ignore the possibility of cooperation between states, and fail to explain or predict the re-engagement between Beijing and New Delhi in the post-Cold War era. Many earlier studies assumed that any improvement of relations between the two sides would involve a settlement of the boundary problem (Lamb 1964: 2, Rao 1968: 2). Belying such arguments, China and India have agreed to expand contacts and cooperation in many fields with a high frequency of government-to-government exchanges and a significant increase in bilateral trade, even if there is still no foreseeable final solution to the border dispute.

In order to offer some fresh insight into this topic, this book will take account of the constructivist understanding of international relations in order to develop an alternative approach to that of the existing literature. Thus, the constraints to the development of Sino-Indian relations will be studied in terms of mutual perceptions and expectations, particularly the perception of threat. In addition, as Indian scholars pointed out, India needs to get a first-hand pulse of China for formulating its China policy instead of relying on western sources (Singh 2011: 38). Considering that Sino-Indian studies in English suffer from a sparseness in the Chinese perspective compared to the Indian one, an attempt will be made to make greater use of Chinese language sources in order to fill this information gap.

Regarding perception studies, Robert Jervis has identified perception as a variable in analysing international politics and foreign policies. He explored the process of perception and identified common forms of misperception, which are perceptions of centralization, overestimating one's importance as influence and target, the influence of desire and fears on perception, and cognitive dissonance (Jervis 1976). His pioneering study has thus provided a foundation in this area.

This book tries to narrow the focus on the perception of threat to understand China–India interactions. Threat perception refers to perceived intent and perceived capability of an opponent. In this book, threat perception is defined as an expectation of harm to assets or values of the state (Baldwin 1971: 71–8, Maoz 1990: 13). The loss or damage caused by a perceived threat might be in the areas of military, economic, strategic, national sovereignty and national prestige.

There are three major sources of threat perception. The first one is historical enmity. States tend to rely on past experiences and interactions to forecast how other states will behave. As David Singer states, historical memories easily help to transform vague suspicion into concrete hostility (Singer 1958: 93). Moreover, the existence of historical enmity will often amplify present perceptions of threat (Buzan *et al.* 1998: 59). The second source of threat perception is the sense of separate identity. Since a state's identity informs its interests and preference, states which do not hold a shared identity are uncertain as to each other's intentions and plots. On the contrary, a sense of shared identity can reduce the perception of threat (Rousseau 2006: 213–14). A power gap between the competing states is the third major source of the threat perception. A substantial gap in power between the competing states will increase the sense of insecurity for the state with less power.

In addition to illustrate the perceptions of threat between India and China, this book tries to understand how China and India interact under their own threat perception. A state will not mobilize available resources against a threat if it does not perceive the existence of threat. On the contrary, the threat perception will encourage a state to take counter-measures against its perceived threat. Several counter-measures for dealing with the threat are often discussed, such as the following.

The first is balancing. Internal balancing is to increase one's own strength and to reduce vulnerability; external balancing is used to ally with states which share common concerns (Buzan *et al.* 1998). However, an increase in capabilities, especially militarily, may intensify the security dilemma and is not conducive to a reduction in the perception of threat.

According to Stephen M. Walt's 'balance of threat' discourse, which modified the popular balance of power theory, a state's alliance behaviour is determined by the threat they perceive from other states. That is, a state aims for balance against perceived threats rather than against the most powerful states (Walt 1987: 21–6). T.V. Paul has proposed the concept of 'soft balancing' as a variant of the traditional 'hard balancing', which is based on countervailing alliances and arms build-ups. According to his idea, soft balancing involves tacit balancing short of formal alliances. The features of soft balancing are limited arms build-up, *ad hoc* cooperative exercises, or collaboration in regional or international institutions (Brooks and Wohlforth 2005: 72–3, Paul 2005: 46–71).

The second way to deal with threat perception is to bandwagon the perceived threat (appeasement of or subordination to the main source of threat) (Buzan *et al.* 1998: 58). Weak and small states are more likely to 'jump on the bandwagon' with the rising threat in order to protect their own security (Waltz 1979: 123–8). The third option to reduce the threat perception is a policy of constructive engagement, such as conducting Confidence-Building Measures (CBMs) to reduce both military capability and estimated military intent.[2]

Threat perceptions vary in degrees. David Singer even tried to define threat perception in a quasi-mathematical form: Threat Perception = Estimated Capability × Estimated Intent (Singer 1958: 93). Zeev Maoz also attempted to measure the magnitude of threat perception by listing the comparison indexes, which include (a) the nature and scope of assets perceived to be affected, (b) their relative importance to the decision maker, (c) the perceived extent of loss to each other's assets or values, (d) the likelihood of loss, and (e) the scope of currently possessed assets (Maoz 1990: 13). This book is not conducting a quantitative analysis for threat perception, but has taken note that threat perceptions vary in intensity. That is, the perception of threat between two competing states are most likely asymmetrical.

After reviewing the above-mentioned studies, this book thus develops an analytical framework based on the asymmetrical perception of threat. The theoretical hypothesis developed by this book is that the asymmetry in threat perceptions will result in a symmetrizing process to reduce the threat perception. The state with a higher perception of threat will tend to change the *status quo* in order to reach a more favourable balance of threat. Counter-measures taken by the state may involve options of balancing, bandwagoning, or CBMs. On the contrary, the state with a lower perception of threat will prefer to maintain the status quo. However, this book will argue, to maintain status quo is not the best strategy as asymmetrical threat perceptions will drive the opponent state to change the intensity of threat perception. This asymmetry can be summarised as follows: the higher the threat perception, the higher the probability that the state with intensified threat perception will take hard balancing measures to reduce threat perception.

The China Threat with Indian Characteristics

With the fall of USSR, China's security environment became more favourable. However, China's security concerns soon increased as it was targeted as a challenge to the new post-Cold War status quo. China's dramatic economic growth and its modernizing military power have not only attracted attention on the world stage, they have also invited suspicion and are sometimes perceived as posing a threat. Indian Defence Minister, A.K. Antony, argued, 'We (Indians) cannot lose sight of the fact that China has been improving its military and physical infrastructure. In fact, there has been an increasing assertiveness on the part of China. We are taking all the necessary steps to upgrade our capabilities' (*The Indian Express* 2010).

Given that China has had nuisance value to some countries, exacerbated regional conflicts and refuses to comply with some international norms, it is feared that a strong China may pursue an expansionist policy to recapture the land and rights to which it lays claim. In the words of Zheng Yongnian, there is a concern that a rising China may seek 'revenge' for the actions of western imperialists (Zheng 1998: 5). That is, many in the West tend to see a rising China as the main potential threat to international peace and stability in the post-Soviet era.

As well as listing China as a major source of uncertainty in the post-Soviet era, some commentators in the West have gone further and bluntly called for a containment policy. The Chinese feel disappointed when they are targeted as a 'threat', and feel that the real aim of the 'China threat' theory is to thwart China's bid for its rightful place in the world. Furthermore, the 'China threat' discourse is seen as a strategy targeted at sowing discord between China and the other Asia-Pacific countries, especially at harming China's relations with its neighbours (Ren 1996: 10–11). The Chinese maintain that the 'China threat' theory has overshadowed China's relations with its neighbours (Wang 1997: 7–8).

China is aware that many countries fret about the security implications of a rising China. Thus, it has been busy informing the international community that it wants peace abroad so that it can concentrate on economic development at home. Chinese leaders have reiterated that China needs a surrounding environment conducive to stability and development. On the military front, Beijing has argued that it pursues a defensive policy aimed at resisting outside invasion, safeguarding national territorial, air and marine integrity, and maintaining national unity and security; that its military expenditure remains at a relatively low level and China has no overseas military bases (Ren 1996: 10–11). In keeping with the 'peaceful development' argument, China has also claimed that its rise is a 'peaceful' one (Jiang and Xia: 2004).

The Chinese side acknowledge that India has long been suspicious of China's strength. That was why the late Chinese leader Deng Xiaoping repeatedly told the Indians that neither China nor India posed a threat to each other. For example, in a meeting with an Indian parliamentary leader, Subramaniam Swamy, Deng Xiaoping tried to allay India's suspicious about China. He dismissed the possibility of another Sino-Indian border war, saying that the Chinese army could not cross Tibet to attack India because of the lack of oxygen at that altitude. He also claimed, 'we do not have many troops and we also do not see any threat from your side to China' (*The Times* 1981: 4).

In the early 1990s, the defence establishments in Beijing and New Delhi finally resumed the exchanges on defence and security matters. In order to maintain peace and tranquillity along the disputed border, the two countries concluded two agreements on CBMs in 1993 and 1996. However, there are many Indians who are still attached to the idea of a permanent enmity against China. Although China has argued that it will not harm the existing peaceful international environment even at the risk of its own development programme, and emphasizes that China and India do not pose any threat to each other, Indian defence planners remain very cautious about China's strength and intentions. The efforts to develop a friendship between the two countries are also hindered by the accumulated and long-standing distrust that remains embedded in the minds of the Indian strategic community. In Indian eyes, the Chinese betrayed India's friendship and committed an aggression to occupy India's territory.

Thus, as this book seeks to illustrate, despite China's assurances, India continues to perceive China as a serious threat. That is why India's nuclear tests took place amidst rising anti-China rhetoric from a section of the Indian establishment. However, India's perception of the 'China threat' is quite different from the Western view. The 'China threat' theory circulated in the West is that the rise of China will inevitably destabilize regional security and challenge the vital interests of the countries concerned. It is believed that a stronger China will be intent on challenging the present international order dominated by western and developed countries and will thus confront the countries concerned.[3] However, the Indians do not consider a belligerent China as a merely imagined scenario, as Western strategic analysts do, but argue that China has frequently been a hostile and disagreeable neighbour, as India has already suffered from China's expansionism and containment. In contrast to the West's concerns about the intention of a future China, India's 'China threat' syndrome probably has its roots in the history of the 1950s and1960s, much before the West's 'China threat' theory of the 1990s.

It is no secret that, after the 1962 border war, Indian strategic thinkers treated China as a potential rival and not as a partner. Just as Alka Acharya has observed, mutual perception between China and India are still being shaped by the shadows cast by the 1962 war that ended in China's favour (Acharya 2008: 24). The annual reports of the Indian Ministry of Defence have long been guardedly articulating the view that China is India's most potent threat (Joshi 1998). The humiliating defeat of the 1962 border war, China's takeover of Tibet, and China's strategic links with India's smaller neighbours have all been rich sources of the 'China threat' perception.

Beijing, for its part, has not expended much energy in its relations with India because of its perception of India's marginal role and influence in international affairs. To Chinese officials, India has not yet reached the position that merits much attention from the Chinese side. The main foci of Chinese interests and security concerns lie elsewhere, despite India being China's second largest neighbour.

Asymmetrical Perceptions of Threat in China–India Relations

The Indians have not altered their position that China is the major threat to India. On the other hand, Beijing does not take India seriously. Although India is acknowledged to be a rising power, Beijing has not identified India as an immediate adversary. What may make Beijing take notice is if India becomes an important part of an international strategy to contain China. So far, though, China's perceived threat from India is far less than that from other countries, such as the US.

Paying more attention to the interactive culture between China and India, therefore, the first aim of the book is to point out the existence of an asymmetrical threat perception. Indeed, the threat perception between two states may often be asymmetrical. However, as John Garver's study has shown, India tends to be deeply apprehensive about the threats from China, while China appears comparatively unconcerned about the threat from India (Garver 2002b: 109–34). Such an asymmetry is both apparent and remarkable, especially considering that India and China share a similar type of international identity—both are big and populous developing countries and regional powers with considerable economic, military, and political potential.

The second contention in this study is that Sino-Indian relations are constrained by the asymmetry of their threat perceptions. Walt (1987: 21–6) argued that states aim for balance against perceived threats rather than against the most powerful states. A perceived threat could therefore affect a state's behaviour and preference in dealings with its counterpart country. In general, China does not perceive India as a serious security threat; it considers the status quo to be favourable and wants to maintain the status quo between the two countries. On the contrary, India perceives China as a serious security and tries to reduce the sense of insecurity by adopting counter-measures, such as developing nuclear weapons, allying itself with other countries, or constructive CBMs.

Third, this book will argue, the asymmetrical nature of the relationship has made it difficult for China and India to forge a relationship based on shared knowledge and to set a common agenda around which their expectations could converge. The Chinese side has ignored the asymmetry and is in no mood to share India's expectations and concerns. Instead, it argues that India suffers from a 'victim' syndrome.

Further, the book will demonstrate that the imbalance in the perception of threat will result in a dilemma for India. On the one hand, India will be on a perennial quest for changes in Sino-Indian relations, such as a final resolution of the border issue and securing the nuclear deterrent against China. On the other hand, some Indian strategists deem that India has no real bargaining leverage with China (Pant 2010: 9). As a result, India is also very cautious not to anger China, sometimes with self-imposed conditions because of the fear of its perceived threat from China.

In order to address the aforementioned objectives, the following chapters will examine the major issues of China–India relations. Chapter 1 discusses the nuclear dimension in China–India relations. As India has secured a new identity as a nuclear-weapons state, the nuclear issue has emerged as a late but significant issue between the two countries. India's nuclear tests and its securing of nuclear weapons altered not only the hard power structure between China and India, but also the ideational structure. Chinese leaders have had to reassess the implications of nuclear India's challenge to China's security environment, and to take account of India's enhanced international status derived from its possession of nuclear weapons. Beijing also has to deal with the 'China threat' theory as perceived by Indian strategic planners and its use by them to justify India's move against the international nuclear non-proliferation regime. Of particular concerns to Beijing are the ways in which its expectations about the trajectory of Sino-Indian relations were suddenly undermined by India.

The Tibet issue is still a sensitive and intractable issue for China's diplomacy. Chapter 2 provides a brief account of China's 'liberation' of

Tibet, and points out India's special role and Tibet's significance for China. As will be suggested in this chapter, the Chinese are not satisfied with India's approach to the Tibet issue, particularly its accommodation of the Dalai Lama and the government-in-exile. Although the Indian side has said in explicit terms that Tibet is a part of China and has stated that the Dalai Lama cannot carry out political activities in India, Beijing remains intensely suspicious of India's Tibetan policy, and levels the criticism that India has been very reluctant to recognize Chinese sovereignty over Tibet. On the other hand, India has adopted a cautious approach in dealing with the Tibet issue, and faces a dilemma about playing the 'Tibet card'.

Chapter 3 will deal with the long-standing boundary question. China and India have paid a high price for the unresolved border dispute, which significantly undermined relations between the two countries throughout most of the Cold War period and even sparked a war. However, development under the mechanism of the border talks shows that the border dispute, even if far from being resolved, can be managed properly. The legacy of the border dispute, including the 1962 war and CBMs, will be identified. This chapter then further discusses the work that has been done on delineating the Line of Actual Control (LAC). The following section will focus on the recent efforts and problems regarding an earlier solution. The establishment of the Special Representative mechanism, the Sikkim Issue, and the Tawang controversy will also be discussed.

Chapter 4 will focus on the geopolitical context of the China–India relationship. As regional powers, neither China nor India will ever give up their efforts to maximize their respective influence in the region. New Delhi keeps a wary eye on China's ties with its South Asian neighbours, especially its arms transfers to Pakistan and military cooperation with Myanmar. While Beijing has quarrels with some of its marine neighbours over the South China Sea, New Delhi has embarked on a 'Look-East' policy to engage Association of South East Asian Nations (ASEAN) states. This chapter, which deals with these aspects of geo-politics, also analyses the sub-regional economic cooperation and anti-terrorism campaign to explore the possible cooperation related to the complex region.

Chapter 5 assesses the development of China–India relations in the global context. The Indo-American alliance, the China–India–Russia strategic triangle, and the Chindia idea are scrutinized. This chapter refers to possible trends, cooperative or competitive, in China–India relations. The Indo-American alliance is seen as part of a global strategy against China, while the China–Russia–India strategic triangle and Chindia suggest a cooperative model for China and India to forge a new international order.

The concluding remarks summarize the findings of the book, and conclude that the asymmetry in China's and India's threat perceptions is an unstable factor for bilateral relations. Based on the asymmetrical threat perceptions, this book thus provides a new perspective for understanding China–India relations.

Notes

1. For the text of Vajpayee's letter, see *The New York Times* (1998a: A12).
2. For more analysis on how CBMs work, see Krepon (1998).
3. See, for example, Bernstein and Munro (1997: 18–32).

1 The Nuclear Dimension in India–China Relations

WHEN CHINA SUCCESSFULLY EXPLODED its first atomic bomb in October 1964, it opened up a new dimension in Sino-Indian relations—the nuclear dimension. New Delhi had tried to appeal to the US and the USSR for some form of protection from China's nuclear threat, but had failed to achieve any reassurance.[1] In the light of these developments, the threat of China's nuclear capability has continued to be an important driving force behind India's nuclear weapons programme.

However, India remained in an ambiguous nuclear limbo, and had to choose between being a nuclear power and being a non-nuclear state. Although India detonated its own nuclear device under Indira Gandhi's administration in May 1974, it maintained that the test was merely for peaceful purposes and it was reluctant to manufacture nuclear weapons.

India's ambiguity towards developing nuclear weapons may have been seen as one strategic option for the Indian leaders, but it failed to come to terms with the perceived threat to India arising from China's nuclear capability. By May 1998, India's deep-seated suspicions were reinforced by the possibility of China's nuclear coercion, the latters' clandestine support for Pakistan's nuclear weapons programme, and the enhanced international status China derived from nuclear weapons. Yet none of these concerns were taken into account by the Chinese side.

The failure to achieve a satisfactory solution to its security concerns regarding China's nuclear threat clearly spurred India's decision to move more surely down the road to nuclear weaponization. In May 1998, India finally discarded its ambiguous stance and proclaimed itself a 'nuclear-weapons state' after conducting five nuclear tests.

Unlike the 1974 tests, India in 1998 clearly identified the 'China threat' as its rationale for exploding nuclear devices. For Beijing, an India equipped with nuclear weapons presented a totally different challenge. India's possession of nuclear weapons altered the hard power structure and played a decisive role in building up a new military balance between China and India. Moreover, India's new identity as a nuclear power would reshape the ideational structure between India and China. People not only needed to reassess the implications of nuclear India's challenge to China's security environment, but also needed to take account of India's enhanced international status derived from its possession of nuclear weapons. Meanwhile, Beijing had to deal with the 'China threat' theory used by Indian strategic planners for justifying India's move against the international nuclear non-proliferation regime. Of particular concern to Beijing were the ways in which its expectations about developing Sino-Indian relations were shattered and rejected by the Indian side. Facing the new situation, China felt obliged to re-evaluate and reconstruct its India policy.

This chapter will illustrate the theory that India sees the possession of nuclear weapons as a kind of status symbol of a great power and a deterrent against security threat. Similarly, China also sees nuclear weapons in this way. The difference is that India has considered China as one of the major reasons to develop a nuclear deterrent as it identifies China as the major security threat, while China's nuclear weapons are not necessarily directed against India. Thus, this chapter argues that in relation to each other, there is an asymmetrical perception of nuclear threat. Moreover, India seeks to catch up with China in terms of international status and influence by developing nuclear weapons. The China–India security dilemma is further driven by perceptions of great power status deriving from the possession of nuclear power.

To understand the impact of nuclear weapons issues on Sino-Indian relations, this chapter will first retrace the role of nuclear deterrence as a factor in Sino-Indian relations before the 1998 tests to highlight how the nuclear issue has contributed to the formation of a perception of threat in India. The chapter then analyses India's rationale for the 1998 tests, and China's reactions to India's nuclear tests. The following section focuses on how China evaluates India's nuclear weapons programme and India's status as a nuclear-weapons state. This chapter concludes that India's 1998 nuclear tests constitute a turning point for Sino-Indian relations in the post-Cold War era. Although India has not been able to balance the perception of threat posed by the possession of nuclear weapons, its potential nuclear challenge to China's security environment and enhanced international status deriving from the possession of nuclear weapons has allowed the creation of a more favourable framework for India to deal with China–India relations.

Nuclear Deterrence in China–India Relations before 1998

One main characteristic of Sino-Indian nuclear relations prior to India's 1998 nuclear tests, according to John Garver's observation, was the 'asymmetry' in terms of the motives for nuclearization and the perceived nuclear threat (Garver 2001: 313–15). Before 1998, for Beijing, the main concerns about a nuclear threat came first from the US and then the USSR. Although a hostile relationship between China and India meant that China became a potential nuclear threat to India, Chinese leaders did not feel it necessary to launch a nuclear attack against India (Chen 1999b). That is, China's nuclear deterrent was not directed towards India.

On the other hand, the Indian side has perceived a clear nuclear threat from China since 1964. Three sources of concern, at least, have contributed to the construction of this perception. The first came from the scenario that China could use its nuclear capability to blackmail or coerce India. The second arose from China's stance towards nuclear proliferation due to its assistance to Pakistan. The third source, less linked with nuclear issues, came from China's political and diplomatic status as a nuclear power (Wu and Song 1998). The conventional wisdom in India is that, partly due to its possession of nuclear weapons, China edged out India and secured a higher international status. This might undermine India's prestige and leadership amongst the Asian and developing countries. These concerns related to China's nuclear power motivated India to consider the nuclear option.

China's Nuclear Strength and Posture

China successfully conducted its first nuclear test in October 1964, becoming the world's fifth nuclear power. Since then, China's nuclear forces have grown steadily, with advanced nuclear warheads and delivery systems. In July 1966, the Second Artillery Corps was established as China's strategic nuclear force. China has conducted 45 tests, and the last of them being held on July 29 July 1996. As regards delivery systems,

China launched a Dongfeng-2 (DF-2) Medium-Range Ballistic Missile (MRBM) in October 1966, and then developed a series of Surface-to-Surface Missiles (SSMs), Intercontinental Ballistic Missiles (ICBMs), and Submarine-Launched Ballistic Missiles (SLBMs). Despite these advances, around the end of the Cold War, China's nuclear force was in fact seen as minimal in quantity and deficient in accuracy, credibility, and survivability.

China, in 2006, officially published the details of its nuclear policy to the effect that it was pursuing a self-defensive strategy. The White Paper on China's national defence in 2006 said that China's nuclear strategy is designed to deter other countries from using or threatening to use nuclear weapons against China. Thus, China aims at building a lean but effective nuclear force and conducts a 'limited development' of nuclear weapons (SCIO 2006). In general, China claims that it tries to maintain a nuclear doctrine of 'minimum deterrence', thus securing only the capabilities necessary to maintain a credible nuclear deterrent.

In addition, China was the first country to commit to the policy of no-first-use of nuclear weapons. It also unconditionally undertook not to use or threaten to use nuclear weapons against non-nuclear weapon states or nuclear-weapon-free zones.[2] Given Beijing's commitment to the no-first-use principle, a non-nuclear India was, in theory, free from the threat of being attacked by China's first nuclear strike and should not have seen itself as the main target on the radar screen of China's nuclear weapons. In fact, China had decided to develop nuclear weapons as early as 1955, a time when China and India still shared a mood of optimism over the possibility of a friendly bilateral relationship. The perceived threat from the US was the main reason prompting China to develop its own nuclear weapons.

Although India was not the main cause for China's nuclear weapons programme, Indian strategic analysts had to consider the scenario that India might suffer another humiliating defeat like the 1962 war in case China exploited its nuclear advantage *vis-à-vis* India (Joeck 1997: 37). In response to China's nuclear weapons, therefore, there was an increasing outcry within the Indian domestic polity for the immediate weaponization of the country's nuclear capability (Ghose 2007: 985–6). India's concerns were further aggravated by a series of nuclear tests that China conducted between 1964 and 1974. In fact, throughout the Cold War era, the most visible nuclear threat pressure to Indians came from the US in the early

1970s. Washington sent the nuclear-armed USS *Enterprise* to the Bay of Bengal during the Bangladesh war in 1971 as a signal warning India not to escalate the war. However, as far as the Indian side was concerned, even though China did not consider India as a reason for developing nuclear weapons, the perceived nuclear threat from China was too imminent to ignore for the Indians because of the worsening relationship following the 1962 war. That is, India's perception is linked to the security dilemma, under which a state is keen to enhance its own power in order to defeat the perceived threat. Since India suspected China's intentions, it sensed the need to enhance its military power in order to 'prepare for the worst'.[3]

India finally conducted its first nuclear test in 1974 (Pokhran I), but it took a very different approach from that of China towards developing a nuclear weapons programme. As China went down the route of cultivating nuclear weapons, the Indian government's position was that the 1974 explosion in Pokhran was for 'peaceful purposes'.[4] India thus discontinued its nuclear weapons development after demonstrating nuclear capability, despite keeping the nuclear option open.[5] India's self-restraint posture on nuclear weapons was not much appreciated by many strategists, but instead was seen to be too ambiguous and moralistic to constitute a credible deterrent. As a result, Beijing did not need to worry much about India's nuclear ability. This partly explains why the nuclear issue was not a serious issue between the two countries until the late 1980s.

The Sino-Pakistani Nuclear Nexus

The most controversial aspect of China's nuclear policy was its position towards non-proliferation. Only since the late 1980s has China adjusted its foreign policy orientation to actively take part in the nuclear non-proliferation regime. China joined the International Atomic Energy Agency (IAEA) in 1985, more than two decades after going nuclear, and agreed to place its civilian nuclear facilities under IAEA safeguards in 1988. In 1992, it acceded to the Treaty on the Non-Proliferation of Nuclear Weapons (NPT). In addition, China joined the Zangger Committee in October 1997 and joined the Nuclear Suppliers Group (NSG) in June 2004. In September 2004, China officially submitted its application for membership of the Missile Technology Control Regime (MTCR). China was also among the first countries to sign the Comprehensive Test Ban Treaty (CTBT) in 1996.

Beijing stressed that it had signed all international treaties and joined all relevant organizations in the field of non-proliferation, and had faithfully honoured all the attendant obligations. China also claimed that it firmly opposed the proliferation of Weapons of Mass Destruction (WMD) and their means of delivery and had actively participated in the international non-proliferation process (SCIO 2003, 2005). However, the international community has long been suspicious of China's actual performance on its nuclear proliferation claims and its connection with the nuclear programmes of states like Pakistan, North Korea, and Iran.

As far as Sino-Indian nuclear relations are concerned, China's assistance to Pakistan's weapons programme has been a cause of grave concern for India's security. In the late 1970s, the media published evidence of China's aid for Pakistan's nuclear programme.[6] Since then, apart from the conventional military equipment, there have been continued reports that China had been assisting Pakistan in developing its missile and nuclear capabilities to compensate for its deficit in weaponry *vis-à-vis* India.[7] It was surmised that, in 1983, China had transferred a complete nuclear weapons design and sufficient uranium to build a nuclear weapon to Pakistan (Chandy 2000: 316–17), and that China supplied nuclear-capable M-11 missiles to Pakistan between 1992 and 1994 (Baweja and Hussain 1998: 38). With Chinese assistance, Pakistan was believed to have moved toward serial production of solid-propellant Short-Range Ballistic Missiles (SRBMs), such as the Shaheen-I and Haider-I (*The Hindu* 2001a, *Dawn* 2002). Not surprisingly, Indian Defence Minister George Fernandes has accused China of being the 'mother' of Ghauri, Pakistan's intermediate range ballistic missile (IRBM) (*Associated Press* 1998).

China did not deny its military ties with Pakistan, but repudiated the argument that it had supplied Pakistan with nuclear expertise and long-range missiles. Chinese officials have only confessed that they have provided some conventional weapons, including a few short-range tactical missiles. On the issue of missile technology transfers, Chinese officials claimed that China had voluntarily observed the main guidelines and parameters of MTCR, and had not exported any missiles capable of reaching a range over 300 km or with a payload of over 500 kg.[8] Repudiating the report about China's missile transfer to Pakistan, Chinese Foreign Ministry officials also stressed that China had no intention of assisting any country in any way to develop ballistic missiles that could be used to carry nuclear weapons.[9]

Similarly, the typical response of Beijing to claims of China's assistance to Pakistan's nuclear weapons ability was a denial of any knowledge of the nuclear weapons technology transfer. Although a considerable number of reports suggested otherwise, the Chinese maintained that their nuclear cooperation with Pakistan was confined to 'peaceful purposes', and that it was all under IAEA supervision (Ram 1998a: 15). Some Chinese scholars even argued that Pakistani nuclear technology came from the western world (Ye 1999: 9). Refuting reports of having received any assistance from China in developing missiles, Pakistan said that its missile programme was 'totally indigenous' (*Xinhua* 2002a).

To China's and Pakistan's embarrassment, however, Iftikhar Ahmed Khan, Pakistan's former intelligence official and military attaché at the Pakistani Embassy in China, confirmed China's assistance in developing Pakistan's nuclear bombs.[10] Abdul Qadeer Khan, known as the father of Pakistan's nuclear weapons programme, also revealed that China had gifted Pakistan 50 kg of weapons-grade uranium in 1982, and also supplied a blueprint for a simple bomb that significantly speeded up Pakistan's nuclear programme (*The Times of India* 2009a: 15). International society, to a great extent, holds China responsible for the nuclear proliferation in Pakistan, irrespective of China's attempts at self-justification.

Despite China's protestations of innocence, China's transfer to Pakistan, particularly of missiles and nuclear expertise, was perceived as hostile by India. Given the tension and conflict between India and Pakistan, the possible nuclear threat from Pakistan loomed even larger than the one from China. Not surprisingly, India had repeatedly raised the issue of nuclear and missile assistance from China to Pakistan during its interactions with China, but Beijing did not deal with India's concerns seriously.

As a result, even as Beijing worked to improve relations with India by exchanging visits, expanding trade, and maintaining peace and tranquillity along the disputed border, the perceived threat from China, in terms of its nuclear coercion, did not evaporate, but remained embedded in the minds of the Indian strategic community. On the other hand, China did not feel so much pressure from the Indian side. Such an asymmetry in the perception of threat thus encouraged New Delhi to fashion a revisionist security agenda, if China continued to ignore New Delhi's concerns.

India's Pokhran II Nuclear Tests

India's Reasons for Conducting Pokhran II

China's nuclear capability, its nuclear connection with Pakistan, and the nuclear-state status constituted an imperative incentive for Indian leaders to develop India's own nuclear weapons. However, India's nuclear weapons programme remained dormant between 1974 and 1998. The next two decades after the 1974 test saw India continue its efforts to keep disarmament in focus in international fora. India maintained an ambiguous stance, showing its nuclear capability and keeping the nuclear option open without building a nuclear arsenal.

In fact, successive Indian governments had, over time, tried to restore the nuclear tests. As the former Indian Defence Minister (and later President), R. Venkataraman recalled, India was ready with full preparations for an underground nuclear test in 1983, but was dissuaded from going ahead by external pressure (*The Indian Express* 1998a). A similar attempt to carry out new nuclear tests was made in 1995 but halted by the US. The then American Ambassador to India, Frank Wisner, showed satellite photographs that India was preparing for a nuclear test to Indian officials, and asked the Indian side to halt the programme (*The New York Times* 1998b).

It was the Hindu nationalist BJP, which won the general elections in 1998, that decided to end the long-standing ambiguity over the nuclear option. Although the BJP had called for nuclear bombs since the 1980s and had included the nuclear option in its electoral manifestoes, the issue about the nuclear weapons programme did not figure significantly in the elections. Therefore, very few people had expected that India would soon conduct nuclear tests when the BJP came to office. However, the BJP-led government lost no time in surprising the world in May 1998 by conducting five rounds of nuclear tests in Pokhran in the northern state of Rajasthan. These nuclear tests were known as Pokhran II because India had already conducted a nuclear test in 1974 at the same site. In the following weeks, Pakistan detonated its own six nuclear blasts, symbolically one more test than India's, in the Chagai hills. Given the long-standing tension between India and Pakistan, there was increasing concern that the subcontinent was embroiled in an overt nuclear confrontation.

The reasons for the BJP government to go nuclear were mixed and have been well-detailed in numerous studies.[11] To put it simply, three main factors were behind the decision: India's perception of its security needs, domestic political considerations, and the ambition to make India a world-recognized great power. China might not have played a part in the domestic factor behind India's decision to develop nuclear weapons, but was a major factor in shaping India's security perception, and found itself relevant in India's pursuit of becoming a major world power.

The irony is that since India had been an advocate of nuclear disarmament and a nuclear weapons-free world for decades, the Indian government needed to find some reasons to justify its shift in position. Soon after the first round of nuclear tests in May 1998, Indian Prime Minister Atal Bihari Vajpayee wrote letters to the heads of some other countries explaining India's rationale for conducting the tests. In his letter to the US President Bill Clinton, Vajpayee argued that India shared borders with a nuclear-weapons state that had committed armed aggression against India in 1962. He also explained that India had an unresolved border dispute with one neighbour, which had also materially helped its neighbouring adversary.[12]

The statement was a clear reference to China, although Vajpayee did not name it directly. This parlance, in fact, also reflected New Delhi's perception and assessment of the post-Cold War security environment: the end of the Cold War had done little to ameliorate India's security concerns, and China was seen as the major contributor to the destabilization of India's security environment.

The letter then reminded people that the Indian Defence Minister, George Fernandes, had earlier commented on the 'China threat' theory, when he warned that India was encircled by Chinese military and naval activity. He argued that China had extended 11 airfields in Tibet, which posed a threat to India's security, and had set up electronic surveillance installations on the Coco islands, just 40 km off the northern tip of India's Andaman and Nicobar islands, to observe Indian missile trials and other exercises. Furthermore, in an interview with the Indian media, he publicly termed China as India's 'potential threat number one', stressing that the potential threat from China was greater than that from Pakistan (*The Indian Express* 1998d). In his view, 'there is a reluctance to face the reality that China's intentions need to be questioned.' Further, he argued that India had made the mistake of underplaying or ignoring the potential threat from China, and had been forced to pay the price in the 1960s (*Press Trust of India* [*PTI*] 1998). He then called for 'tough decisions' to counter the potential threat from China (*The Indian Express* 1998d).

Fernandes' comments on China had evoked sharp criticism from Beijing, which had officially protested to New Delhi twice in less than a month (*The Hindu* 1998g: 1). China's Foreign Ministry spokesman described Fernandes' utterances as 'ridiculous and not worthy of refutation', but his statements had seriously sabotaged the atmosphere for improving relations (*The Hindu* 1998h: 1). Initially, the Chinese government did not equate Defence Minister Fernandes' views with the position of the BJP government, because the Indian side tried to present his rhetoric as being just an individual statement of opinion. After the publication of Vajpayee's letter, however, Beijing was astonished to learn that the idea of permanent suspicion of China was not limited to just a few members of the BJP government. It seemed logical for Beijing to associate Defence Minister Fernandes' 'China threat' discourse as a prelude for exploding the nuclear weapons.

The Indian posture that China was the principal motive for the decision to go nuclear represented a setback for China's policy towards India. Over the decade before India's nuclear tests of 1998, the Chinese side had been confident of engaging India and had concluded that the relationship had gradually improved. In contradiction to what Beijing might have expected, the improvement of Sino-Indian relations in the 1990s did not relieve India's concerns about the military balance between India and China and its security environment. On the contrary, the rise of China and China's relations with other South Asian states, especially the surreptitious military transfer to Pakistan, had led Indian leaders to conclude that the early 1990s was a greatly troubling period (Singh 2006: 112). Given the continuing deterioration in the conventional balance in favour of China, India came to believe that developing nuclear weapons was a better option to assert and establish strategic autonomy *vis-à-vis* China. Just as the Indian President A.P.J. Abdul Kalam claimed, 'when we were surrounded by nuclear armed countries, we didn't have any alternative but to become a nuclear weapon state' (*The Hindu* 2005c). That is, the nuclear weapon was considered as an instrument to eliminate India's 'China threat' perception.

China's Reactions to the Pokhran II Nuclear Tests

Like other countries, China was surprised by India's nuclear tests. However, what annoyed China most was not the fact that the Pokhran II tests endangered the nuclear non-proliferation regime or triggered a nuclear arms race in the subcontinent, but India's use of the 'China threat' as justification for resuming testing.

In fact, some Chinese scholars conceded that it was difficult to deny India's right to conduct nuclear tests. The senior Chinese scholar Ye Zhengjia, a former diplomat once assigned to India and then a research fellow at the Foreign Ministry's Institute of International Studies, argued that it was India's sovereign right to decide whether to have nuclear weapons or not (Ram 1998c). Another well-known Chinese nationalist scholar, Wang Xiaodong, also stated frankly that he could not find a just reason to oppose India conducting nuclear tests (Wang 1999a). However, India's use of what Chinese observers and commentators called the 'China threat' theory as the excuse did enrage China.

The differences were well-illustrated by the official statements from Beijing. China's initial reaction to India's first round of nuclear tests on 11 May 1998 was seen as relatively mild and cautious, as it expressed only 'serious concerns' (*Renmin Ribao* 1998a: 3). However, after learning the content of Vajpayees' letter, published on 13 May, Beijing became indignant. China soon adjusted its earlier tone and strongly condemned India's nuclear tests (*Renmin Ribao* 1998c: 4). The then Chinese Foreign Ministry spokesman explained the change in China's attitude towards India's nuclear tests. As he said, China had exercised restraint in expressing its position by merely expressing regret about the first round of tests. On 13 May, after India had conducted its second round of nuclear tests and the Prime Minister had sent a letter to President Clinton alleging that China posed a threat, China raised its voice against India's nuclear tests by issuing a strongly worded statement.[13] The Chinese statement read:

> In disregard of the strong opposition of the international community, the Indian government conducted two more nuclear tests on May 13 following May 11 nuclear tests. The Chinese government is deeply shocked by this and hereby expresses its strong condemnation [...] The Indian government, which itself has undermined the international effort in banning nuclear tests so as to obtain the hegemony in South Asia in defiance of the world opinion, has even maliciously accused China as posing a nuclear threat to India. This is utterly groundless. This gratuitous accusation by India against China is solely for the purpose of finding excuses for the development of its nuclear weapons. (*Renmin Ribao* 1998a: 1)

Beijing also launched a propaganda campaign against India. As a symbolic protest, China's state-owned *Renmin Ribao* (*People's Daily*) published two commentator's articles on 15 and 19 May condemning the nuclear tests (Renmin Ribao 1998d: 14, 1998c: 14). Some Chinese scholars argued that India was trying to present a 'China threat' scenario to extract mileage out of the ideological differences between China and the West while New Delhi was masking its own contradictions with the West to lessen the extent of any possible sanctions (*The Hindu* 1998a: 14). Some others considered that India's nuclear tests and Vajpayee's testimony exposed India's suspicious mind and animosity towards China.

Therefore, the initial task for Beijing in response to India's nuclear tests was to refute the 'China threat' discourse proposed by India, instead of echoing the Western concerns about nuclear proliferation. China stressed that it was ridiculous to suggest that China could pose a threat to any other country because China had no military bases and not a single soldier outside its borders. Moreover, the Chinese side argued that China was the only country among the five nuclear powers to have promised not to use nuclear weapons against non-nuclear weapon states and nuclear-free zones.[14]

The then Chinese Ambassador to India, Zhou Gang even said that 'China, being a socialist country, does not believe in posing a threat to any neighbouring nations, let alone India. [...] The slogan *Hindi Chini Bhai Bhai* is still very popular with the people of China' (*The Indian Express* 1998b), though this defence sounded unpersuasive. Claiming that Beijing's defence policy was defensive in nature, Zhou said that any fear of a 'China threat' was entirely unfounded and was fabricated with ulterior motives (*PTI* 1999a).

Stressing that their nuclear tests were more 'legitimate' than India's, China also argued that the circumstances and context in which China conducted its first tests in October 1964 were totally different from those prevailing in 1998. The Chinese stressed that their nuclear weapons programme was developed when China faced threats from the superpowers. China's nuclear weapons were acquired and developed against the background of the monopoly of the former USSR and the US, the Chinese argued, while India faced no such threat from China.

Beijing aimed to clear its name as a motive for the Indian nuclear tests, repeatedly arguing that India's nuclear tests had nothing to do with India *versus* China, but were related to India's ambition to dominate

South Asia. In a statement on India's nuclear tests, China accused India of pursuing a hegemonistic ambition in South Asia and triggering a new round of the arms race in the subcontinent (*Renmin Ribao* 1998a: 1).

Meanwhile, Chinese officials began to list India's 'China threat' theory as the main irritant in Sino-Indian relations. For example, the then Chinese Ambassador to India, Zhou Gang, argued that the main cause for the upset in Sino-Indian relations was that some personalities in India had accused China of posing a threat to India's security so as to justify India's nuclear tests (*PTI* 1999a). The official Chinese line was that a prerequisite for the development of healthy Sino-Indian relations was the understanding that neither side constituted a threat to the other, and that the basis of their relationship were the Five Principles of Peaceful Coexistence jointly initiated by the two countries.[15]

Not satisfied with New Delhi's responses, Beijing asked the Indian side to take concrete steps to declare that China did not constitute a threat to India. As well as suspending the border dialogue, military exchanges also remained dormant in the wake of the Pokhran II tests. Moreover, calls began to be made for a change in China's policy towards India. Chinese scholar Song Dexin, for example, argued that it was imperative for China to chart an alternative policy instead of sticking to the policy of 'good neighbours' because India still treated China as a threat and held on to a Cold War mentality (Song 1999: 36–42). In a warning tone, another senior Chinese South Asian specialist, Ma Jiali, said, 'If India regards China as a rival or enemy, it is possible for China to be that way' (Ram 1998a). Despite the re-normalization process that had taken place since the late 1980s, Sino-Indian relations were not as optimistic as they seemed on the surface.

China's Adjusted Posture

The deadlock between Beijing and New Delhi following the nuclear tests has prompted China and India to modify their approaches to dealing with their bilateral relations. It was not in the interest of India to return to a relationship of conflict with China. Although Prime Minister Vajpayee cited China as the reason behind the decision to test, it was not India's intention to go nuclear at the cost of Sino-Indian rapprochement. In some respects the Chinese were right to say that New Delhi used China as the rationale for going nuclear, in effect playing the 'China threat' card to ease Western pressure in the wake of the nuclear tests (*The Indian Express*

1998c). Yet New Delhi appeared to have expected Vajpayee's letter to remain confidential, and was upset when US officials leaked it to the press. India's tactic of mentioning China as a threat then became a diplomatic stumbling block, as the tone and content of Vajpayee's letter soon caused China to harden its position toward India's nuclear tests.

In order to mend relations, the Indian side took several initiatives to placate the Chinese. First was the statement by Brajesh Mishra, the Principal Secretary to the Prime Minister, who said that India wanted to have 'the best of relations' with China and urged China to return to dialogue (*Australia Associated Press* 1998). This was followed by Vajpayee's statement that some misunderstandings between China and India had been created only due to the 'distorted version of statements' appearing in the media (Lok Sabha Debates 1998: 394). However, Beijing expected a more credible commitment from New Delhi.

As part of the plan to manage the situation in the wake of the nuclear tests, in December 1998, Jaswant Singh was appointed Minister for External Affairs, the portfolio previously retained by Prime Minister Vajpayee himself. Aware of the importance of engaging China, the new minister lost no time in seeking a revival of talks with China. He asked the Chinese side to return to the negotiating table, and argued that China should help India 'untie the knot' through frequent consultations and talks (*The Hindu* 1998b). The Chinese side expressed its appreciation of his statement, but did not make any commitment (*Renmin Ribao* 1998b: 4).

In February 1999, Indian officials were sent to Beijing in an attempt to urge their counterparts to restart the dialogue on the boundary problem. The official visit brought about a positive result with an announcement by the Chinese Foreign Minister Tang Jiaxuan just a few weeks later, that the Chinese side had recently acknowledged the statements issued by Indian leaders that China posed no threat to India (*Renmin Ribao* 1999d: 1). Tang's announcement came as the first positive signal of China's desire to put behind it the bitterness that had arisen in the wake of India's nuclear tests. During Indian External Affairs Minister Singh's visit to China in June 1999, he endorsed China's argument that the precondition for developing China–India relations was that neither side saw the other as a threat (*Renmin Ribao* 1999a: 4).

Despite India's efforts to engage China, the reason behind the softening of Beijing's rigid stance towards New Delhi came partly from India's diplomatic success in allaying international suspicion about its nuclear tests. In July 1998, for example, the ASEAN Regional Forum (ARF) decided not to condemn India's nuclear tests, ignoring China's displeasure. India also successfully repaired its relations with most of the major powers by conducting formal consultations and resuming high-level visits. Eight rounds of dialogue between India and the US were held between June 1998 and January 1999. Indian Prime Minister Vajpayee visited France in September 1998. The visit was followed by the first meeting of the Indo-French Strategic Dialogue in October 1998. Russian Prime Minister Yevgeny Primakov visited India in December 1998, and Indian President K.R. Narayanan visited Germany between 6 and 10 September 1998. Brajesh Mishra, the Principal Secretary to Prime Minister and later India's National Security Advisor, visited the UK and France in June 1998 and January 1999, respectively. The India–Japan Foreign Office consultation was conducted in January 1999. As other major powers had been conducting official dialogues with India, China became increasingly isolated at the international level in continuing to urge New Delhi to abandon its nuclear programme. It was against this background that China began to moderate its position on India, although it was still angry with the way in which India allayed suspicions by using the 'China threat' as justification for its nuclear tests.

Following the trend to restore the pre-Pokhran II relationship, at the 12th Joint Working Group (JWG) meeting on the boundary problem in April 2000, Beijing and New Delhi agreed to resume high-level military interactions, which had been suspended after India's nuclear tests in May 1998. Chinese Foreign Minister Tang Jiaxuan visited India in July 2000, followed by Lieutenant General Tian Shugen, Vice-President of the Academy of Military Science, in August 2000. It was the first exchange between the two armies after the People's Liberation Army (PLA) Chief of General Staff Fu Quanyou had visited India in April–May 1998. Subsequently, two Indian naval ships paid a goodwill visit to China in September 2000. Clearly, there was a positive shift in the tone and content of the bilateral relationship.

Despite its resentment of India's nuclear tests, China did not want to adopt a course of conflict and a hostile policy posture. Still, China did not see India as a serious security threat, and was not willing to escalate tensions between the two countries, if this would have an adverse effect on its domestic development. In pursuing the goal of rising in peace and building a well-off society, the Chinese leadership strived to improve

China's relations with the major powers, neighbouring countries and the Third World (Zheng 2005, Wang 2004).

Officials in Beijing argued that there were no serious problems between India and China and no fundamental conflict of interest, but that a lack of communication and contact had sometimes led to misunderstanding.[16] In other words, Beijing was expressing confidence that India's suspicion about China could be dispelled if both sides increased exchanges in various fields. There was a growing recognition that mutual understanding between the two countries was not enough and needed to be improved. This point was shared with New Delhi.

A comprehensive dialogue mechanism was formed with the aim of promoting an improvement of and a development in bilateral relations through dialogue. Despite the existing negotiation mechanism on boundary problems, a security dialogue was established in June 1999 during Indian External Affairs Minister Singh's visit to China. Three rounds of dialogue were held between March 2000 and September 2002. An India–China Eminent Persons Group was constituted during Indian President Narayanan's state visit to China in May–June 2000, and the first meeting of this group took place in New Delhi on 17–18 September 2001. The group was expected to serve as an important advisory agency for the two governments. The India–China dialogue mechanism on counter-terrorism was established during Chinese Premier Zhu Rongji's visit to India in January 2002 to address concerns in the wake of the September 11 events. The first meeting was held in New Delhi on 23 April 2002.

The dialogue mechanism appeared to be a new feature of Sino-Indian relations in the post-Pokhran era, but it was still questionable whether both sides could make use of it to enhance mutual understanding and further strengthen bilateral relations. Despite the assumption that it is seeking a stable and friendly relationship with India, Beijing needs to keep pace with the changes when fashioning its India policy. In fairness, the so-called 'constructive partnership of cooperation oriented towards the twenty-first century' had not worked out as satisfactorily as hoped since its proclamation.[17] Despite the continued engagement, China remained more cautious about India's perception of China. For example, a *Renmin Ribao* commentary article published in 2001 criticized the 'China threat' content in the annual report of India's Ministry of Defence (Zhao 2001). It reflected that China was still sensitive to the 'China threat' discourse.

On the other hand, China showed flexibility in its policy towards India. The major figures of the BJP-led government, including Prime Minister Vajpayee, Deputy Prime Minister and Home Minister Lal Krishna Advani, and Defence Minister Fernandes were all considered as hardliners by the Chinese and as such were not popular in either political or academic circles in China,[18] but Beijing still invited them to visit China.

Beijing's flexibility bore some much-needed fruit. During Indian Prime Minister Vajpayee's visit to China from 22 to 27 June 2003, both sides issued a 'Declaration on Principles for Relations and Comprehensive Cooperation', which stated, 'The two countries are not a threat to each other. Neither side shall use or threaten to use force against the other.' Chinese experts evaluated the clause as a *de facto* non-war pact (*Xinhua* 2003). It was a diplomatic effort by Beijing to mend what it saw as the damage done by India's use of the 'China threat' discourse to justify its development of a nuclear weapons programme.

Apparently, China considers India to have made a public apology by declaring that it did not see China as a threat. India's low-profile attitude in dealing with the 'China threat' after the nuclear tests fostered a perception of benign intentions and thus reduced the perception of threat in the eyes of China, and thus influenced the degree to which China would like to take a softer approach toward India.

India's Nuclear Doctrine and Posture

Although China and India showed willingness and a capability to manage the diplomatic aftershock of India's nuclear tests, suspicions and distrust still remained. With India's emergence as a nuclear power in its neighbourhood, for the Chinese, a more significant question that needed to be answered was whether a nuclear India would undermine China's security.

In fact, the Chinese have not ignored India's military power in their assessment of Sino-Indian relations. The Chinese analyst Chen Fengjun identified India's military capability as the most noticeable component of its national strength (Chen 1999a: 6–7). However, few in China had taken India seriously or treated India as a strategic threat before India transformed into a nuclear-weapons power. Such a mindset was dramatically changed as India has been empowered by nuclear weapons. In assessing India's nuclear weapons programme, the major concern for

China was that China lost most of its nuclear superiority against India. No matter how credible India's nuclear weapons are, the Chinese perceive India's nuclear weapons as an unpleasant factor in its security environment. The quantitative and qualitative improvement of India's nuclear forces has led to an increased perception of threat in China. As a result, China is still very reluctant to recognize India's status as a nuclear state and tries to underline the illegitimacy of India's nuclear weapons programme.

India's Nuclear Deterrent against China

Since Indian strategists had branded China's and Pakistan's nuclear capability as the main security imperative in the development of a nuclear weapons programme, the implication was that New Delhi intended to use its nuclear weapons to counterbalance China's strength. In other words, India's possession of nuclear weapons had made an impact on China's and Pakistan's strategic environment.

In the case of Pakistan, it was well-recognized that India had previously enjoyed massive superiority over Pakistan in conventional military strength. However, Pakistan had taken the same step to conduct tests and to declare itself a nuclear-weapons state on the heels of India's nuclear blasts. India has not substantially increased its strategic advantage *vis-à-vis* Pakistan. Ironically, as a result, the option of joining the nuclear club had to some extent neutralized India's conventional military strength against Pakistan, since Pakistan was also armed with a nuclear deterrent. Worse, there were no signs that the nuclearization of India and Pakistan could effectively help to reduce the long-standing conflict between the two countries. Months after India and Pakistan had declared themselves nuclear states, the two countries engaged in a major military confrontation between May and July 1999 in the Kargil district of the disputed Kashmir region. The conflict was, in fact, the first direct military confrontation between India and Pakistan in nearly 30 years, and thus was considered by some as the fourth Indo-Pakistan war. The Kargil conflict proved that the nuclear deterrent did not work to make military confrontation between India and Pakistan less likely. In the view of many, the subcontinent became less secure as a result of the tit-for-tat nuclear tests by India and Pakistan. After the nuclear tests of 1998, the Indian Nobel prize laureate Professor Amartya Sen, speaking in a sardonic tone, argued that, 'Bangladesh is probably now the safest country to live in, in the subcontinent' (Sen 2005: 258).

The tension between India and Pakistan in fact did not serve China's interests either. Beijing had always been reluctant to be dragged into an India–Pakistan military stand-off, and had concerns about the possibility of a Pakistan–India nuclear holocaust. Besides, it also worried about the impact of a nuclear confrontation in its neighbourhood. That was one of the reasons why, instead of supporting Islamabad's adventure, China asked both India and Pakistan to show restraint during the Kargil crisis.

In addition to the possible India–Pakistan nuclear conflict, for Beijing, a more critical question was whether a nuclear-armed India posed a threat or a serious challenge to China's security. China had become a member of the nuclear club decades before India and its nuclear weapons programme remained many years in advance of India's. However, India's decision to go down the route of developing nuclear weapons has neutralized China's perceived superiority in terms of military strength. Rationally, China will no longer be able to use nuclear blackmail and coercion against India, because the latter is also equipped with nuclear strike ability. Just as Shanta Nedungadi Verma of Delhi University suggested, 'With India being a nuclear power, Beijing would not like to antagonise India beyond a certain point' (Kumar and Sengupta 2000). This is why the then Indian External Minister Jaswant Singh argued that nuclear tests acquired for India 'strategic space' and rewarded it with strategic autonomy (*The Hindu* 1999a: 13)

Indeed, some analysts in China were very confident that India remained unable to pose a threat to China. For example, the senior Chinese scholar Ye Zhengjia once said that China was not very worried about India's targeting China (Ram 1998c). Chen Fengjun of Peking University also expressed the belief that India did not constitute a serious threat to China (*Zhongguo Shibao* 2000). Even so, China has kept an eye on India's nuclear build-up and has tried to interpret India's real intentions toward China in the context of the nuclear issue. Before the nuclear tests, Chinese analysts deemed that China's western frontier was quite stable and peaceful (Ye *et al.*1997: 429–50). However, India's nuclear tests changed that optimistic view.

Despite lacking a detailed analysis about how India's nuclear weapons programme would affect China's security environment, Chinese scholars identify India's nuclear weapons as a negative factor. The conclusion is that South Asia is no longer a region that poses only a minimum threat to China's security. Instead, the view is that South Asia might become a region with the greatest potential threat to China (Yang 2003: 165). Contrary to their earlier optimism, the Chinese have become more cautious, seeing Sino-Indian relations as an 'unstable' factor in China's security environment (Song 1999: 36–42).

India's Nuclear Doctrine

Conducting nuclear tests indicates that a country is willing to take the step to cross the nuclear threshold, but is not necessarily proof of a country's capacity for mass destruction, nor a nuclear deterrent. The effectiveness and the credibility of nuclear deterrence hinges on guidance mentioning the conditions and possible scenarios under which the nuclear weapons will be used. Another significant factor contributing to the nuclear deterrent is the delivery system. In the case of China and India, in order to examine its implications for China–India relations it is imperative to contemplate India's nuclear strategy and its development.

Although Indian officials made some statements about its nuclear arms immediately after Pokhran II, exactly how India might stage a nuclear strike was still largely a matter of speculation. That is why the Indian attitude towards nuclear weaponization was characterized by ambiguity and uncertainty by some Indian pundits (Sen 2005: 260–2). In fact, it took a nuclear India 15 months to release its first formal declaration on the subject of its nuclear weapons policy, the draft Report of the National Security Advisory Board on Indian Nuclear Doctrine, which was issued on 17 August 1999, and in essence was adopted by the Indian government as official policy in January 2003.

The document appeared to be an attempt to reassure the world that India has a responsible and considered nuclear arms policy, and is determined to build up an assured nuclear retaliation. According to the doctrine, the fundamental purpose of Indian nuclear weapons is to deter the use and threat of use of nuclear weapons by any state or entity against India and its forces. India forswears first use of nuclear weapons and maintains a 'minimum credible deterrent'. Meanwhile, it promises not to be the first to initiate a nuclear strike, although it will respond with punitive retaliation if the deterrent fails. India also claims that it will not resort to the use of or threat to use nuclear weapons against states that do not possess nuclear weapons, or are not aligned with nuclear-weapons powers. In March 2011, Indian External Affairs Minister S.M. Krishna asserted that there would be no revision of India's no-first-use nuclear doctrine and remained committed to maintaining credible minimum nuclear deterrence (*The Hindu* 2011a).

Similar to China's nuclear position, one element of India's nuclear doctrine is that it unequivocally renounces the first use of nuclear weapons. The commitment to no-first-use has explicitly underscored India's lack of any intention to use nuclear weapons as a tool of pre-emptive policy and its intention to use them instead simply to dissuade attempts by any state at nuclear blackmail. Though it is tempting to dismiss the no-first-use commitment as an empty promise, and although the efficiency of the no-first-use policy is also questioned by some analysts, the deterrent nature of India's nuclear doctrine appears clear. In effect, then, the principal role of India's nuclear force is to protect the nation from the prospect of nuclear blackmail and coercion at the hands of countries such as China or Pakistan.

Since the Chinese side also claims that China will not be the first to use nuclear weapons, the no-first-use principle has become a set of double safety valves between China and India to avoid a direct nuclear clash. Even though the two countries are equipped with nuclear weapons, a nuclear war between China and India therefore remains less likely.

As was noted earlier, among the five nuclear weapon states, China was the first country to commit to no-first-use of nuclear weapons. The Chinese even proposed that all nuclear-weapon states should commit themselves to the no-first-use of nuclear weapons before the goal of complete prohibition and thorough destruction of nuclear weapons is achieved, and should abandon the policies of nuclear deterrence based on the first use of nuclear weapons and reduce the role of nuclear weapons in their national security policy. China has also called for a multilateral treaty among nuclear-weapon states on a mutual policy of no-first-use of nuclear weapons against each other. In January 1994, China formally presented a draft text of the Treaty on the No-First-Use of Nuclear Weapons to the other four nuclear-weapons states. At the same time, China also worked vigorously on arrangements among nuclear-weapon states (NSWs) on the mutual no-first-use of nuclear weapons and the mutual de-targeting of nuclear weapons at each other. In September 1994, China and Russia declared that they would not be the first to use nuclear weapons against each other and would not aim their strategic nuclear weapons at each other. In June 1998, China and the US declared the de-targeting of their nuclear weapons against each other. In May

2000, China and the other four nuclear weapons states issued a joint statement declaring that their nuclear weapons are not aimed at each other (SCIO 2005).

Meanwhile, India reached an agreement on nuclear CBMs with Pakistan. As early as in 1988, India and Pakistan agreed that they would not attack each other's nuclear facilities and would annually exchange a list of civilian nuclear facilities. During PM Vajpayee's visit to Lahore in February 1999, India and Pakistan agreed to negotiate a range of CBMs. The two sides undertook to provide each other with advance notification in respect of ballistic missile tests. India has also held expert-level talks on CBMs with Pakistan since June 2004, trying to find ways to achieve nuclear risk reduction.

However, no similar agreement has been reached between China and India. Some Chinese scholars had suggested before Pokhran II, that all nuclear countries should reach an agreement undertaking not to be the first to use nuclear weapons under any circumstances (Liu and Zheng 1997: 6). After India's nuclear tests in 1998, Chinese academics soon ruled out a similar agreement between India and China (*Frontline* 1998a). Such a position contradicts China's existing policy and shows that China remains unwilling to recognize India's nuclear status.

The Indians acknowledged that differences existed in Sino-Indian relations, especially on the nuclear issue, so they used the first-ever security dialogue to explain India's nuclear policy. However, Chinese officials diplomatically maintained their tough stance and asked India to implement in earnest the UN Security Council Resolution 1172 and to renounce its nuclear weapons programme (*PTI* 2000c).

As a new initiative to deal with the new nuclear order in South Asia, India's External Affairs Minister, K. Natwar Singh, suggested in June 2004 that India, Pakistan, and China should develop a common nuclear doctrine. Definitely, it was too early to expect China and India to sit together to coordinate their nuclear strategy. The use of nuclear capability is related to strategic deterrence and is at the heart of military strength. While China and India still endeavour to address conventional CBMs to avoid conflicts, it is still premature to turn our attention to the nuclear CBMs.

Moreover, it is not easy for either side to reach a compromise on all nuclear issues. China insisted that India should join the NPT and CTBT unconditionally and oppose the American proposal of a Theatre Missile

Defence (TMD) system. On the contrary, India considers the NPT and CTBT as being against its own national interests and supports the TMD. However, Natwar Singh's idea underscored India's new Congress government's policy of cooperation towards China. India's self-chosen belief in itself as a responsible and rational nuclear-weapons power, as its nuclear doctrine tries to manifest, would help to minimise the risk of nuclear and missile conflict with Pakistan and China.

Since the prevention of any nuclear war in the neighbourhood is also in China's interests, the experiment to coordinate their positions and stop squabbling over bilateral differences should have won approval from Beijing. The Chinese side considered Singh's proposal a goodwill gesture, but chose not to react so far, because it has not been in favour of according nuclear status to India and bringing it on a par with China. Accepting the proposal for a common nuclear doctrine even in principle would mean acknowledging India as a nuclear power, which China did not intend to do. Chinese Assistant Foreign Minister Shen Guofang instead asked the international community to keep to the spirit and principles enshrined in the NPT as well as the consensus reached in the UN Security Council resolution 1172 (*Dawn* 2004). There was yet no sign that Beijing accepted the reality and would stop asking India to renounce its nuclear weapons programme.

Although the two sides have begun to include civil nuclear cooperation on the agenda, currently China has no intention of discussing the nuclear CBMs such as de-targeting each other to avoid any endorsement of India's nuclear status. The Chinese leaders also avoid making any reference to India's *de facto* status as a nuclear-weapons state.

India's Nuclear and Missile Programme

Part of India's nuclear doctrine, such as the no-first-use principle, underlined the value of reducing the risk of a nuclear war with China. However, part of the doctrine also emphasized the need to maintain a credible minimum nuclear deterrent against China.

According to its nuclear doctrine, India needs to develop an effective deterrent against a potential adversary and ensure that India can and will retaliate with sufficient nuclear weapons to inflict destruction and punishment. Indian policymakers appear confident that a small nuclear force capable of surviving a first strike could meet this requirement. That is, India's strategy is a kind of mutual assured destruction. Since a nuclear deterrent cannot be effective unless backed by appropriate delivery systems, the doctrine also recommended that India should develop a 'triad' strategic defence system in which nuclear weapons could be delivered by land-based missiles, aircraft, and submarines.

A decade after Pokhran II, however, India has yet to reach the target of completing its nuclear triad. Though India, in February 2007, successfully test-fired its first-ever SLBM, the K-15 (Sagarika), it is currently limited to SSMs and fighters to carry nuclear weapons. Since India has a relatively limited capability to launch nuclear weapons from planes and submarines, the surface-based missiles, especially the Agni series, are at the very core of the Indian nuclear programme and have attracted much more attention.

The Agni missile is part of the Integrated Guided Missile Development Programme (IGMDP) launched by India in 1983. Under the scheme, India first test-fired the 700-km Agni in May 1989, but suspended further testing after three test flights in 1994. Only after Pokhran II, in order to acquire a credible nuclear deterrent, did India decide to restore the testing to further advance the missile programmes relentlessly.

On 11 April 1999, ignoring US appeals for restraint in testing weapons, India ended five years of uncertainty by successfully test-firing an Agni-II missile with a range of around 2,000 km. The testing of the Agni-II missile raised fears of a new arms race in South Asia, as Pakistan soon test-fired its Hatf-V (Ghauri-II) missile, which has the capability to cover almost the whole territory of India (*The Indian Express* 1999a). Although some analysts may be tempted to assess the test-firing of Agni missiles in the context of Indo-Pakistani relations, as a deterrent against Pakistan, Agni-I has sufficient range and Agni-II does not pose any major additional threat to Pakistan. On the contrary, it is China that needs to worry about the development of Agni-II.

With this type of nuclear-capable missile, India's nuclear warheads could reach targets inside China. The Chinese side was aware of the China-specific feature of the missile. Meanwhile, Beijing rebuked India for deliberately playing the 'China threat' card as a reason for test-firing Agni-II (Gu 1999: 6). The Chinese side also condemned the Agni-II tests, saying that it was a violation of the UN Security Council resolution 1172 and warned that it might trigger a new arms race in South Asia (*Renmin Ribao* 1999b: 4). A Chinese commentator warned that India's statement regarding China as the target of attack in fact ran counter to Indian leaders' expression of their attitude that China and India did not constitute a threat to each other. As a result, the Chinese said it was difficult to believe in the sincerity of India, which had repeatedly expressed its willingness to improve its relationship with China (Gu 1999: 6).

The Indian side, however, showed no signs of compromising over the development of the nuclear weapons programme, and insisted that it would undertake all necessary steps to ensure it maintained a credible minimum nuclear deterrent. As the then Indian Defence Minister Fernandes said, the test of Agni-II was 'an effort to acquire a credible minimum deterrent needed for India's security' (*The Hindu* 2001b: 1). Indian Prime Minister Vajpayee also said that India would not accept any restraints on its research and development capabilities, and that his government decided 'to maintain the deployment of a deterrent that is both minimum but credible' (*Xinhua* 1998).

Against China's wishes, both the 700-km Agni-I and the 2,000-km range Agni-II have been inducted into the armed forces. Although the Agni-II can reach deep into China, it in fact still does not cover all China's major cities. Therefore, India needed to extend its missile coverage of China, something that would make Indian nuclear strike capability more credible. Around 2002, India began to work on the longer-range Agni-III missile. Although the Agni-III's maiden launch in July 2006 failed, it was followed by three other successful test-firings in April 2007, May 2008, and February 2010.

The new missiles gave a boost to India's nuclear deterrent capability *vis-à-vis* China, as they are capable of striking targets deep inside China, such as Beijing and Shanghai. Although Indian officials have claimed that the missile testing was not country-specific, the Agni-III missile has once again revealed the China-specific nature of India's nuclear strategic concerns. Almost all the Indian media chorused that India had finally achieved credibility in its nuclear deterrent posture *vis-à-vis* China, something which it had been striving towards for quite some time. India has inched closer towards building a 'minimum credible nuclear deterrent' against China since Pokhran II.

Chinese strategic analysts also deemed that the Agni-II and Agni-III are China-specific missiles. However, despite the diplomatic statements, Beijing did not take serious steps to interrupt India's nuclear weapons programme. Beijing also did not respond to the Indian tests by entering into an arms race, one of the major reasons being that China's nuclear and missile arsenal is still in a different league from India's.

It was reported in June 2011 that the Agni-III missile had already been inducted into the armed forces (*The Times of India* 2011a: 13). On 15 November 2011, India successfully test-fired the Agni-IV with a strike range of about 4,000 km. It was followed by a test-fire of the over 5,000-km range Agni-V on 19 April 2012 in a bid to join the super-exclusive ICBM club that counts just the US, Russia, China, France, and the UK as its members. Meanwhile, India would also like to have SLBMs. However, India's stark asymmetry *vis-à-vis* China in terms of delivery capability remains. China already has a wide array of missiles. In the surface-to-surface category, China's arsenal includes the DF-4 (Chinese Surface-to-Surface-3) with a range of 4,850 km, the DF-5/5A (CSS-4) with a 13,000-km range, the DF-31 (under development and tested) with a range of 8,000 km, and the DF-41 with a range of 12,000 km (*The Hindustan Times* 2008a: 10). China also owns the Ju Lang (JL)-1 and is developing the 7,200-km range JL-2 SLBM. Thus, China's nuclear strike ability is still far ahead of India's.

It is true that India needs more time to counter the stark strategic imbalance with China in terms of nuclear and missile arsenals. However, the narrowing of the military asymmetry with China provided a significant boost for India, even if the strike range of India's missiles is still much less than those of Chinese ones. As India moves closer towards building a credible nuclear deterrent against China, it gains more faith in its ability to deal with China without making humiliating concessions.

In other words, although India is still in the process of building and deploying a nuclear arsenal capable of threatening China militarily, India's perception of a 'China threat' seems to have abated. Ironically, an India empowered with a nuclear military force may not be disadvantageous to the development of Sino-Indian relations. Although Chinese missiles can target any major city in India, the Indian side has deemed that it is sufficiently empowered to dissuade China from any aggression. That is why some analysts in India have argued that the development of missiles reflects a strategic mindset that seeks to augment military capability as a way of keeping the peace (*The Hindu* 2008a: 12).

Fortunately, all this activity on the missile front has not adversely affected the overtures of efforts to reduce sources of tension between India and China. However, it has not assuaged apprehensions either in the region or globally. Even before the 1998 nuclear tests, some analysts in China were aware that India's nuclear weapons programme was targeting

China (Ye *et al.* 1997: 430). As India is determined to develop and deploy a credible minimum nuclear deterrent, it has established the ability to strike well beyond its immediate border zone. As a result, India's nuclear capability constitutes a negative factor in China's security environment. In the long run, as India's nuclear strike capability becomes more credible, Beijing will find it imperative to take India's nuclear and missile capabilities more seriously.

India's Status as a Nuclear-Weapon State (NWS)

At least two implications stem from India attaining an identity as an NWS. First, it would help India to break the nuclear monopoly, and share the same privileges as the five nuclear states. Second, it is considered as a step toward making India a world power. Despite the perception and concerns from the 'China threat', another motivation behind India's decision to cross the nuclear threshold is a desire to secure the status of being a major power.

After Pokhran II, India considered itself a fully-fledged nuclear power. However, it seemed more difficult for India to muscle its way into the world nuclear order than it had expected. India's wish to be acknowledged as a *de jure* NWS, alongside the five recognized nuclear powers, was not accepted by the international community.

Great Power Status and India's Nuclear Capability

Some Indians were of the opinion that India shared similar characteristics with China, but its international status was inferior to that of China. The reason, they tended to conclude, was the lack of nuclear weapons and not having UN Security Council membership. As a result, many saw being identified as an NWS as the entry card to the exclusive club of major world powers. The popular logic within India was that if India possesses its own nuclear weapons, it would follow China and other NSWs to be recognized as a major player in the international community and secure higher international status. Robert Ross' study has provided an interesting comparison. He found that Chinese nationalism drives a widespread popular demand for construction of an aircraft carrier and a large blue-water navy, which are seen as traditional symbols of great power status. That is, the desire to be recognized as a great power, rather than security, is the reason behind China's naval ambition (Ross 2009: 46–81). Namely, countries such as China and India tend to go after status symbols of great power, such as aircraft carriers or nuclear weapons to enhance their international standing.

Chinese leaders do in fact believe in the correlation between international status and the possession of nuclear weapons. Deng Xiaoping in the late 1980s argued that were it not for the atomic bomb, the hydrogen bomb, and the satellites, China would not have its present international standing as a great, influential country (Deng 1988). With the same logic, China is aware of India's embracing nuclear weapons as a step towards becoming a great power. However, it has refused to accord India this status as an NWS to prevent India from sharing an international status similar to its own.

The 1998 tests can certainly be read as a signal of New Delhi's ambitions of securing the status of a great power. Although some analysts in New Delhi hoped the possession of nuclear weapons would give India membership of the club of great powers, Pokhran II did not advance the cause of India's putative elevation to permanent membership of the UN Security Council. The possession of nuclear weapons did not automatically grant India any symbolic status, such as a seat on the UN Security Council. Nowadays, nuclear weapons are not the only factor contributing to the status of a great power. The reason is not so difficult to understand if account is taken of Pakistan also having nuclear weapons. Pakistan is the first Islamic state and might be seen as a representative of the Islamic world in the nuclear club, but it is unlikely that Pakistan can ever move up the league table of great powers. That is, India's rise as a world power might be widely expected, but it is not yet fully assured of that status even after becoming a nuclear power (Luce 2006: 262–3).

Part of the opposition to granting nuclear status to India comes from the concern that the recognition of India's status as an NWS would further damage the international nuclear non-proliferation regime. India used to argue that since New Delhi had not signed the CTBT or joined the NPT, it had not broken any international agreements by choosing to test nuclear devices. In addition, India had identified the CTBT and NPT as being discriminatory in character. India argued that the NPT in 1960 granted a monopoly over nuclear weapon powers to various states, including China, and denied this capability to the rest. Even after the nuclear tests of 1998, the Indian side was still reluctant to accede to the nuclear non-proliferation regime. The Indian argument for not signing the CTBT or NPT was as follows: 'If India is not recognised as a nuclear weapon state and does not enjoy an equal status with the five nuclear weapon power states, then it will have to bear the obligations and will not have any benefit' (Mukherjee 1998: 10). Even so, India's Pokhran II nuclear tests still received much criticism which questioned the timing and rationale of the tests. All this while an international campaign went on against India and Pakistan, both of which faced sanctions and international isolation.

The concerns about the international nuclear non-proliferation regime thus provided China with a warranty against India's nuclear weapons. China argued, India's nuclear weapons programme is 'nothing but an outrageous contempt for the common will of the international community for the Comprehensive Ban on nuclear tests and a hard blow to the international efforts to prevent nuclear weapon proliferation' (*The Hindu* 1998i: 1). At the international diplomatic level, China also tried to persuade the international community to put pressure on India to desist from nuclearization on the grounds that India was undermining the global non-proliferation regime.

Given China's controversial role in building the nuclear and missile capabilities of Pakistan, China's condemnation of and concern over India's nuclear programme was unlikely to have much credibility. However, it was not difficult for China to garner international support to halt India's nuclear programme, as India's and Pakistan's nuclear tests did deliver a blow to the nuclear non-proliferation regime. The UN Security Council passed Resolution 1172 on 6 June 1998, calling on India to cease the development of ballistic missiles capable of delivering nuclear weapons. Under the cloak of the resolution, Beijing toughened its opposition to India's nuclear programme, asking India to fulfil all the requirements of Resolution 1172 and to renounce its nuclear weapons programmes.

China was also opposed to any deal that would allow India to maintain a 'minimum nuclear deterrent' in return for joining the CTBT. China has adopted the view that it would be a direct violation of the Security Council Resolution 1172 to negotiate, or even discuss, with India its insistence on maintaining a minimum nuclear deterrence capability (*The Hindu* 1999d: 14). Since India had become able to target China with nuclear weapons, whether the Indian side decided to sign the CTBT was seen as a factor in China's security (Zhang 1999: 15). China asked India to sign and ratify the CTBT and adhere to the NPT unconditionally. As a result, among the five nuclear powers, China was seen as the country that had adopted the toughest line in the wake of the tests. Meanwhile, Chinese academics ruled out the proposal to conclude an agreement that neither side would use nuclear weapons against the other (*Frontline* 1998a).

India was unhappy about China's response, as it argued that Beijing was hardly in a position to preach to India on what it should or should not do, because over the years, China had carried out more than 40 nuclear tests, and even as late as July 1996 had gone on a 'testing spree'.[19] In an equally harsh statement, India referred to China's record of nuclear tests, including those that took place while the CTBT was being finalized, arguing that '[i]f China, with a large nuclear arsenal built with the experience of over 44 tests, felt compelled to test again in July 1996 (when the CTBT was in the final stages) for its own security, then it should be possible to understand the rationale of India conducting a limited number of tests after a 24-year-long period of voluntary restraint' (*The Hindu* 1998j: 1). Thus, the Indians expected the international community would appreciate the compulsion of security behind the nuclear explosion.

To alleviate concerns from the critics, India made a number of moves to demonstrate that it was a responsible nuclear state. These included a voluntary moratorium on testing, offers to convert this moratorium into a formal obligation through negotiations, to abide by some of the provisions of the CTBT, to tighten government control over the export of sensitive materials and technologies and to participate seriously in the Fissile Material Cutoff Treaty (FMCT) negotiations (Dubey 1998: 12). President A.P.J. Abdul Kalam also announced that India would never be a proliferator of weapons of mass destruction even though it was not a signatory to the NPT (*The Hindu* 2005c). Apparently, India tried to convince the international community that India was a responsible nuclear state, and hoped the international community would not use the nuclear non-proliferation concerns as the reason to undermine India's *de jure* status as a nuclear-weapons state.

India–US Nuclear Agreement

Although China had adopted a stubborn position against India's nuclear weapons programme, of greater relevance to New Delhi was the need to modify the reaction of the US, which was leading world opinion in condemnation of India (Singh 2006: 127). In reaction to India's 1974 nuclear test, the US terminated nuclear cooperation with India and proposed the formation of the NSG as a mechanism to control the transfer of nuclear technology. The NSG then prohibited the transfer of nuclear technology to India. The US had successfully thwarted India's plan to conduct nuclear tests in the mid-1990s. In response to the Pokhran II tests, US President Clinton immediately cancelled a scheduled visit to India. The US and a number of its partners also imposed economic sanctions against India, which lasted till 22 September 2001 and was lifted due to the needs of the post-September 11 cooperation on anti-terrorism.

At the same time, however, the Clinton administration realized that Washington had to engage the new *de facto* nuclear power in dialogue. Fourteen rounds of talks on the nuclear issue were held between the US Deputy Secretary Strobe Talbott and Indian External Affairs Minister Jaswant Singh from June 1998 to September 2000.[20] The Indo-American relationship improved over the course of the talks. US President Clinton then visited India in March 2000, and India's then Prime Minister, A.B. Vajpayee, visited Washington in October 2000. Although differences on nuclear proliferation issues were not fully resolved, these engagements allowed the US to gradually recognize India's status as a nuclear state.

India–US relations continued to witness intensive engagement towards a qualitative transformation over the following years. This was well-reflected in their efforts to normalize the nuclear issues between the two countries. In addition, a framework for dialogue was established across a spectrum of issues. There were also intensive interactions at a high level, and joint military exercises increased in frequency.

US President George W. Bush and Indian Prime Minister Vajpayee announced in January 2004 the joint statement 'Next Steps in the Strategic Partnership' (NSSP) that described the vision for the Indo-US strategic relationship, including an expansion of cooperation or dialogue on civilian nuclear activities. The move was termed an important 'milestone' or 'manifestation of the qualitative change' in India–US relations (MEA 2004: 88, 198). In addition, NSSP marked an important shift in the nuclear dialogue between India and the US.

In July 2005, Indian Prime Minister Manmohan Singh and US President George W. Bush ended the long-standing nuclear dispute between the two nations, which had lasted since May 1998, by agreeing to cooperate in the area of civilian nuclear energy. In a joint statement, the Bush administration acknowledged India as 'a responsible state with advanced nuclear technology', and committed itself to seeking agreement from Congress to adjust US laws and policies, and working to adjust international regimes to allow full civil nuclear energy cooperation and trade with India. In exchange, New Delhi agreed to segregate civilian and military nuclear facilities and programmes, and voluntarily place its civilian nuclear facilities under IAEA safeguards. India would assume the same responsibilities and practices as other nuclear-weapons states, continuing India's unilateral moratorium on nuclear testing, and would adopt nuclear non-proliferation measures. The statement became a road map for India–US nuclear cooperation.

India and the US finally reached consensus on the nuclear issue in May 2006 during President Bush's three-day visit to India. The two countries agreed on India's plan to separate its civilian and military nuclear reactors, and to put 14 of the 22 existing nuclear reactors under IAEA safeguards. In return, the US and other countries would relax measures restricting the export of advanced nuclear technology and materials to India. The Bush administration would work towards amending US domestic laws to accommodate the policy change. Thereafter, the US Congress in December 2006 passed the Hyde Act, allowing, in principle, nuclear commerce with India.

In July 2007, the two countries announced the finalization of the deal after months of tough negotiations on a bilateral pact, and unveiled the text of the bilateral pact, called the 123 Agreement. The deal helped bring India out of international nuclear isolation. The separation of civilian and military reactors acknowledged that part of India's nuclear facility was for military use, thus implicitly recognizing India as a nuclear-weapons power, but without conferring *de jure* status given the constraints of the NPT. It is a goal which India had been pursuing for a long time.

In order to implement the Indo-US nuclear deal, the US also helped India to secure approval from the 35-member Board of Governors of the IAEA, which agreed with the India-specific safeguards agreement in August 2008. Fourteen of India's 22 existing and future nuclear reactors would be under the IAEA's inspection. In September 2008, the 45-nation NSG granted India a waiver from the existing rules forbidding nuclear trade with a country that had not signed the NPT. India not only could obtain nuclear fuel and technology from the US, but also could access the global market for nuclear fuel and technology. For example, India soon pencilled in nuclear deals with France and Russia in the following months.

That is, the US played a crucial role in ending India's international nuclear isolation, but did not monopolize civil nuclear cooperation with India.

The long-standing constraints on India's acquisition of nuclear fuel and technology had adversely affected its civilian programme. Due to the lack of fuel, Indian reactors were operating at low capacity. If the US is to lead the world in lifting the curbs on nuclear supplies to India, India will be able to use nuclear energy to meet part of its energy demands to sustain its economic growth. Moreover, under the deal with the US, India's military nuclear facility would remain outside of international purview. That is, both India's economy and military would benefit from the ending of nuclear isolation.

The question that arises is why the US so generously helped India to access the nuclear material and gain nuclear status without joining the CTBT and NPT. If it is argued that the deal in fact strengthened global non-proliferation efforts by bringing India into the international non-proliferation fold, it should be pointed out that in contrast to its efforts to push for a nuclear deal with India, the US refused to have a similar deal with Pakistan. Despite the concerns expressed by the non-proliferation community, the deal faced strong opposition from India's Left-wing parties, which ultimately withdrew their parliamentary support for the government led by Prime Minister Manmohan Singh. The deal was criticized as being nothing more than a cementing factor for an Indo-American alliance, with India becoming a junior partner and ally of the US in its long-term Asian strategy, at the cost of India's independent foreign policy and strategic autonomy. Many analysts also deemed that the aim of the nuclear deal was to cultivate India as a power that could limit China's rise.

As negotiations progressed and India debated the merits and demerits of the nuclear deal in the domestic arena, the Chinese also closely assessed and scrutinized the development. There was a great outpouring of analytical views and judgments on the issue within China. As an implicit objection, Beijing continued to argue that there should be no country-specific exemption in a global nuclear regime. Even though the international community is going to recognize India's nuclear status, the Chinese argued, it should not adopt 'double standards' in dealing with India's nuclear issues (Liu 2006: 18).

The Chinese side further pointed out that the Indo-American deal would help India expand its nuclear arsenal. India would fuel its civilian reactors with imported uranium while conserving native uranium fuel for weapons-grade plutonium production. The transfer of advanced technology would also help India advance its missile programme (Liu 2006: 18). For example, India is believed to have added around 20–30 nuclear warheads in 2010 alone, and holds about 80–100 (*The Times of India* 2011b: 9). Some even estimated that India could produce 50 nuclear warheads per year instead of the previous level of 6–10 warheads (Tian 2006: 53–6, 63). The Chinese also suspected Washington's strategic intention of pushing an Indo-American nuclear deal. It was recalled that as early as 1997, a US report had already suggested that Washington could treat a nuclearized India as a valuable partner and cultivate India as a nuclear power against China (Liu 2006: 19).

In fact, New Delhi also needed Beijing's support at the NSG and IAEA, as China is a key member of the two groups. Indian Prime Minister Manmohan Singh had tried to secure China's support while meeting Chinese President Hu Jintao on the sidelines of the G-8 summit in Sapporo, Japan. China was reluctant to give India a firm assurance in this regard, although the Chinese side expressed its willingness to cooperate with India on civilian nuclear use (*The Hindustan Times* 2008b: 11). The Indian side was optimistically hopeful of China's support, as Indian Prime Minister Singh said that he had 'a strong feeling that when the matter comes before the relevant international fora, China will not be a problem' (*The Asian Age* 2008: 3).

Contrary to India's optimistic expectation, however, China made a last-minute objection to India's case at the NSG meeting in September 2008, trying to boycott the resolution of lifting the nuclear embargo on India. The US President, George W. Bush, then made a phone call to the Chinese President, Hu Jintao, to persuade China to compromise on the issue. The Chinese Ambassador to India was also recalled to India's Ministry of External Affairs at midnight for the issue. When New Delhi protested against China's stand in the matter, China insisted that it did not present a hurdle for New Delhi to obtain the unanimous approval of the NSG. This again demonstrated that Beijing and New Delhi did not share a common understanding on certain issues related to their international status and security concerns.

Finally, with the assistance of the US, India obtained some kind of formal recognition of its *de facto* status as a nuclear-weapons state. The psychological advantage that nuclear status would confer is also important for India when dealing with China. The acquisition of the nuclear identity brought India a little closer to being treated on a par with China in terms of its international position.

Nuclear Impact on China–India Relations

To highlight the nuclear issues in China–India relations, this chapter illustrated that China's nuclear capability against India has been a source of India's 'China threat' perception, and contributed to developing the asymmetry of the threat perceptions between the two countries. Moreover, India's nuclear tests and weapons programme could be seen as one of the most dramatic steps adopted by India to reduce the asymmetry in the perception of threat between China and India.

India's nuclear tests of 1998 brought about a new phase in China–India relations. The China factor played a significant role in India's decision to develop nuclear weapons, and the threat to India's security from China was identified by the Indian side as the major motivation for its Pokhran II nuclear tests. Beijing was offended by the series of anti-China statements that had emanated from New Delhi and India's references to the 'China threat' in its initial justification of nuclear tests. On the other hand, India was upset by Beijing's condemnation of the tests and its insistence that India should roll back its nuclear programme and sign the NPT. China opposed acceptance of India's minimum deterrence demand and urged India to renounce its nuclear weapons and join the non-proliferation treaty. The tensions between China and India have been further compounded by the nuclear issue.

It is not easy to estimate the economic and social cost of the nuclear programme, but politically, India has successfully withstood international pressure and sanctions, and has almost been accepted as a fully-fledged nuclear power. No matter whether the subcontinent might be more secure as a result of the nuclear developments or not, India did gain some benefit, including a strategic balance *vis-à-vis* China as well as an enhancement in India's international standing. As C. Raja Mohan has pointed out, 'The new sense of self-confidence *vis-à-vis* China and the prospect of an inevitable strategic parity with Beijing allowed New Delhi to approach its bilateral problems with China in a more practical manner' (Mohan 2007: 1025). Being a nuclear state, India's strength and identity has changed; it has become a more resolute power now, compared to what it was during the years of non-alignment.

The shared understanding is that India's nuclear weapons development has helped reduce the strategic gap between China and India because the nuclear tests and subsequent weapons programme have given India more military strength and self-confidence. Especially, the Indian side has seldom restated the worsening security situation that justified its need for acquiring a nuclear deterrent. However, the asymmetry of the threat perception between the two countries still remains and conditions China–India relations.

In addition, it should be also noted that China still does not worry much about the possibility that India itself presents a serious challenge to China. China is concerned with India's ensuing attempts to maintain a credible nuclear deterrent and to secure a *de jure* nuclear power status, but it feels confident that China's overall strength remains greater than India's. Even though China adhered to a hardline policy towards India's nuclear programme, in fact, it did not take any apparent actions to block India's initiatives. What worries China is India's improved security ties with the US. Since the US must also view China as a potential adversary, there would be a growing convergence of American and Indian objectives in dealing with China.

Notes

1. For example, during the visit to the UK in December 1964, Indian Prime Minister Shastri stated at a press conference that nuclear powers should discuss some kind of guarantee which was needed for the non-nuclear countries. For a detailed analysis, see Noorani (1967: 490–502).
2. For a brief account of China's no-first-use policy, see Kamath (2011: 65–77).
3. For more analysis regarding security dilemma in China–India relations, see Dittmer (2001: 897–906), Garver (2002a: 1–38), and Holslag (2009: 811–40).
4. For Indian government's statement, see *The New York Times* (1975: 1).
5. T.N. Kaul, a senior Indian diplomat had recalled that Indian scientists were capable of producing a cheap atom bomb in 1957, but the then Prime Minister Jawaharlal Nehru did not give them the green light. See, Kaul (1998: 10).
6. See, for example, *Radio Peace and Progress* (1979).
7. For detailed reports, see *Monterey Institute of International Studies* (1999, 2000).
8. See Chinese Foreign Ministry spokesman Zhu Bangzao's remarks in Ram (1998b).

9. The statement is available at http://www.people.com.cn/GB/shizheng/3586/20010809/531588.html (accessed 12 August 2013).

10. See Iftikhar Ahmed Khan's interview with *Pingkuo Jihpao* (*Apple Daily*), Hong Kong, 4 October 2001, available at http://www.renminbao.com/rmb/articles/2001/10/4/16238.html (accessed 12 August 2013).

11. For an analysis of New Delhi's motivations to conduct nuclear tests in 1998, see Synnott (1999: 12–23) and Perkovich (1999: 404–24).

12. For the text of Vajpayee's letter to Clinton, see *The New York Times*, (1998: A 12).

13. Foreign Ministry spokesman Zhu Bangzao's statement, in Ram (1998b).

14. See, for example, 'The Chinese Embassy Responds', in *The Washington Post*, 30 May, 1999, p. B06.

15. See 'Foreign Ministry News Briefings', *Beijing Review*, 5 July 1999, p. 15. These five principles are mutual respect for sovereignty and territorial integrity, mutual non-aggression, non-interference in each other's internal affairs, equality and mutual benefit, and peaceful coexistence.

16. See Chinese Vice Foreign Minister Wang Yi's statement, in *The Times of India*, 4 October 2002.

17. In December 1996 when Chinese President Jiang Zemin visited India, a new diplomatic initiative was taken as China and India agreed to establish 'a constructive partnership of cooperation oriented towards the twenty-first century' (*mian xiang ershi yi shiji de jianshexing hezuo huoban guanxi*) as the goal of developing bilateral relations.

18. See Qian Feng, '*Yindu, shei dui Zhongguo zui qiang ying*'(Who are the most hard-line figures towards China in India?), *Renmin Wan* (People's website), 5 April 2001. <http://www.people.com.cn/GB/junshi/60/20010405/433542.html>.

19. See, for example, the statement issued by the BJP senior Vice-President, Jana Krishnamurthi, in *The Hindu* (1998c: 11).

20. For an account of this dialogue, see Talbott (2004).

2 The Tibet Issue in Sino-Indian Relations

SINCE THE 1950s, Tibet has been a nettlesome issue in Sino-Indian relations. It may have seemed that the issue was less controversial than other delicate problems, such as border disputes and the Sino-Pakistani military cooperation, because New Delhi had officially recognized Tibet as being part of China since 1954. Furthermore, neither China nor India wants to clash directly on the Tibet issue and so they have reached certain agreements over Tibet's status. However, the issue of Tibet remains unsettled, and this has resulted in the accumulation of a culture of distrust between China and India.

For China, the Tibet issue is an internal matter in which no foreign country has any right to interfere. The Chinese have argued that India has officially recognized Chinese claims over Tibet since 1954 when the two countries signed an agreement regarding trade and intercourse between the Tibet region and India. Therefore, if India keeps its promise to adhere to the Five Principles of Peaceful Coexistence, as the Chinese believe they should, the Tibet issue will not come up in the agenda of Sino-Indian relations.[1] However, the interactions over the last decade seemed to be against such an expectation. India's sincerity in honouring its commitment is frequently questioned by the Chinese side, which has repeatedly expressed concerns about the anti-China activities of exiled Tibetans in India.[2]

As will be suggested in this chapter, however, the Chinese have failed to engage India in a worthwhile dialogue on the Tibet issue, especially regarding India's treatment of the exiled Tibetan leader, the Dalai Lama, and the Tibetan government-in-exile. Given its own considerations, India cannot always conform to China's demand to stand away from the Tibet issue. More significantly, the Tibet issue is identified as strategic leverage against China. As the Indian side is still obsessed with the security threat from China, the Tibet issue is one of the bargaining chips India can use when dealing with China. India's particular role in the Tibet issue, especially India's hosting of the Dalai Lama and tens of thousands of his followers, gives New Delhi a say in the matter.

Not surprisingly, given that China sees Indian involvement in Tibetan issues—even sympathy or moral support towards the Tibetans—as a misconduct that breaches the spirit of the Five Principles of Peaceful Coexistence and interferes in China's internal affairs, the Tibet issue began to undermine the mutual trust between China and India.

In fact, New Delhi has been very cautious of playing the Tibet card against China. Many Indian strategists have acknowledged the strategic significance of the Tibet issue. Given the asymmetrical perception of threat, however, India has not been confident enough to use the leverage offered by the Tibet issue, as the Indians are worried China will retaliate against India. As a result, India's Tibetan policy has been characterized by ambivalence. Mostly, New Delhi avoids angering Beijing by limiting the Tibetans' anti-China protests in India, and endorses China's official claims over Tibet by not supporting Tibetan independence in public. On the other hand, it sees the benefits of making Tibet an autonomous region, and allows the Tibetan government-in-exile to operate in India. Furthermore, India is reluctant to comply with China's demands to abandon its influence over the Tibetan question. As India is still concerned with a possible threat from China to its security, the Tibet issue is an important source of leverage against China.

The Chinese are not satisfied with India's dealing on and attitude to the Tibetan question, but they also expect to marginalize the Tibet issue in Sino-Indian relations in order to avoid India's involvement. Beijing's continued suspicion about India's sincerity and intentions on the Tibetan question has contributed to the formation of a culture of distrust between the two sides, which is also one of the features of Sino-Indian relations. Unless Beijing and the Tibetans reach a final agreement on Tibet's relations with China, India's role and involvement in the Tibetan question will still be seen as a thorn in Beijing's side.

To illustrate further the significance of the Tibet issue in Sino-Indian relations, this chapter will analyse China's concerns regarding Tibet, and discuss the peculiar role the Tibet issue plays. This chapter will then delve into India's debate over playing the Tibet card against China. Although

China and India have reached some consensus, this chapter will conclude that the issue is still far from being completely resolved. The Tibet issue will continue to emerge and affect China–India relations.

India's and China's Tibetan Questions

Since the signing of the 'Seventeen-Point Agreement for the Peaceful Liberation of Tibet' on 23 May 1951, Tibet has been under the control of the Chinese authorities. However, the Chinese side failed to settle the Tibetan question completely, as Beijing did not forge a benign relationship with the Tibetans after the so-called 'peaceful liberation'. The Tibetan leader—the Dalai Lama—and his followers, chose to go into exile in India instead of cooperating with Beijing after the 1959 uprising. With India's consent, a Tibetan government-in-exile was established in India in 1960, aiming to call into question China's claims and its control over Tibet.

Traditionally, Tibet was a society that comprised the unification of state and Tibetan Buddhism; the Dalai Lama is seen as the incarnation of the Buddhist God of Compassion. Therefore, the Dalai Lama has more charisma for the religious-minded Tibetans than the atheist communist regime of China. Thus, the aim of Beijing's policy is to eradicate the influence of the Dalai Lama in the Tibet region. Unsatisfied with the Dalai Lama's stance and policy, since 1993, Beijing has refused to hold official dialogues with him on the grounds that he was not sincere in the dialogue, but aimed to split Tibet from the motherland. Informal contact was also severed after November 1998. Currently, Tibet's status and relationship with China are still debated in the international arena, and remain a sensitive and intractable issue for China's diplomacy.

As regards the ownership of Tibet, the Chinese argue that the central government of China has continuously exercised sovereignty over Tibet since the region was officially incorporated into the territory of China's Yuan Dynasty (1271–1368). The Chinese government termed its military march into Tibet in 1950 as 'peaceful liberation' (SCIO 1992, CPC Tibet Autonomous Regional Party Committee and People's Government of the Tibet Autonomous Region 2001: 6).

However, the opposite view has been successfully promoted outside China. The Tibetans and their supporters claim that before the PLA marched into Tibet, Tibet had been an independent state. Repudiating China's claims over Tibet, the Tibetan side argues that the traditional relationship between China and Tibet was a religious priest–patron one, which was established during China's Yuan Dynasty (The Government of Tibet in Exile 1993). Such a relationship, from the Tibetan perspective, was mainly of a religious nature and did not suggest that Tibet was a vassal state of the Chinese (Shakya 1999: xxiii).

Aware of the power gap between Beijing and the Tibetan government-in-exile, the Dalai Lama chose an indirect approach to challenge Beijing's control over Tibet by accusing China of damaging Tibet's ethnic culture, religious belief, and ecological environment. The Dalai Lama also rejected the Chinese accusation that he was splitting Tibet from the 'motherland', saying that he called only for 'self-rule' or 'high degree autonomy' in Tibet, which was inscribed in China's constitution. In other words, the Dalai Lama has agreed to end activities aimed at establishing Tibet's independence, but he has demanded that Beijing should grant 'authentic' autonomy to Tibet.[3] As early as 1987, the Dalai Lama proposed a Five-Point Peace Plan at a Congressional Human Rights Caucus in Washington DC. The aim of the plan was to make Tibet an international peace zone, calling for an end to China's use of Tibet as a site for nuclear weapons production and the dumping of nuclear waste. Later, the plan was repeated at the European Parliament in Strasbourg, France. The Dalai Lama stressed that the aim was to preserve Tibet's unique culture and religion. Although under great pressure, the Dalai Lama has strictly adhered to a policy of non-violence in his approach to Beijing.

However, the Chinese have doubted the sincerity of the Dalai Lama's suggestion for the 'genuine autonomy' of Tibet within China, partly because the Dalai Lama still refuses to accept the argument that Tibet has been part of China for several hundred years. A Chinese diplomat argued that if the Dalai Lama does not recognize that Tibet was part of China before 1951, then the logical consequence would be as follows: 'The action of the People's Liberation Army in 1951 was an illegal aggression; Tibet now is an "occupied country"; the Dalai Lama has been forced to agree that Tibet can be within China; and, finally, Tibetans have the definite right to declare Tibetan independence when the opportunity arises in the future' (Mao 2008: 13).

Furthermore, Beijing suspects that the 'genuine autonomy' proposed by the Tibetan government-in-exile would be the first step on the path towards independence (Mao 2008: 13). Despite irregularly scheduled contact and dialogue between Beijing and Dharamsala, there is no breakthrough on the Tibetan question.

China's 'Liberation' of Tibet

During the early 1950s, China's 'liberation' of Tibet appeared to be the only issue that might worsen Sino-Indian relations. In October 1950, Beijing dispatched troops into Tibet to 'liberate' the region. The Tibetan authority was then compelled to send representatives to Beijing to negotiate its status and relationship with the new China. On 23 May 1951, the Chinese and Tibetan deputations signed the 'Seventeen-Point Agreement for the Peaceful Liberation of Tibet'. The agreement stated that the Tibetan people would return to 'the big family of the Motherland', Beijing would not alter the existing political system in Tibet, and promised that the Tibetan people would have the right to exercise national regional autonomy under the leadership of China's central government.

Chinese military action against Tibet came as a shock to the Indians. When India became independent in 1947, it inherited the existing treaty rights and obligations of British India regarding Tibet (Sandhu 1988: 85). It also wanted to continue British policy toward Tibet, namely, treating Tibet as an autonomous buffer region between India and China, while recognizing Chinese suzerainty, but not sovereignty over Tibet (Norbu 1997: 1079). Although the Indian leadership did not give a detailed definition of the 'suzerainty', the core element of its Tibetan policy was to maintain Tibet's autonomy.[4] India then sent several notes to the Chinese government to lodge protests about the situation in Tibet.

Despite these diplomatic gestures, however, India was not willing to confront China over the issue. The Indian Prime Minister, Jawaharlal Nehru, said in Parliament on 12 February 1951, that he would not allow the event to affect India's policy or desire to maintain friendly relations with China. He even had no intention of letting the development affect India's China policy in general, and the policy regarding the admission of China into the United Nations in particular (Gopal 1993: 335).

Despite the diplomatic protest, Nehru was unwilling to assist Tibetan independence at the expense of Sino-Indian relations. It seemed that Nehru, from the beginning, believed that China would take possession of the whole of Tibet and no other external force, including India, could change that. In November 1950, Nehru suggested that 'it may be taken for granted that China will take possession, in a political sense at least, of the whole of Tibet. There is no likelihood whatsoever of Tibet being able to resist this or stop it. It is equally unlikely that any foreign power can prevent it. We cannot do so' (Gopal 1993: 343). He then denied the possibility of Indian military intervention in Tibet by arguing that India had neither the resources nor the inclination to send armed assistance to Tibet (Gopal 1993: 335).

India's policy of non-intervention in the Tibet issue was strengthened when China's takeover of Tibet was legalized by the conclusion of the 'Seventeen-Point Agreement'. India soon accepted China's claim over Tibet by refusing to sponsor the Tibetan appeal to the UN against the PLA's invasion. In order to solve India's inherited historical rights regarding Tibet, such as the deployment of military guards, China and India began negotiations in December 1953. The two countries finally signed the agreement regarding trade and intercourse between India and Tibet in April 1954, setting up the legal framework for India's relations with post-'liberation' Tibet. India finally agreed to accept China's sovereignty over Tibet while using the term the 'Tibet region of China'.

India's reluctance to become involved in the China–Tibet imbroglio was still clear in 1956 when the Dalai Lama and the Panchen Lama visited India to attend the celebrations of the 2,500th anniversary of the birth of the Buddha. The young Dalai Lama was considering seeking exile in India. Aware of the situation, Chinese Premier Zhou Enlai flew to India to persuade him to return to Tibet. Meanwhile, Nehru told Zhou that he would not tempt the Dalai Lama to stay in India, but he would grant him asylum if he asked for it. In fact, Nehru himself urged the Dalai Lama to return to Tibet and cooperate with Beijing on the basis of the 'Seventeen-Point Agreement'. Nehru also told the Dalai Lama that India was not prepared to support Tibet's independence (The Fourteenth Dalai Lama 1990: 56). The crisis then ended when the Dalai Lama agreed to return to Tibet.

India's reluctant attitude and caution did not prevent the Tibetan question from being a controversial issue between China and India, and the Tibet issue continued to test Sino-Indian friendship. In May 1959, the PLA moved into Lhasa to quell the most serious revolt since the 'peaceful liberation', and there were rumours among the Tibetans that the PLA would harm the Dalai Lama. As a result, the Dalai Lama and his associates decided to escape from Tibet. With foreign assistance, especially of the US Central Intelligence Agency (CIA), the Dalai Lama successfully fled to India and asked for political asylum (The Fourteenth Dalai Lama 1990: 151–7). New Delhi soon granted asylum to the Dalai Lama and his followers. Nehru's daughter, Indira Gandhi, was involved in setting up an all-party Central Relief Committee for the Tibetan refugees (Adams and Whitehead 1997: 176–7).

India was still not willing to challenge China over the Tibet issue; hence, India abstained from voting on the UN General Assembly resolution that criticized the Chinese for the violation of human rights in Tibet. The Indian government hoped that such an abstention would facilitate eventual conciliatory efforts towards a peaceful solution of the Tibetan problem.

However, the Dalai Lama's exile sparked a wave of sympathy towards Tibet and condemnation of China among the Indian public. In order to find a peaceful resolution to the Tibet issue, Nehru tried to play the role of mediator and requested Beijing to send the Panchen Lama, the second highest ranking leader in Tibet, or any other Chinese representative, to come to India to meet the Dalai Lama and discuss the situation of Tibet (Sandhu 1988: 114). However, Beijing rejected the proposal. To Beijing, the Tibet issue was entirely an internal issue, and China was not prepared to allow a third party to become involved.

Furthermore, China was very displeased with India's condemnation in the wake of the Dalai Lama's exile. It began to suspect that the Indian government had masterminded the event. Earlier, China had used to accuse the 'imperialist, Chiang bandit clan, and foreign reactionary' of splitting Tibet. But Mao Zedong then ordered the Chinese official publicists also identify 'Indian expansionists' as one of the forces that wished to separate Tibet from China (Wu 1999: 198). This was the first warning that Chinese leaders had changed their minds about India in the wake of the deterioration of the Tibetan question. However, China also held the possibility of maintaining an amiable and stable relationship with India, because it did not want India to become another security concern along the border.

The 1959 uprising in Tibet resulted in the exodus of the Dalai Lama and his followers across the Himalayas, and later the establishment of the Tibetan government-in-exile in Dharamsala, a town in Himachal Pradesh, the northern state of India. Although the Indian government officially regards Tibet as a part of China, there is continuing speculation in China regarding India's sincerity. In contradiction to its promise that anti-China political activities by the Tibetans are not permitted on Indian soil, India has not prevented the exiled Tibetans from running a government-in-exile in Dharamsala, which continues to mount international pressure to deny China's rules and claims over Tibet. It is also self-deceptive to suggest that the Dalai Lama is merely treated as a religious leader, because he is indeed the pivot of the Tibetan government-in-exile, not to mention that the Dalai Lama's status in the international society was further promoted when he received the Nobel Peace Prize in 1989.

This is why China maintains that India has failed to observe the Five Principles of Peaceful Coexistence and its promise regarding Tibet. From the Chinese point of view, since India has recognized Chinese sovereignty over Tibet, no matter how the Indian side tries to justify providing accommodation to the exiled Tibetan group, India has violated the agreement. China has repeatedly expressed its concerns about the anti-China activities by the exiled Tibetans in India, as the Dalai Lama continues to campaign for Tibetan rights from India where the government-in-exile is based.

Today, there are more than 1,30,000 Tibetan refugees rehabilitated in India. The presence of the Tibetan government-in-exile and the Tibetan diaspora on Indian soil give India a peculiar role and position on the Tibet issue, which cannot be replaced by any other country, irrespective of China's views on the matter. Any activities by the Dalai Lama and the government-in-exile will inevitably remind Beijing that it is India that shelters the 'anti-China' Tibetans.

India's Peculiar Role in the Tibet Issue

Although China seems to have sufficient confidence to quell any threat emanating from nationalism or religious fundamentalism and the challenge to its territorial integrity, the outcome has not always been as it has expected. To a great extent, the international assistance to the exiled Tibetans has aggravated the existing pressures emanating from Tibet's disaffections. With the approach of 'non-violence' and an emphasis on Tibet's unique culture, the Dalai Lama and his Tibetan government-in-exile have successfully mounted an international propaganda campaign against China's claims and rule over Tibet. The overseas visits of Chinese leaders are often marred by protests organized by pro-Tibetan independence groups, especially when the leaders travel to India or to Western countries. The Tibetan demonstrators always gain a significant amount of international publicity, while China's image and 'face' are badly tarnished by the media coverage. The award of the Nobel Peace Prize in 1989 to the Dalai Lama was seen in China as part of the international conspiracy. Therefore, the Chinese used to attribute their failure to crack down on the Tibetan separatist sentiment to the internationalization of the Tibet issue and to foreign interference. In the eyes of the Chinese, the Tibet issue is not a product of Tibetan nationalism, but has been incubated by anti-China forces. China argued that there was no such word as 'independence' in the Tibetan vocabulary before the British invasion, and stressed that foreign intervention in Tibet was at the root of the Tibet problem (*PTI* 2004a). The Chinese side has also criticized the international pressure promoting negotiations between the Chinese government and the Dalai Lama, arguing it represents interference in China's internal affairs and the use of Tibet as leverage against China. Not surprisingly, China has asked other countries to respect China's sovereignty and territorial integrity and not to provide a platform for the Dalai Lama to conduct anti-China activities.

In an attempt to refurbish China's image abroad, China's State Council has issued many policy papers on Tibet, including *Tibet—Its Ownership and the Human Rights Situation* (1992), *New Progress in Human Rights in the Tibet Autonomous Region* (1998), *The Development of Tibetan Culture* (2000), *Tibet's March Toward Modernization* (2001), *Ecological Improvement and Environmental Protection in Tibet* (2003), *Regional Ethnic Autonomy in Tibet* (2004), *Protection and Development of Tibetan Culture* (2008), and *Sixty Years Since Peaceful Liberation of Tibet* (2011). The frequency and length of the White Papers on Tibet highlight China's concerns about the Tibetan question, and China's eagerness to win international understanding to reverse the current sympathetic trend towards the Dalai Lama and the Tibetan government-in-exile.

In general, China is more concerned with the US support for the Dalai Lama's activities than with the support offered by other foreign countries.[5] China saw the US policy towards Tibet as part of America's strategy of containing China. However, unlike other foreign countries, India plays a peculiar role in the Tibetan question, which cannot be ignored.

As China saw India's sheltering the Dalai Lama as a breach of the spirit of the Five Principles of Peaceful Coexistence to interfere in China's internal affairs, the Tibet issue began to shatter the mutual trust between China and India. In retaliation to India's Tibet policy, China encouraged the Naga and Mizo rebellions in northeast India. The overt support continued until the late 1970s.

On the other hand, India has been cautious in handling the Tibet issue. In October 1987, when a riot broke out in Tibet and caused the death of at least six Tibetans, India soon declared that the disturbance was an internal affair of China and decided not to exploit China's strategic vulnerability. The Indian army then took precautionary measures on the Ladakh–Tibet border to prevent the arrival of any refugees. A spokesman from India's Ministry of External Affairs stated that India did not recognize any government-in-exile and considered the Dalai Lama a religious leader and temporal head of the Tibetans. The major reason for this policy stance was that border talks were scheduled for November that year (Ali 1988: 13–14, Delfs 1987: 8–10).

In fact, despite its supposed commitment to the above policy, the Indian side is very reluctant to comply with China's demands on the Tibet issue or to accept China's policy towards Tibet. In addition to the role as host to the exiled Tibetans, there are several sound reasons for India to pay more attention to the Tibet issue in many of its actions, sometimes at the risk of angering China.

First, it is religious sentiment that inspires Indians' sympathy for the Tibetans. Ancient India was the birthplace of Tibetan Buddhism, which has been the pillar of Tibetan politics and society. The Indians see Buddhism as one of India's religions, and some Hindus view it as part of their 'religious geography' and 'the repository of lost Indian treasures and culture' (Norbu 1997: 1089). The Dalai Lama himself has also described Hinduism and Tibetan Buddhism as twin sisters (*The Hindu* 2001i: 9), and has suggested that India and Tibet are bound more by spiritual relations than by political ones (*The Hindu* 2002f). That is, while some Western countries are fascinated by the mystical element of Tibetan Buddhism, it is the emotion of religious kinship that affects the Indians when dealing with the Tibet issue. Therefore, the Indian government cannot ignore the Indian public's support and sympathy towards the exiled Tibetans and is not able to crack down on all exiled Tibetan's activities as Beijing wishes, even though those activities are seen as unfriendly or anti-China by the Chinese side. However, China denounces the claimed cultural significance between India and Tibet. The Chinese side argue that India has exaggerated the India–Tibet affinity (Yi *et al.* 1997: 445).

Second, India is a democracy which allows the free expression of a variety of opinions. In India, opinions regarding the Tibet issue range from those seeking Tibet's independence to those who exhort the government to rein in the Tibetan government-in-exile. This freedom of expression is integral to the Indian ethos. No matter how uncomfortable and uneasy the Chinese government feels about the pro-Tibetan voice and the movement of freedom of Tibetan protestors, the Indian government cannot restrict the freedom to voice support for the Tibetan independence movement. Nor can the Indian government ban the opposition and retired officials from engaging with the so-called 'Dalai clique'.[6] Rejecting the attitude of the Chinese authorities, senior Indian diplomats have argued that it is impossible for India 'to abandon its democratic norms to meet Chinese concerns relating to the presence of the Dalai Lama' (Ranganathan and Khanna 2000: 176). Indian parliamentary politics have also opened a door for the Tibetan lobby. It has been said that the Dalai Lama's advisers have supported certain Indian politicians at the time of elections (Swamy 2001: 25). The Chinese apparently understand that the freedom of expression is guaranteed in India, but they cannot accept that the right is extended to the Tibetan exiles as well (*The Times of India* 2008a).

Third, and perhaps most importantly, India's ambivalent Tibet policy stems from its concerns over the geo-strategic implications of China's takeover of Tibet. Explaining the strategic importance of Tibet, George Ginsburgs and Michael Mathos suggested, 'He who holds Tibet dominates the Himalayan piedmont; he who dominates the Himalayan piedmont threatens the Indian subcontinent and may well have all of South Asia within his reach, and with that all of Asia' (Ginsburgs and Mathos 1964: 210). The argument may appear simplistic, but reflects Tibet's geopolitical significance. If Tibet is controlled by an unfriendly force, it is believed to pose a direct threat to India. Unfortunately, China seemed to be such a case. China's acquisition of Tibet made it India's biggest neighbour, and India's defeat in the 1962 war with China proved that the Chinese acquisition of Tibet was a menace to India's security. The Dalai Lama has also reminded India that since China's occupation of Tibet, the Tibet–India border has become one of the most fortified regions between the two countries (*PTI* 2004b). By the late 1970s, the Indians were worried about a two-front attack from Tibet in the east and Pakistan in the west.

India's security concern about the threat from Tibet is heightened by the fact that China has built up a military arsenal in Tibet. Once a militarily weak buffer zone between empires, Tibet has now been militarized to the point of containing at least 1,20,000 Chinese troops and 10 military airfields (Wang 1998c: 128). In 2008, Indian Army Chief General Deepak Kapoor admitted that China's military modernization and improvement of the infrastructure in Tibet could affect India's security in the long term (*The Indian Express* 2008a). Although India is concerned with the Chinese military build-up in Tibet, China has maintained that its military deployments in Tibet are not open to discussion.

Another factor of concern to India about Tibet is the emplacement of Chinese nuclear-tipped missiles in Tibet. Of the countries bordering Tibet, India might be the possible target of China's nuclear weapons. These missiles are capable of reaching all Indian cities, and thus Tibet is considered a serious threat to India (Kanwal 2000: 1591–628).

The same strategic considerations over Tibet's geostrategic value made the Indian side watchful of China's Grand Western Development project. Although China attempted to give an economic colour to the infrastructure development in this region, the Indian side expressed concerns over the security implications. Some Indian strategic analysts saw China's mega-infrastructure build-up in the Tibet region as 'tentacles' that not only strengthened China's grip on these restive regions and enabled it to further exploit natural resources, but also advance its capability to move troops and weapons stockpiled in its other neighbouring military regions.[7] They argued that these strategic links, including the rebuilding of the Lhasa–Beijing Highway, would double China's military deployment and multiply the missile deployment in Tibet. Therefore, they concluded that China's Tibet-related western development would affect India's strategic environment and increase India's vulnerability (Kapila 2001). Since China and India are still far from being friendly partners, any Chinese move to consolidate its hold on Tibet serves to aggravate the Indian strategic analysts.

Although the Indian side remains very concerned about China's takeover of Tibet, from Nehru's administration onward, the Indian government has clearly acknowledged the fact that Tibet is under China's control and it is very difficult for India alone to help Tibet split from China. In addition, the Indian leaders need to take account of India's own domestic situation if India wants to accommodate Tibet's independence. Like China's far-flung communities of Tibet and Xinjiang, India's Northeast and Kashmir are it's weak spots. China was accused of sponsoring Naga and Mizo insurgencies in India's Northeast by the late 1970s. It also backed Pakistan's stand on the Kashmir issue. Any Indian public support for Tibetan independence would possibly result in China taking revenge by interfering in India's domestic discord, especially the agitation in Kashmir and the northeast region. Obviously, China will not allow the secessionist movement of the Tibetans to succeed, and will not weaken its hold on Tibet. Even if making Tibet a security buffer would serve India's interests, the Indian side has to be very cautious about any mention of Tibet's independence. As a result, although India has a particular role and special relationship with Tibet, the Indian government has avoided supporting Tibetan independence in public.

Tibet's Significance to China

The Tibetans have won international sympathy and garnered a certain amount of support against Beijing. No matter how great the international pressure is, however, China finds it unacceptable to give up its claims to Tibet. Explaining briefly why Tibet is significant for China's territorial integrity, the then Chinese President Jiang Zemin said that Tibet was of importance to China's grand western development strategy, national unity, social stability, and the unification and security of the motherland, and is related to China's national image and international struggle.[8] In sum, this statement reflects how the Tibet issue is associated with China's concerns regarding state sovereignty, territorial integrity, and peripheral security.

According to Chinese President Hu Jintao, Beijing's conflict with the 'Dalai clique' is not an ethnic problem, a religious problem, or a human rights problem. He claimed that it was a problem concerning the need to safeguard national unification or to avoid splitting the motherland (*The Associated Press* 2008). The Tibet Autonomous Region (TAR) covers an area of 1.2 million sq km, accounting for one-eighth of the total area of China and one-third the size of India. It is the second-largest of China's autonomous regions and provinces after Xinjiang. The 'Greater Tibet' proposed by the Tibetan government-in-exile covers even larger areas, including the TAR, the whole of Qinghai Province, half of Sichuan Province, one-third of Gansu Province, one-fourth of Yunnan Province, and one-fifth of the Xinjiang Uyghur Autonomous Region. It spans about 2.4 million sq km, nearly one quarter of China's territory (Mao 2008: 13). No Chinese leader could afford the political cost of losing such a vast area of land, particularly under the pressure of Chinese nationalism.

China also cannot ignore Tibet's geographical significance to its security when considering the Tibetan question. In fact, modern history demonstrates that the internationalization of the Tibet issue is due to its geographical significance, which has turned this region into a point of contention between various powers since the mid-eighteenth century. With an average elevation of 4,000 m above sea level and sharing borders with India, Nepal, Bhutan, and Myanmar, the enormous Tibet region has been seen by the Chinese as a backdoor and adds immense depth to China's defence. Conversely, if Tibet is out of Chinese control, China's 'new' southwest frontier would recede approximately 1,000 km from the present Tibet–India border, leaving China's southwest region open to greater external danger. Chinese experts on Tibet believe that, were Tibet to gain independence, it would ally itself with India. As a result, the Chinese argue, the Indian military would advance, thus posing an immediate threat to the Chinese heartland 'without firing a shot' (Wang 1998c: 140). Were this to happen, China's soft underbelly of vulnerability would be exposed to foreign powers.

China's security concerns to its west have intensified since the US launched the global war against the Taliban regime in Afghanistan in 2001. Some neighbouring Central Asian states are forging new strategic ties with the US while India, Pakistan, and even Nepal have been cooperating with the US. Against this background, Tibet's strategic value becomes more apparent because it still secures a strategic depth for the Chinese heartland. From the Chinese perspective, they have to prevent Tibet from sliding into the embrace of other countries whereupon it could be used as a cat's paw to check China.

The Chinese have tried to quash the Tibetan separatists' sentiment with a mixed approach: a blend of economic development and religious repression. China expected that its 'strike hard' campaign, combined with economic development, could reduce the Dalai Lama's magnetism and inspiration to the Tibetan people and their desire for independence. However, it resulted in the Tibetan government-in-exile accusing China of secretly adopting a Nazi-style 'final solution' to end Tibetan resistance to China's rule. The plans allegedly include further flooding of Tibet with Chinese settlers and manipulation of senior religious circles to create divisions among Tibetans overseas (*Far Eastern Economic Review* 1993: 14).

It would appear, however, that in the final analysis, China's policy regarding Tibet has not been very successful. For example, the 2008 Beijing Olympic torch relay was hampered by Tibetan protesters. Until now, Tibetans have been fleeing to India from Tibet every year. Beijing remains unable to win the hearts of the Tibetan people. Although China claims that it has broken the Tibetan independence movement, the spokesman for the Ministry of National Defence, Hu Changming, admitted that China faces an independence movement in Tibet that forms a major security threat to China (*PTI* 2009). After six decades of rule in Tibet, aspirations of Tibetan separatists and the ethnic tension between the Hans and the Tibetans continue to cause concern to Beijing. In March 2008, the demonstration for the 49th anniversary of the failed 1959 Tibetan uprising against Beijing's rule led to the most serious and violent riots in the region for decades. Since 27 February 2009, nearly 100 people in Tibet have immolated themselves to protest Chinese rule (*International Campaign for Tibet* 2012). These events highlight how the Tibet issue continues to cause concern to Beijing even though it seems unlikely that Tibet could split away from China in the near future.

Renewed Challenges

China–India Agreements on the Tibet Issue

A new phase of Sino-Indian relations started with Indian Prime Minister Rajiv Gandhi's China visit in 1988. The two countries also agreed to accommodate each other on the Tibet issue. The Chinese side expressed concern over anti-China activities by some Tibetan elements in India, while the Indian side 'reiterated the longstanding and consistent policy of the Government of India that Tibet is an autonomous region of China and that anti-China political activities by Tibetan elements are not permitted on Indian soil' (Ministry of Foreign Affairs of the PRC 1988).

This discourse, that 'Tibet is an autonomous region' then became India's official answer in response to the Tibetan question, and has been confirmed by the Indian side repeatedly in subsequent high-level exchanges. For example, when Chinese Premier Li Peng visited India in 1991, the position was written into the 'Sino-Indian *Communiqué*'.

Semantic nuances may, however, be noted. The Indian side holds that its 'long-standing and consistent policy' is that Tibet is 'an autonomous region of China'; this does not echo China's usage that Tibet is 'an inalienable part of China'. China maintains that India reconfirmed its promised position that Tibet belongs to China and thus disappointed the Tibetan government-in-exile (Zhao 2000: 319). According to John W.

Garver, the use of the phrase 'autonomous region' reminded Beijing of the promise it made in 1954–7, when India endorsed China's ownership of Tibet (Garver 2001: 72).

Even if India is not clandestinely encouraging Tibet to move towards independence, the Indian side is in favour of Tibet's claim to a higher degree of autonomy. Tibet as a peaceful zone, a non-nuclear zone, or a zone of *ahimsa* (non-violence) proposed by the Dalai Lama (*PTI* 2004b), will serve India's geo-strategic interests and reduce India's threat perception of China. That is why the Indian government prefers Tibet to be an 'autonomous region' with reference to Tibet as part of China. Since India is not willing to give up the Tibetan cause and does not wish to annoy Beijing over the Tibet issue, one of the best options for India to address the Tibetan question is to endorse the proposal of a 'high degree of autonomy'. As a result, preserving Tibet's autonomous status has become the core element of India's Tibet policy.

However, China has rejected the Dalai Lama's goal of implementing 'real autonomy' in Tibet, arguing he is in fact seeking independence in the guise of autonomy. Beijing even snubbed the Dalai Lama's proposal for adopting a 'one country, two systems' formula to solve the Tibetan question, an approach that Beijing has implemented in Hong Kong and Macao (SCIO 2004).

Beijing, in seeking a good neighbourly policy, and hoping to improve relations with India, is willing to shelve the differences between the two countries. Thus, it hoped to encourage India to keep its promise to stand aloof from the Tibet imbroglio. As a positive gesture, Beijing tended to play down India's role in the Tibet problem. In its White Paper *Tibet—Its Ownership and Human Rights Situation*, issued in September 1992, Beijing made no reference to India's involvement in the Tibet independence movement and 'the Dalai Clique's separatist activities', but maintained that the issue was concocted by old and new imperialists, i.e., the British Empire and the US (SCIO 1992).

This was a far cry from Beijing's previous official stand. In fact, some Chinese still continued to criticize India's involvement in the Tibetan independence movement. For example, the former Chinese ambassador to India, Yang Gongsu, has repeatedly accused India of supporting the 1959 uprising (Yang 1992; Zhang 2008b). Interestingly, some in India also acknowledge that India participated in the Khampa rebellion sponsored by the CIA in the early 1950s. Eric Gonsalves, a veteran Indian diplomat, admitted that India was a participant in Western efforts to destabilize China through Tibet (Gonsalves 1998). Subramanian Swamy, President of India's Janata Party and a former Indian minister, also revealed that, in the 1980s, the Indian government raised an 8,000-strong commando group of Tibetans, the members of which woke up every morning in special camps with cries of 'Long live the Dalai Lama. We shall liberate Tibet' (Swamy 2001: 26). It is naïve to suggest that Beijing was not aware of these activities. In contrast to its public silence on India's involvement, the Chinese government, in fact, remained very attentive to the India–Tibet linkage. A confidential Chinese document, revealed by the Tibetan government-in-exile, identified that India's support for the Dalai Lama's group was the most 'odious' among that of foreign countries.[9] Therefore, this White Paper's silence on India's involvement was a clear demonstration of China's resolve not to let the Tibet issue become an obstacle to the Sino-Indian rapprochement.

Beijing's cautious treatment of the Tibet issue in Sino-Indian relations signals that the Chinese would like to develop relations in other fields while shelving the differences between India and China. On the other hand, they also hoped to encourage India to extricate itself from the Tibet embroilment while stressing that common interests outweighed the differences. In addition, from the Chinese perspective, the Tibetan question is an internal affair and not open to negotiations by any third party. That is why the Director–General of the Asia Department of the Chinese Foreign Ministry, Fu Ying, argued that the Tibet issue was not on the agenda because 'it is not a bilateral problem between China and India' (*PTI* 2002). For Beijing, overemphasis on India's role in the Tibet issue would only give India greater leverage against China, and contribute to the internationalization of the Tibet issue.

The continuous effort to reduce the significance of the Tibetan question in China–India relations were seen during Indian Prime Minister Narasimha Rao's visit to China in 1993. The Tibetan question received a relatively perfunctory treatment in the talks between the Indian Prime Minister Rao and the Chinese leaders as they focused on the border talks (Kaye 1993: 13). Similarly, during Chinese President Jiang Zemin's state visit to India in 1996, the Tibet issue was raised only during the meeting between Chinese Foreign Minister Qian Qichen and his Indian counterpart Inder Kumar Gujral (*Xinhua* 1996a). These developments reflected that China and India shared the common aspiration to marginalize the Tibet issues while improving relations in other fields.

Impact of India's Nuclear Tests on the Tibet Issue

Sino-Indian relations seemed to reach a new high as China and India agreed to establish a constructive partnership of cooperation oriented towards the twenty-first century during Chinese President Jiang Zemin's visit to India in 1997. Although Beijing was satisfied with the new tenor of India–China relations, their differences over Tibet were far from being resolved, but rather were shelved. China's good neighbourly policy towards India was dealt a serious blow by India's detonation of nuclear devices in 1998. Despite years of mistrust and frosty forbearance, Beijing was not so blind as not to notice that the Indian side had accommodated the activities of exiled Tibetans. The nuclear tests and subsequent missile programme not only delayed the normalization process of Sino-Indian relations in general, but also triggered China's unhappiness about India's management of the Tibet issue. In contrast to the previous silence, China criticized India's approach towards the Tibetan problem again.

The Dalai Lama's comments on India's nuclear tests had been a new source of tension between China and India. Commenting on India's nuclear tests, the Dalai Lama said that he was saddened to hear about the series of nuclear tests conducted by India, but argued that as long as some of the major world powers continued to possess nuclear weapons, it was not right to condemn India's nuclear tests outright (*The Indian Express* 1998e). The Dalai Lama's statement in defence of India's right to test and bear nuclear arms took the same line the Indian government used to rebut critics. Although the Dalai Lama also endorsed the call made by China for a ban on nuclear weapons by all countries, his decision not to condemn India's nuclear blasts was a new source of dissatisfaction for Beijing.

The state-owned *Renmin Ribao* soon carried a commentator's article further criticizing India, saying that India had played a 'disgraceful' role in the Tibet issue and that the Indian authority concerned had let the Chinese people down (*Renmin Ribao* 1998f: 4). In an article rebuking India's nuclear tests, the state-run news agency, *Xinhua*, condemned that India allowed the Dalai Lama's group to conduct separatist activities, and claimed that there was an underhand relationship between India and Tibet (Xinhua Agency Commentary 1998: 4).

China felt even more uncomfortable after Indian Prime Minister Vajpayee held a meeting with the Dalai Lama and Defence Minister Fernandes promised to adhere to the notion of China's suzerainty over Tibet. China reacted strongly and expressed 'deep resentment and regret' over the meeting between Vajpayee and the Dalai Lama, saying it violated the commitment of the Indian side not to allow the Dalai to engage in anti-China political activities in India and claiming that the event amounted to interference by New Delhi in China's internal affairs (*The Hindu* 1998d: 1). Meanwhile, Chinese strategists were concerned with this development and argued that India, anti-China forces in the West and the Dalai Lama were using these opportunities to challenge China's sovereignty over Tibet.

The issue of secessionist movements in India was also raised for consideration as a counter to India promoting the 'Tibet card'. There was speculation that China would not hesitate to use the 'Kashmir card' if India played the 'Tibet card' against China. There was also a minority view in the Chinese government that India's problem areas such as Punjab and the northeastern region should also be placed at the forefront of diplomatic affairs if India continued to play the 'Tibet card' (Cherian 1998). Chinese scholars also linked the Kashmir cause to the Tibet issue, in an attempt to encourage India to step away from the Tibet issue. Senior Chinese scholar Ye Zhengjia stated that 'India has its problems—in the north-eastern region, in Kashmir, in Punjab. On Tibet, it's the same kind of problem. If we interfere with each other, there can be no friendship, no normal relationship' (Ram 1988c: 18).

On the other hand, India's nuclear tests and the war against terror unleashed new strategic uncertainties for China on its southwestern frontiers, and further highlighted Tibet's strategic value. Some Chinese strategic analysts argued China's security environment in the southwest had suffered because India's nuclear tests posed a potential threat to Tibet. Assessing the Chinese security environment after India's nuclear tests, the Chinese strategic analyst Zhang Wenmu concluded that China's security concerns were 'urgent in the east, serious in the west' (*dong ji xi zhong*), and cautioned against India's desire to include Tibet in an India-controlled union (Zhang 1998: 108).

China's immediate and harsh criticism of India's Tibet policy after India's 1998 nuclear tests proved that India's assistance to the Dalai Lama's government remained a thorn in the flesh in Beijing's side, and could easily arouse the indignation of the Chinese. Again, it exposed Tibet as an unresolved issue between China and India. China, in fact, has been very suspicious of India's real policy towards Tibet, although the Indian side reiterates that its long-standing and consistent position that Tibet is an autonomous region of China and that it does not allow Tibetans to engage in anti-China political activities in India.

The Karmapa Event

While Chinese suspicions over India's intentions regarding Tibet deepened after India's nuclear tests, the Tibet issue was further compounded by the 17th Karmapa Lama Ugyen Trinley Dorje's flight from Tibet to India in January 2000. The Karmapa Lama is the spiritual leader of the Kagyu lineage of Tibetan Buddhism and ranks third in importance in Tibet's Buddhist hierarchy, second only to the Dalai Lama and Panchen Lama.[10] More significantly, unlike the controversial selection of the 11th Panchen Lama, he has been recognized by both Beijing and the Dalai Lama, and therefore, possesses legitimacy. The fact that the 14-year-old Lama had received Beijing's patriotic education and had still decided to escape certainly caused China considerable embarrassment. The Karmapa's flight not only suggested the failure of China's patriotic education to indoctrinate the Tibetan leader, but also showed that the destabilizing influences in Tibet would continue to pose significant political and other kinds of obstacles in China's quest to defend its sovereignty and territorial integrity.

The Karmapa's flight also once again drew international attention to China's dubious record in Tibet. In a bid to counteract the effect of the event and to 'save face', China claimed that the young Karmapa had gone abroad to retrieve religious artefacts, musical instruments, and ritual black hats that had been used by the previous Karmapa Lama and had been left in the Rumtek monastery in Sikkim. The Chinese stressed that his Indian sojourn 'did not mean to betray the state, the nation, the monastery, and the leadership' (*The Associated Press* 2000).

More importantly, the Karmapa's decision to leave China and to join the Dalai Lama's side was damaging to Beijing's assumption that the Tibet issue would naturally be resolved when the present Dalai Lama was out of the picture. Before the Karmapa's departure, Beijing had tried to push forward the Karmapa Lama to replace the Dalai Lama as an alternative leader to the Tibetans. However, now the situation has been gradually reversed. Not only can the Karmapa not be used as a tool against the Dalai Lama, but there is a new belief that the Karmapa could be the transitional successor to the Dalai Lama, who is now in his seventies (*The Times of India* 2008c: 19).

It was believed that Beijing was playing a 'waiting game' with the Dalai Lama to win ultimate control over Tibet. A senior Chinese official was quoted as saying that the Chinese did not need to engage in dialogue with the Dalai Lama because it would be 10 years, at the most, before the Tibetan leader died. The Chinese official argued that, when the Dalai Lama died, the issue of Tibet would be resolved forever (Gyari 2000: 28). That is, in the eyes of Beijing, the Tibetan question is the equivalent of 'the Dalai Lama question'. Beijing believed the Tibetan question would cease to exist once the present Dalai Lama had passed away.

Indeed, regarding the confrontation between Beijing and the Tibetan government-in-exile, time is on the side of the Chinese. In the TAR, Han immigrants are expected to outnumber the Tibetans in the next few years. Meanwhile, the young generations of exiled Tibetans are losing their original Tibetan identity, and developing a new identity that is closer to that of their host countries. Kesang Takla, Secretary for the Department of Information and International Relations of the Tibetan government-in-exile, admitted that more and more Tibetans in India are gradually considering themselves as Indians (Lin 2000). The Chinese might be happy to see the exiled Tibetans neutralized by host states and alienating themselves from Tibet, while the aboriginal Tibetans are diluted by the external immigrants. With the lack of a significant figure with the charisma and the iconic international status of the present Dalai Lama, the Tibetan government-in-exile will find it more difficult to inspire the Tibetans to rise against China. It will also be an arduous task for the successor of the present Dalai Lama to consolidate the different factions within Tibetan Buddhism. As the Dalai Lama himself agreed, 'If the Dalai Lama is simply replaced by another senior lama, then the other sects will not agree' (*Taipei Times* 2001). It is also likely that the new leader will not be able to restrain the violence-prone factions, such as the Tibetan Youth Congress, which is infamous for its appeal to use violent means to promote the Tibetan independence movement. A leadership vacuum in the wake of the Dalai Lama's death will inevitably lead to the collapse and split of the Tibetan government-in-exile. This is the scenario Beijing anticipates.

Some media reports have also revealed that the Chinese government has already set up a task force to search for the next reincarnation of the Dalai Lama (*The Indian Express* 2000a). Just as it selected his own reincarnation of the Panchen Lama in 1995 and the Reting Lama reincarnation in December 1999 without the Dalai Lama's blessings, Beijing will attempt to appoint its own favourite reincarnation of the next Dalai Lama. Though Beijing's appointee may not be accepted by all Tibetans, it will benefit Beijing because the 'two Dalai Lamas' controversy could undermine the legitimacy and influence of the one accepted by the Tibetan government-in-exile.

Aware of the change in the wake of the Karmapa's departure, Beijing found it less credible to use its own puppet Panchen Lama as a symbol to legalize its rule over Tibet since neither the Dalai Lama, the Karmapa Lama nor the two major leaders of the Sakya sect were on its side. Therefore, Beijing was obliged to take the initiative of resuming contact with the Dalai Lama. The Dalai Lama's elder brother, Gyalo Thondup, who had long been an emissary between Beijing and Dharamsala, was invited to visit Beijing in October 2000. He visited China again in July 2002 and was permitted to enter Tibet for the first time since 1959. Just several weeks later, two high-level figures from the Tibetan government-in-exile, the Dalai Lama's special envoy to the US, Lodi Gyaltsen Gyari, and his envoy to Europe, Kelsang Gyaltsen arrived in Beijing and then visited Tibet. Although Chinese officials still declined to recognize this visit as official contact, in reality, the visit carried great significance and sparked hopes of the resumption of a formal dialogue between the Dalai Lama and Beijing. The Dharamsala delegation was allowed to visit China and hold eight rounds of meetings with Beijing officials between May 2003 and January 2010. Although there was no significant breakthrough, China has recognized that there was some kind of contact between the central government and the Dalai Lama.

However, it is unlikely that China has shown flexibility on the issue of Tibetan independence. While receiving the delegation from the Dalai Lama, Beijing still took a hardline attitude towards the Dalai Lama by blocking him from making any visits outside India. Some analysts were wondering whether discreet international pressure, particularly from Washington, might have been the major factor in encouraging Beijing to resume the dialogue. However, the resumption of high-level contact between the two sides indicated that Beijing was aware that it could not merely depend on the 'waiting for a natural resolution' approach to solve the Tibet issue.

The Karmapa Lama arrived at a time when New Delhi was trying to mend fences with Beijing in the wake of the 1998 nuclear tests. In fact, the Indians were more confounded than excited by the Karmapa's unforeseen arrival although India supports Tibet's autonomy. Such confusion was well-reflected in the initial reactions of major Indian newspapers.[11] Some were worried that it might be a deliberate plot by the Chinese to disturb India's domestic peace, while others welcomed him to stay.[12]

The dilemma for the Indian government was whether to grant the Karmapa Lama political asylum. The Indian Defence Minister Fernandes, a known hardliner towards China, was the first high-ranking Indian official to say that the Karmapa Lama could stay in India. In fact, from the Indian perspective, granting the Karmapa Lama sanctuary on humanitarian grounds did not signify any change in India's Tibet policy,[13] because India had already sheltered the Dalai Lama and tens of thousands of exiled Tibetans. However, China also made it plain that it did not want the Karmapa Lama to obtain political asylum in India. China expressed a hope that India would adhere to its commitments in this regard, especially the policy of mutual respect and non-interference in each other's internal affairs of the Five Principles of Peaceful Coexistence. Beijing also expected that the Karmapa Lama would not be allowed to engage in political activities and that New Delhi would not allow him to be used by other foreign powers in strategies or plots against China.[14]

India took a cautious attitude towards the Karmapa's arrival and did not want to provoke Beijing. As a result, New Delhi played down the issue of political asylum by granting only refugee status to the Karmapa Lama. More significantly, the decision was made one year after the Karmapa's arrival and, currently, he is still prevented from visiting Sikkim, where another Karmapa Lama resides.[15] As a low-profile protest, the Chinese called off a medical delegation which was scheduled to visit India to assist the victims of the Gujarat earthquake.

The Karmapa issue provided a new opportunity for China and India to measure the importance of the Tibet issue in Sino-Indian relations and reconsider their approaches. The Indian government's statecraft in managing the Karmapa issue once again proved their reluctance to challenge Beijing directly over the Tibet issue. However, India's decision to host the Karmapa Lama also revealed that India would not conform to all of China's expectations over the Tibet issue, but would continue to accommodate exiled Tibetans. Furthermore, the event once again reminded people that India is the host to the Tibetan government-in-exile and plays a particular role in the China–Tibet embroilment, as international media also took notice of the possibility that the Karmapa might continue the Dalai Lama's political mission (Biema 2008). As a result, it was inevitable that India's sheltering of the Karmapa and the Karmapa's presence in India would affect China–Tibet–India interactions, especially in the post-Dalai Lama period. On the other hand, China's dilemma is that it does not want the Tibet issue to become a bilateral issue, but it has not been able to marginalize India's role either.

The Tibet Card

India's Self-restraint Approach

In the wake of new developments, such as the Karmapa's stay in India, China felt it imperative to bring the Tibet issue to the China–India agenda. An initial shift was seen during Chinese Premier Zhu Rongji's visit to India in January 2002. The most contentious issues that came up in discussions between the two sides were the Dalai Lama and the activities of Tibetan refugees in India (*The Times of India* 2002a). Beijing understood that it needed to raise the Tibet issue with New Delhi rather than applying the cool-down policy by ignoring India's role.

Indian Prime Minister Vajpayee's visit to China in 2003 marked another effort by both sides to improve relations despite the controversy caused by India's nuclear tests. A new document, the 'Declaration on Principles for Relations and Comprehensive Cooperation between the Republic of India and the People's Republic of China', was signed to mark their progress in an effort in finding common ground in bilateral relations. Again, the Tibetan problem became a significant topic for discussion between the two sides. On the Tibet issue, the declaration stated, 'The Indian side recognizes that the Tibet Autonomous Region is part of the territory of the People's Republic of China and reiterates that it does not allow Tibetans to engage in anti-China political activities in India'. In fact, just before Vajpayee's visit, the Indian side had decided to ignore both the Tibet and Sikkim issues and concentrate on economics and border clarification (Chawla 2003). Nonetheless, Beijing was not satisfied with a repetition of India's previous stance, and wanted India to make a more categorical commitment to recognize Tibet as an inalienable part of China.

By signing the statement, India had, for the first time, used the official Chinese description, the 'Tibet Autonomous Region', to refer to Tibet and acknowledged it as part of the territory of the People's Republic of China (see Table 2.1). In essence, the new discourse did not represent any change in India's Tibet policy, but the Chinese side soon expressed its appreciation for India's support in stating its policy in black and white. The state-run *Xinhua* news agency lost no time in hailing India's apparent recognition of Tibet as part of China. The spokesman of the Chinese Foreign Ministry, Kong Quan, then affirmed that India's stand on Tibet helped to 'enhance confidence and defuse suspicions' (*The Hindu* 2003a).

On the other hand, however, from the Indian perspective, the declaration did not represent any shift in India's position either on Tibet or on the presence of the Dalai Lama or other Tibetan refugees in India. Indian Prime Minister Vajpayee stressed that 'there is no change in our decades-old policy', because 'Indians have never doubted that the Tibet Autonomous Region is a part of the territory of the People's Republic of China' (*PTI* 2003a).

Literally, the declaration regarding Tibet replaced the reference to 'Tibet' with the phrase 'Tibet Autonomous Region'. However, since India had already recognized Chinese sovereignty over Tibet, there was no substantive change in India's stand. In other words, the new discourse on Tibet was notional rather than substantive.

To conclude, it would appear that the new reference to Tibet in the joint declaration reflected Beijing's growing nervousness about Tibet, due to a series of new developments, including the Karmapa's escape and India's nuclear tests.

The subsequent high-level visits saw Beijing and New Delhi satisfied with the new discourse on Tibet. The 2005 'Joint Statement' by China and India and the 2006 'Joint Declaration' by India and China stated that 'The Indian side reiterates that it has recognized the Tibet Autonomous Region as part of the territory of the People's Republic of China and that it does not allow Tibetans to engage in anti-China political activities in India', and that 'The Chinese side expressed its appreciation for the Indian positions'. With the issuing of such statements on the Tibetan question, both China and India might have thought again that they had reached consensus over the handling of the Tibet issue.

Table 2.1 Indian Statements on Tibet

Date	Document	Description
29 April 1954	The Agreement between India and China on Trade and Intercourse between Tibet Region of China and India.	Desirous of promoting trade and cultural intercourse between the Tibet Region of China and India and of facilitating pilgrimage and travel by the peoples of China and India.
2 August 1958	Notes sent by the Ministry of External Affairs to the Embassy of China in India.	The Government of India recognizes that the Tibetan region is part of the People's Republic of China.
23 December 1988	India–China Joint Press *Communiqué*.	The Chinese side expresses concern over anti-China activities by some Tibetan elements in India. The Indian side reiterates the long-standing and consistent policy of the Government of India that Tibet is an autonomous region of China and that anti-China political activities by Tibetan elements are not permitted on Indian soil.
16 December 1991	India–China Joint *Communiqué*.	The Chinese side expresses concern about the continued activities in India by some Tibetans against their motherland and reiterates that Tibet is an inalienable part of Chinese territory and that it is firmly opposed to any attempt or action aimed at splitting China and bringing about the 'independence of Tibet'. The Indian side reiterates its long-standing and consistent position that Tibet is an autonomous region of China and that it does not allow Tibetans to engage in anti-China political activities in India.
23 June 2003	Declaration on Principles for Relations and Comprehensive Cooperation between the Republic of India and the People's Republic of China.	The Indian side recognizes that the Tibet Autonomous Region is part of the territory of the People's Republic of China and reiterates that it does not allow Tibetans to engage in anti-China political activities in India. The Chinese side expresses its appreciation for the Indian position and reiterates that it is firmly opposed to any attempt or action aimed at splitting China and bringing about 'independence of Tibet'.

Table 2.1 *(Cont'd)*

Date	Document	Description
11 April 2005	Joint Statement of the Republic of India and the People's Republic of China.	The Indian side reiterates that it recognizes the Tibet Autonomous Region as part of the territory of the People's Republic of China and that it does not allow Tibetans to engage in anti-China political activities in India. The Indian side recalls that India was among the first countries to recognize that there is one China and its one-China policy remains unaltered. The Indian side states it will continue to abide by its one-China policy. The Chinese side expresses its appreciation for the Indian position.
21 November 2006	Joint Declaration by the Republic of India and the People's Republic of China.	The Indian side reiterates that it has recognized the Tibet Autonomous Region as part of the territory of the People's Republic of China, and that it does not allow Tibetans to engage in anti-China political activities in India. The Chinese side expresses its appreciation for the Indian position.
15 January 2008	A Shared Vision for the 21st Century of the Republic of India and the People's Republic of China.	(There is no mention of Tibet).
16 December 2010	Joint *Communiqué* of the Republic of India and the People's Republic of China.	(There is no mention of Tibet).

Source: Author.

The mixture of India's denial of any change and China's delight with the new formulation indicated that their understandings and expectations did not converge. The Indian government still refused to endorse China's argument that Tibet is an integral and 'inalienable' part of Chinese territory. However, because of fears about China's aggressive reactions, New Delhi usually bowed to Chinese pressure to curb Tibetan activities while allowing the Tibetan government-in-exile to operate in India. For example, India's Cabinet Secretariat was reported to have issued a circular asking all ministers to keep away from a function to congratulate the Dalai Lama after he had been honoured with the Gold Medal bestowed by the US Congress (*PTI* 2007).

In March 2008, some exiled Tibetans organised the 'Return March to Tibet' to mark the anniversary of China's 1959 crackdown in Tibet. They planned to reach Tibet by travelling on foot from Dharamsala to Tibet's border to protest China's rule over Tibet by the time the Beijing Olympics began on 8 August of that year. For China, the initiative was a serious provocation. Indian police arrested approximately 100 Tibetans to stop the march. Later on, a fresh riot followed by an anti-government protest erupted in Lhasa on 14 March 2008, leading to a massive crackdown. The PLA was moved into Lhasa to maintain order. The Chinese government accused 'the Dalai clique' of orchestrating the protests in Tibet.

In New Delhi, demonstrations had also been seen outside the Chinese Embassy. The Tibetan exiles repeatedly tried to storm the Chinese embassy and were detained by the Indian police. Meanwhile, a group of Tibetan students, who planned to hold a candlelight vigil at the India Gate, were stopped from doing so by Indian police. In addition, the Indian Ambassador to Beijing, Nirupama Rao, was summoned after midnight by the Chinese Foreign Ministry, which wished to express China's concerns over these demonstrations by Tibetans at the Chinese embassy in New Delhi. The fact that she was summoned after midnight was seen in New Delhi as an unfriendly gesture.

To avoid embarrassing China, India imposed a series of restrictions on Tibetan activists and protesters. India's Foreign Minister, Pranab Mukherjee, even publicly warned the Dalai Lama, saying that India would continue to offer him hospitality, but that he and his followers should not engage in any political activity or any action that could adversely affect relations between India and China during his stay in India (*The Hindu* 2008b).

India also made great efforts to reassure Beijing that the Olympic Torch Relay in New Delhi would pass off smoothly under the cover of massive security. As a result, the Chinese government lauded India for its handling of the Tibet issues. The Chinese Ambassador to India, Zhang Yan, proclaimed that China appreciated these goodwill gestures (Zhang 2008). India's self-restraint and muted response to the protests in Tibet might have made Beijing feel comfortable and might have earned praise from Beijing, but within India, a section of the media described the government's kowtowing to China as 'chicken-hearted' (Suraiya 2008: 18). The former Defence Minister, George Fernandes, also said, 'It is a disgrace that China should say that India has done well' (*The Times of India* 2008d: 14).

Given India's use of extreme caution regarding the Olympic torch relay in New Delhi, the Chinese may have felt slightly more confident. India was not, however, entirely toeing the Chinese line. In early 2008, the exiled Karmapa Lama travelled to the US. It was the first time the Indian government allowed him to travel outside India in the eight years since he had escaped from Tibet (*The Times of India* 2008c: 19). As the Olympic torch relay turned into a public relations disaster for China, the Karmapa's trip to the US had the potential to ruin Sino-Indian relations; it was a sign that India did not give up its influence over the Tibet issue.

The visit to China by the Indian External Affairs Minister, Pranab Mukherjee, in June 2008, after the turmoil regarding Tibet, was another example that China and India were willing to make further concessions on the issue. However, the talks between Mukherjee and his Chinese counterpart, Yang Jiechi, were not able to break new ground; instead the two ministers became vexed with the differences, including those regarding the Tibet issue. It seems that Chinese officials expressed their objections about the media coverage given to the Dalai Lama and the Tibetan youth movement (*The Times of India* 2008f: 18). As a result, the two sides found it difficult to concentrate on other areas where the two countries could have common interests.

Tibet's 'India Card'

As far as Beijing is concerned, it would like to avoid Tibet playing a central role in India's strategies *vis-à-vis* China. Indian policymakers also want to downplay the Tibetan factor in China–India relations as it seeks to improve relations with China. However, India's peculiar role in the Tibet issue cannot be ignored; India has been dragged into the Tibet issue even though New Delhi is very mindful of managing the prickly and difficult relationship with China. Recent interactions between Beijing–Dharamsala–Delhi show that such a trend is still a factor in Sino-Indian relations.

After the sixth round of talks between Beijing and Dharamsala in 2007, there were no plans to hold further talks in the immediate future.

However, because of the riots of March 2008 in Tibet, both sides held the seventh and eighth rounds of talks in July and November 2008, respectively (Hsu 2008, *The New York Times* 2008). Ironically, the only consensus between Beijing and Dharamsala was that the talks failed to make progress on the contentious Tibet issue and both sides vowed not to compromise on the status of Tibet. The Tibetans' frustration and disappointment over the fruitless talks with Beijing mounted.

The Dalai Lama admitted that his attempts to secure greater autonomy for the region through negotiation with the Chinese government had not succeeded. He then called a gathering of around 600 Tibetan leaders for a six-day special meeting in November 2008 to discuss the direction and the future strategy of the Tibetan movement against Chinese rule; the issue was whether to continue following the middle way for Tibetan autonomy, or to press for complete independence and self-determination.

As Tibetans became frustrated at the lack of progress in the talks with Beijing, the Dalai Lama directly asked New Delhi to help resolve the crisis at the centre of strained border ties between Asia's two biggest nations. He argued, 'India and Tibet have the relationship of a "*guru* and *chela*" (master and disciple), and when the chela is in trouble, the guru must look after him' (*The Times of India* 2008g: 11). The Dalai Lama even called himself a 'son of India' and pointed out that Tibetans have developed very close ties with India over the years (*IANS* 2009a). Moreover, the Dalai Lama voiced his support for New Delhi over the boundary problem, arguing that China should accept the reality that Arunachal Pradesh belongs to India, and should shed its rigid stand and find a mutual solution to the border dispute (*UNI* 2009). However, he also termed India's attitude towards the Tibet issue as overcautious despite the help and support India had offered the Tibetans over the years (*The Indian Express* 2008b).

The Dalai Lama's direct plea for India's involvement in the Tibet issue presented the Indian government with a dilemma. There are varied perceptions in India about the benefit or otherwise of the Tibet card. C. Raja Mohan commented that when there is relative tranquillity in Tibet, India and China have reasonably good relations. *Vice-versa*, he argued, when Sino-Tibetan tensions rise, India's relationship with China deteriorates. The current restiveness in Tibet and the collapse of the talks between the exiled Tibetan leadership and Beijing are likely to affect New Delhi adversely (Raja Mohan 2008).

Besides, Srikanth Kondapalli of Jawaharlal Nehru University noted that India's Ministry of External Affairs viewed Tibet as a liability as, in his opinion, it was India's decision to grant asylum to the Dalai Lama that led to China's attack on India (*The Times of India* 2008h: 10). Sometimes, India's special links with Tibet have compelled New Delhi to be involved in the Tibet issue even if it wishes to avoid it. In the view of K. Subrahmanyam, a senior Indian strategic affairs analyst, 'Tibet is not a card politically and strategically, but India has an obligation to the Tibetan people and their culture' (*The Times of India* 2008h: 10).

Beijing will not recognize India's moral obligation over the Tibet issue. On the contrary, it views India as taking advantage of its relations with Tibet. China has long suspected the real intention of foreign countries for helping the exiled Tibetans. Some Chinese have argued that the Dalai Lama's crowning glory comes from the value that he represents as a focus of anti-China forces (The Human Rights Society of China 2001: 5). Any assistance can be seen as part of a grand plan to weaken or contain China. Seen from a broader perspective, the Tibet issue could provide New Delhi with politico–military options in the future to ally itself with other countries to discomfit China strategically.

Thus, the Chinese side also worries that the Tibetan question has become a platform on which anti-China forces could work together to contain China. For example, China criticized the Dalai Lama for being a tool that allows the US to contain China, and deemed the US as the mastermind behind the Tibetan separatist activities (The Human Rights Society of China 2001: 5). Particularly, since India has a particular position and influence over the Tibet issue, some Chinese researchers have warned that the Tibet issue may bring the US and India closer together because any country wanting to play the 'Tibet card' will have to take action on Indian soil. In fact, some Chinese scholars have also warned that India is likely to play the 'Tibet card' to please the US (Liu 1996: 12). China worries that the US and India may conspire to support exiled Tibetans, which would cast a new question mark over China's security environment.

India's Strategic Ambiguity on Tibet

Although India has occasionally reined-in its anti-China activities, the Chinese side still suspects India's sincerity and considers India's actions to be a sort of political tactic. As Rajiv Sikri, a former secretary in India's Ministry of External Affairs, said, China remains uncertain and anxious about India's Tibet policy despite extracting significant concessions from India on Tibet (Sikri 2008). On the one hand, New Delhi recognizes that Tibet is an autonomous region of China, but on the other hand, it allows exiled Tibetans to conduct 'anti-China political activities' in India. It seems reasonable for the Chinese side to conclude that India has been involved in double-dealing and using Tibet as a trump card to be played against China.

The Indian strategic community has appeared divided on how to tackle the Tibetan problem while New Delhi has tended to maintain an ambiguous posture towards Tibet. Some Indian strategic analysts have candidly argued, 'If it becomes necessary, India should also be ready to play the Tibet card' (Kanwal 2000). However, the Indian government is very cautious in dealing with the Tibet issue, and avoids giving the impression that they use the issue as possible leverage against China. Some Indian analysts have argued that, despite the dramatic rise in international support for exiled Tibetans since the late 1980s, New Delhi has consciously refused to take advantage of the situation and has done nothing to raise political hackles in Beijing (Mohan 2003). That is why Brahma Chellaney of the Centre for Policy Research criticized the Indian position by stating that 'India continues to sit on the sidelines and does not examine the implication of the Tibetan card' (Gupta 2002: 60).

However, India does see and has used the Tibetan question as a *quid pro quo* in its negotiations with China. Such a strategy can be traced back to Nehru's period. Nehru informally proposed a deal to Zhou Enlai: India would give up its claims over Tibet if China would in return respect the *status quo* on the border (Norbu 1997: 1087). Furthermore, India has publicly played the Tibet card at least twice in recent times since the 1980s. Srikanth Kondapalli points out that in 1987 and 2003, when China began supplying arms to the Royal Nepalese Army, India played the Tibet card. In 2003, the Indian Foreign Secretary, Shyam Sharan, went to Dharamsala to meet the Dalai Lama as a message to China that it should not interfere in India's 'backyard' (*The Times of India* 2008h: 10).

Even if the Indian side did not treat the Tibet issue as a card to be played against China, it still saw New Delhi's stance towards the Tibet issue as a bargaining chip and as a means of forcing China's reciprocity. Many Indian scholars maintain that the settlement of the border and the status of Tibet are interlinked issues. That is, India will reserve ambiguities in its Tibetan policy as long as there is no definitive settlement of the boundary (Sikri 2008). Yet, any assistance India renders to the Dalai Lama and his government, from the point of view of the Chinese, is part of the effort to cripple China. Sino-Indian relations thus suffer.

The Chinese side has also argued that, with an improvement in Sino-Indian relations, the Indian government would take a hard-line toward the Tibetan separatists whereas if bilateral relations were to deteriorate, the Indian side would accommodate Tibetan separatists to pressure China. The Chinese side made the criticism that every time the Indian side wants China to make concessions over a territorial dispute or India feels threatened by China, some Indian political figure will publicly support the cause of Tibetan independence (Yang 2002: 40). In sum and substance, the Chinese accuse India of holding a 'dark mentality' toward the Tibet issue by playing the 'Tibet card' against China (Sun 2002: 50–1). Dominated by this thinking, the Chinese side finds it difficult to trust New Delhi over the Tibetan question.

Entering the Post-Dalai Lama Era

The Tibet issue has been an endless source of friction between China and India, and has also been a significant factor in shaping their mutual threat perceptions. The incorporation of Tibet into the People's Republic of China (PRC) in 1950 brought China and India face-to-face across the Himalayas. Therefore, the Indian strategic community has long seen China's takeover of Tibet and its build-up there as a threat to India's security. On the other hand, India can use Tibet to gain strategic leverage against China because it has a special influence on the Tibetan question.

India has officially recognized Tibet as a part of China by signing the 1954 agreement, which speaks of the 'Tibet region of China'. In the post-Cold War era, both China and India have made certain efforts towards improving relations. On the surface, political disagreement over the Tibet issue seems to have been put aside to pave the way for more cooperation in other fields. Meanwhile, New Delhi has not supported Tibetan independence in public. The Tibet issue can hardly ignite a major military conflict between China and India. The consensus between Beijing and New Delhi is that the Tibet issue should not be allowed to become an obstacle to greater cooperation. Both sides are unwilling to adopt a conflictual course or hostile policy posture towards each other.

Since an independent Tibet is not currently a possibility, India is constantly in search of ways to show support for a higher level of autonomy in Tibet. To some extent, India's position of not supporting Tibet's independence is a way to alleviate China's concerns. However, the distrust continues to prevail between the two countries over the issues of India giving shelter to the Dalai Lama and his followers, and India's supporting the Dalai Lama's 'real autonomy'.

The Tibet issue also reflects India's dilemma under the system of asymmetrical threat perceptions. India can use the Tibet issue as a trump card to increase pressure on China, but it is worried about China's possible punitive reactions. That is, the asymmetry in threat perceptions has made India very cautious of taking counter-measures. Nevertheless, the Indians will keep playing the Tibet card as an option, albeit reluctantly. It can be safely argued that for most Indians and India's current crop of leaders, their support to the Tibetan claim does not show any malice toward China, because the Indian government has not attempted to stir up a rebellion against China's rule. However, India's mild stance does not meet Chinese expectations.

Compared to other issues between China and India, Tibet is one of the few issues that has irked China more than it has troubled India. Beijing intentionally applied a cool-down policy to ignore India's role in order to reduce the significance of the Tibetan question in Sino-Indian relations and to encourage India to stay away from the issue. Although China and India seemed to have already found some common ground on the Tibet issue, as mentioned in some joint diplomatic documents, both sides have failed to agree on a healthy way to address each other's concerns relating to the Tibet issue. There is no denying that India still plays host to the Dalai Lama and the Tibetan government-in-exile, and thereby occupies a crucial position in the tortured politics of the Tibet issue. The repeated mention of the Tibet issue in bilateral *communiqués* indicates that the India–Tibet linkage remains a concern to Beijing.

The Chinese side naturally resents the Indian interest in Tibetan affairs, and sees India's warm reception of the Dalai Lama as a violation of a cardinal principle of non-interference in one another's internal affairs. Rather, the Chinese have tended to interpret India's assistance to the exiled Tibetan as India's wish to treat Tibet as an instrument against China. According to the Chinese perception, the only way to remove the Tibetan question from the agenda of Sino-Indian relations is for the Indian side to keep its promise and follow the Five Principles of Peaceful Coexistence.

An unexpected event regarding the Karmapa Lama happened in January 2011 as nearly US$ 1.6 million in foreign currencies was found following a raid in his monastery in Dharamsala. Indian police suspected that the money, which included notes in Chinese Yuan as well as other currencies, was an indication of the Karmapa's secret links with the Chinese government. Some media reports also suspected that the Karmapa might be a Chinese agent or spy.[16] Karmapa's reputation and influence were undermined by the allegation. Worse, the Indian authority is keeping a mistrustful attitude toward him. As a result, the young Karmapa Lama may not be able to become the next Tibetan leader as most people expected.

Facing the new development that the Karmapa Lama might not be able to fill the political void after the Dalai Lama dies, the Dalai Lama in March 2011 decided to unveil his 'post-Dalai Lama blueprint'. He decided to devolve his political powers to the democratically elected leadership, instead of other religious leaders. The decision was later endorsed by the amendment of Tibetan Charter. As a result, most of the Dalai Lama's executive powers rested with Lobsang Sangay, who was newly-elected as Kalon Tripa (Tibetan Prime Minister) in April 2011. As Tibetan Parliament-in-exile spokesman Tenzin Norbu said, the Kalon Tripa's new responsibilities included the selection of representatives and special envoys to hold talks with China (*The Asian Age* 2011). China denounced the Dalai Lama's political retirement as a trick to deceive the international community, and refused to have a dialogue with the newly-elected Tibetan leader, saying they would only meet the representatives of the Dalai Lama (*The Hindustan Times* 2011: 19, *BBC News* 2011). However, the Dalai Lama now could use his charisma to strengthen the democratic establishment against Beijing as a long-term arrangement (Fang 2011). That meant China–Tibet relations had gradually entered the 'post-Dalai Lama period'.

The discord over Tibet will be a constant that both sides must address, as India's hosting of Tibetan *émigrés* and the Tibetan government-in-exile will continue to affect the course of Sino-Indian relations. Any discord in bilateral relations could easily make their mutual distrust re-emerge, and the Tibetan question will once again take centre-stage.

Notes

1. The Five Principles of Peaceful Coexistence are mutual respect for sovereignty and territorial integrity, mutual non-aggression, non-interference in each other's internal affairs, equality and mutual benefit, and peaceful coexistence, as guiding principles in their bilateral relations. The Five Principles of Peaceful Coexistence were first put forward by the late Chinese Premier Zhou Enlai when he met with an Indian delegation on 31 December 1953. These principles were then incorporated into the Preamble of the 'Agreement Between the People's Republic of China and the Republic of India on Trade and Intercourse Between Tibet Region of China and India', and were further advocated in the respective joint statements enunciated by Premier Zhou Enlai and his Indian and Burmese counterparts during his visit to the two countries in June 1954.

2. For the Chinese view that the Indian side has violated its promise by supporting the Tibetans, see Wang (1998b:129–51) and Zhao (2000: 103–40).

3. For further details, see the Fourteenth Dalai Lama's (1998) address to the members of the European Parliament, Strasbourg, France.

4. In his cable to the Indian Ambassador to China, Indian Prime Minister Nehru said, 'Regarding use of the word "sovereignty" or "suzerainty", the question is rather academic [...] Autonomy plus sovereignty leads to suzerainty. Words are not important. What we do attach values to is the autonomy of Tibet'. See Gopal (1993: 350).

5. For a Chinese account of the US support for the Tibet independence movement, see The Human Rights Society of China (2001).

6. China has branded the Dalai Lama and his followers as the 'Dalai clique'. See, for example, Information Office of the State Council of the People's Republic of China (1992).

7. This point of view was shared by the Tibetan government-in-exile. See *The Times of India* (2001a).

8. See Jiang Zeming's statement in the Fourth Tibetan Work Forum, in *Renmin Ribao*, 30 June (2001: 1).

9. See, '*Yuan Yuan Liu Chang De Yin Zang Youyi*' (Long Course and Remote Source of Indo-Tibetan Friendship), *Xizang–Zhiye* (The Website of Tibet), http://www.xizang-zhiye.org/b5/world/guoji/tdguoji06.html (accessed 18 August 2013).

10. There are four main schools of Tibetan Buddhism: the Nyingma, the Sakya, the Kagyu, and the Gelug. The Dalai Lama belongs to the Gelug, or Yellow, sect of Tibetan Buddhism.

11. For an account of major Indian newspapers' responses to the Karmapa issue, see A. Mattoo, 'Imagining China', in Bajpai and Mattoo eds (2000: 14–17).

12. See, for example, *The Hindustan Times*. 2000. 'Beware of a Trap', *The Hindustan Times* (Editorial), 13 January, Available online at http://www.hindustantimes.com/ (accessed 18 August 2013).

13. For this point, see, *The Indian Express*. 2000. 'The Karmapa Conundrum', *The Indian Express* (Editorial), 13 January, available online at http://www.indianexpress.com/Storyold/140390/ (accessed 13 August 2013).

14. See, Chinese Foreign Ministry spokesman Sun Yuxi's statement, in *Press Trust of India*. 2000. 'China warns India against granting asylum to Karmapa', available online at http://www.tibet.ca/en/newsroom/wtn/archive/old?y=2000&m=9&p=22_2 (accessed 10 August 2013).

15. Both Beijing and the Dalai Lama recognized Ugyen Trinley Dorje as the Karmapa Lama. However, Shamar Rinpoche, one the of senior Lamas responsible for finding the reincarnation of the Karmapa, rejected the authenticity of Ugyen Trinley Dorje, and claimed another boy Thaye Dorje to be the real Karmapa.

16. See, for example, *The Hindu*, 2011, 'China Denies Karmapa Links, Tibetans Express Anger', 1 February, available online at http://www.thehindu.com/news/national/article1142446.ece (accessed 13 August 2013).

3 The Sino-Indian Border Problem

THE CHINA–INDIA BORDER covers a distance of some 2,000 km, divided into three sectors: the western, middle, and eastern sectors.[1] The western sector involves the boundary between Kashmir in India, and Tibet and Xinjiang in China. The middle sector runs from the Tibet–Kashmir–Himachal Pradesh border junctions to the Nepal–Tibet–Uttar Pradesh border junction, while the eastern sector starts at the junctions of the China–India–Bhutan border and extends to the junction of China–India–Myanmar border.

Both sides generally agree on the boundary of the middle sector, but serious differences remain regarding the eastern and western sectors, which involve large disputed areas. In the western sector, India accuses China of occupying about 38,000 sq km of Indian territory in Kashmir, in addition to 5,180 sq km ceded by Pakistan to China under the Sino-Pakistan border agreement of 1963. On the other hand, India also argues that Aksai Chin, located in the western sector, is part of India's Ladakh region, but it has been occupied by China since the late 1950s as part of Xinjiang. In the eastern sector, the Chinese claim about 90,000 sq km in India's Arunachal Pradesh region and repudiate the legality of the McMahon Line, which has been considered the Sino-Indian international borderline by the Indian side.[2]

The incompatible claims of the two sides over the disputed territory along the border led to a brief but significant war in October 1962 and strained Sino-Indian relations. Diplomatic relations at the ambassador level were cut off and were restored only in 1976. The two countries have tried to use dialogue to solve the border problem since 1981. Various kinds of official dialogue mechanisms have been proposed, including the eight rounds of Vice-Minister talks between 1981 and 1987, the Joint

Working Group (JWG) meetings, and the Expert Group; the latest are Special Representative Meetings.

Although the Tibet issue had led to a gradual deterioration in China–India relations, it was the border dispute that eventually destroyed the bhai-bhai friendship between Beijing and New Delhi. The deadlock following the border problem ruined the mutual trust. The significance of the boundary issue in China–India relations was well-recognized, as it was seen as the main obstacle to improving bilateral relations.

More importantly, the border dispute and the war have been the major factors leading to the construction of an asymmetrical perception of threat between the two sides. It is no secret that, after the 1962 border war, the Indian strategic thinkers treated China as a potential rival, not as a partner. Annual reports issued by the Indian Ministry of Defence have guardedly articulated the view that China is India's most potent threat (Joshi 1998).

There exists a vast body of literature centred on the 1962 border war, which has provided some insight as to the origins and developments of the border dispute. This chapter will instead focus on evaluating the progress made by new rounds of border talks, particularly after the 1998 nuclear tests, the aim being to shed light on the recent development of the boundary question. This chapter will illustrate that when it comes to forging amicable relations, China and India are burdened with the legacy of the boundary problem, and how the asymmetrical perception of threat regarding the boundary issue has made China and India fashion different approaches toward solving the boundary problem. India tends to be deeply apprehensive of threats stemming from the unresolved Sino-Indian border issue, while China appears less concerned about similar threats from India. The fact that efforts aimed at resolving the boundary dispute have so far borne little fruit has frustrated the two countries, and helped consolidate the mistrustful mindset of the 1960s.

Legacy of the Border Dispute

The 1962 Border War

The border dispute between China and India emerged as China began to lay a 1,200 km road from Xinjiang to Tibet in March 1956. The Chinese opted to construct the road cutting through the Aksai Chin region. Unfortunately, India also claimed the inhospitable mountainous region as a part of northern India. In fact, the Indians did not discover this strategic road until it was completed. Also, Beijing did not mention it during a series of summits with New Delhi.

The basic debate involved in the Sino-Indian border dispute was whether the Sino-Indian frontier had ever been formally demarcated on the ground. According to India, the western border between India and China was demarcated by the 1842 agreement between the Tibet and Kashmir authorities and the eastern border was demarcated by the McMahon Line of the 1913–14 Simla Conference.[3]

However, China maintained that, historically, no agreement on the Sino-Indian boundary had ever been concluded between the Chinese central government and the Indian government. Beijing also claimed that the Chinese central government did not send anybody to participate in the conclusion of the treaties mentioned by India, nor in their subsequent ratification. China found further support in the fact that the British government in 1899 had proposed to delineate this part of the boundary formally with the Chinese central government, but the proposal had already been rejected by the then Chinese government.

Regarding the McMahon Line in the eastern sector, China asserted that it was illegal and a product of British imperialist policy. Moreover, the Chinese argued, the McMahon Line had never been discussed at the Simla Conference, but had been determined by the British and Tibetan representatives through an exchange of secret notes at Delhi in March 1914 (Lawrance 1975: 122–6). The Chinese not only rejected the McMahon Line, but also laid claim to 90,000 sq km in the area shown on the Indian maps.

In fact, by the late 1950s, the Indian side held the belief that there was no border dispute between China and India. During his visit to China in 1954, Indian Prime Minister Nehru had raised a question with Chinese Premier Zhou Enlai, saying that he had discovered some maps published in China that gave a different borderline between the two countries, and Zhou replied that those maps were merely reprints of the old pre-liberation maps and that the authorities concerned had not had the time to revise them yet (Lawrance 1975: 117–22). After the discovery of the Xinjiang–Tibet road, Nehru wrote to Zhou Enlai, trying to remind his counterpart that since no border questions had been raised during the negotiation of the agreement concerning Tibet, the Indians were under the impression that there were no border disputes between India and China; the Indian side assumed that the 1954 Treaty had recognized India's position regarding the India–Tibet border. In other words, the Indian government was of the opinion that the Sino-Indian Agreement of 1954 had settled all outstanding issues between China and India, including the border problem. In his letter of reply to Nehru, however, Zhou pointed out that the border issue did exist, because the Sino-Indian boundary had never been formally delineated. Zhou admitted that the border question had not been raised in 1954 when negotiations were being held between the Chinese and Indian sides for agreement about Tibet, but he explained that it was because 'conditions were not yet ripe for its settlement and the Chinese side, on its part, had had no time to study the question' (Lawrance 1975: 122–6).

Coinciding with the Dalai Lama's exile to India in 1959, the border dispute increased tensions between China and India. From September 1959 to March 1960, around 30 notes, eight letters, and six memoranda were exchanged between New Delhi and Beijing over the boundary problem (Norbu 1997: 1086). As Sino-Indian relations further deteriorated on account of the territorial claims, minor skirmishes between Indian and Chinese troops began to take place at Lonjiu in the eastern sector in August 1959 and at the Kongka Pass in the western sector in October of the same year. China tried to persuade India by linking the border dispute, particularly the McMahon Line, with the imperialist legacy. China claimed that British imperialism constituted the fundamental reason for the dispute over the non-settlement of the Sino-Indian boundary question, and asked India not to follow the imperialist policy.

In April 1960, Chinese Premier Zhou Enlai and Vice-Premier Chen Yi visited India for border talks with Nehru. However, no substantial agreement was reached. At that time, China was still keen to secure India's friendship, as the Chinese thought that China's major threat came from America and its alliance in the East. China proposed that the two sides temporarily maintain the *status quo*, namely, each side would keep the border areas under its jurisdiction for the time being and not go beyond them (Lawrance 1975: 124–5). However, India refused to accept the temporary maintenance of the *status quo* along the border.

Diplomatic efforts to reduce the tension gradually proved a failure as the dispute along the border remained and worsened. In 1961, New Delhi began to adopt a controversial 'Forward Policy', thereby establishing a military presence in the disputed areas as far as possible. A series of measures and statements made by the Indian side further alarmed China.[4] China accused India of taking advantage of China's unilateral cessation of patrol activities to change the *status quo*, and viewed India's movements with misgivings.

The Chinese leader, Mao Zedong, was annoyed with India's uncooperative approach toward solving the boundary question. A military staff officer who was in charge of the border situation reported to Mao that the reason for the Indian government to adopt an 'aggressive' policy was its calculation that China would not dare to counter-attack because of the pressure from America in the East. Mao seemed to agree with this analysis, and then considered that military action might be the only way to stabilize the border and bring India to the negotiating table (Lei 1997: 208–9).

In order to 'teach India a lesson', the Chinese troops launched their 'counter-attack' against India on the morning of 20 October 1962, inflicting a humiliating defeat on India's ill-prepared and ill-equipped troops. As a former Indian diplomat put it, the PLA went through the Indian Army 'like a knife through butter' (Paranjpe 1998: 12). After the military victory pushing back the Indian side, the Chinese Government, on 21 November 1962, surprisingly announced a ceasefire and voluntarily withdrew to positions 20 km behind the line of control that had existed in 1959, and proposed that officials of the two sides hold meetings immediately. In order to create a good atmosphere for reconciliation between the two countries, China released more than 600 Indian personnel and returned the equipment that had been captured during the fighting. However, the Indian side considered the Chinese gestures as only propaganda (*Peking Review* 1963: 10–11). The Indian Parliament passed a resolution urging the government to recover every inch of India's territory lost in the war, which added to the political difficulty of the Indian leaders in securing a compromise border deal with Beijing.

The 1962 war proved Nehru's friendly policy towards China—such as granting diplomatic recognition to Beijing, the Bandung conference and accepting China's claims over Tibet—a failure. The Indians felt that they had been betrayed by the Chinese (Mullik 1971). On the other hand, the Chinese blamed India for the hostile developments. Some senior

Chinese diplomats even complained that India's high-level leaders, with their narrow nationalism, arrogance and egotism, were responsible for the worsening of China–India relations (Liu 2007a: 47). All the euphoria about the Sino-Indian brotherhood dissipated. Haunted by the legacy of border war, Sino-Indian relations since 1962 have been characterized by mutual antagonism, rivalry, distrust, and hostility (Garver 2001; Malik 1995, 2012). Both sides' inability to find a mutually-acceptable proposal impeded the improvement of Sino-Indian relations.

Throughout the Cold War and in the post-Cold War era, the border dispute remained an indelible mark in Sino-Indian relations and China and India continue to hold each other responsible. The military clash is still deeply inscribed in the memory of strategic decision-makers and analysts, if not in public memory, and has acted as an aggravating factor whenever China and India prepare to engage each other. That is why a Chinese scholar urged both sides to 'clarify the facts' about the 1962 conflict in order to normalize their bilateral relations.[5] The reason is simple: no one can make friends with an 'aggressor' or a 'betrayer'.

In fact, the unsolved border dispute places much more pressure on the Indian than on the Chinese side. For Indians, the border war has become a vivid example of the 'China threat', and the unsolved border dispute is a reminder of another possible surprise attack by China. The military defeat also undermined India's national prestige and status in international society. India's credit as a leader among the developing countries was undermined. The historical enmity caused by the 1962 border war then became a significant source of India's threat perception.

Renewed Boundary Talks

While the border dispute became a serious issue between both China and India, Beijing was endeavouring to sign border agreements with Burma and Nepal in 1960, Mongolia in 1962, and Pakistan in 1963. China tried to build up an image of being keen to settle the boundary problem by peaceful negotiation, the implication being that if the boundary negotiation between China and India failed, China should not be blamed.

India's suspicion of China deepened in the wake of China's first nuclear test in October 1964, barely two years after the Sino-Indian war. Undoubtedly, it placed great pressure on the Indians. Tensions continued, as there were border skirmishes in 1965 and 1967. India's annexation of

Sikkim during 1973–5 raised another diplomatic confrontation between the two countries.[6]

In order to promote the idea, Chinese leader Deng Xiaoping also suggested that China and India could adopt a 'one package deal' (*yilanzi jiejue*) to solve the border dispute when Indian Foreign Minister A.B Vajpayee visited Beijing in 1979. He then reiterated the position in an interview to an Indian journal, *Vikrant*. Deng Xiaoping said the package deal meant China would accept the border claimed by India in the eastern sector, namely, the McMahon Line, in return for Indian acceptance of the *status quo* in the western sector (Shen 1987: 88). Since then, the package deal has become one of China's basic principles to settle the longstanding border dispute between the two countries.

On the other hand, India refused to accept the package deal, and supported a separate negotiation of each sector's border, taking into account the specific aspects of each. The Indian side insisted on minor territorial adjustments in the eastern sector and China's unilateral concession in the western sector (Liu 1994: 2). India was more concerned with the effect of the border dispute on its security environment, insisted that a settlement of the border issue was a necessary precondition for improving bilateral relations, and rejected the package proposal.

Since each side merely reiterated its well-known position on the border problem and then dispersed, the eight rounds of border talks between 1981 and 1987 did not lead to a breakthrough or even substantial progress in the solution of the border question. The only achievement was that both sides agreed to maintain stability and tranquillity along the frontier and that the border issue should be resolved through peaceful negotiations and friendly consultations (Liu 1994: 3). However, these talks did not prevent the two countries from engaging in minor border clashes in 1986–7.

The breakthrough visit by Indian Prime Minister Rajiv Gandhi to China in December 1988 broke the impasse in Sino-Indian relations and led to a re-commencement of border negotiations. Regarding the boundary problem, the two sides decided to set up an India–China JWG on the Boundary Question to work out a mutually-acceptable resolution. More importantly, India changed its position to admit that there was a boundary dispute between the two sides, although it did not insist that solving the boundary problem was a precondition for the normalization of Sino-Indian relations (Fang 2002).

From June 1989 until March 2005, 15 sessions of the JWG meetings were held (see Table 3.1). During the visit by the Indian Prime Minister Narasimha Rao to China in September 1993, an India–China Diplomatic and Military Expert Group was created as a subgroup of the JWG. The Expert Group, which was designed to deal with technical details at the Deputy Director-General/Joint Secretary level, met 14 times between February 1994 and June 2002. Although these talks made little progress in reaching a final solution of the border disputes, they were instrumental in establishing a mechanism for regular discussions. More importantly, unlike the previous border talks held between 1981 and 1987, the JWG and Expert Group meetings proved successful in maintaining peace and tranquillity in troubled areas along the Sino-Indian border. That is, to some extent, the dialogue mechanism itself was a kind of CBM, which tied both sides to the negotiation table, and avoided the need to resort to extreme measures.

Besides, the establishment of various dialogue mechanisms on the border problem and the lack of any significant improvement indicated that both sides were willing to solve the problem, but not able to narrow their differences. Fortunately, there were signs that both sides promised to endeavour to maintain peace and tranquillity along the LAC and strengthen cooperation in other fields while working to solve the boundary question. The trend also reflected both sides' willingness to shelve their disputes until there was the possibility of an acceptable resolution.

Confidence-Building Measures along the Border

According to the *Sino-Indian Joint Press Communiqué* issued on 23 December 1988, the aim of the JWG was to seek a mutually-acceptable solution to the Sino-India boundary question. However, from the outset, the JWG focused most of its efforts on initiating CBMs that could maintain peace and tranquillity along the border, instead of discussing possible recommendations to settle the overlapping claims over border areas. This real focus was a clear sign that both sides acknowledged that the time was not yet ripe for reaching an ultimate resolution on territorial adjustment. Aware of the complexity of the border issue, both sides avoided rushing into a border agreement, but aimed at creating a favourable atmosphere conducive to a final settlement of the dispute. The two countries agreed that CBMs were not only of vital importance to safeguarding peace and tranquillity along the disputed border, but would

Table 3.1 India–China Joint Working Group Meetings

	Date	Event	Place	Major Development
1989	30 June–4 July	1st meeting	Beijing	The two sides promised to make efforts to maintain peace and tranquillity along the LAC
1990	30–31 August	2nd meeting	New Delhi	Military border personnel would meet from time to time at an appropriate level.
1991	12–14 May	3rd meeting	Beijing	The two sides exchanged views on how to maintain peace and tranquillity along the LAC.
1992	20–21 February	4th meeting	New Delhi	The two sides agreed that military border personnel would hold regular meetings in the eastern and western sectors in June and October every year. They also agreed to establish telephone links and discussed the issue of prior notification of military exercises.
1992	27–29 October	5th meeting	Beijing	The two sides continued to discuss measures to maintain peace and tranquillity in the regions along the LAC, but no progress was made.
1993	24–27 June	6th meeting	New Delhi	The two sides initiated the 1993 CBMs Agreement.
1994	6–7 July	7th meeting	Beijing	The two sides agreed in principle to the setting up of more points for meetings between border personnel.
1995	18–20 August	8th meeting	New Delhi	The two sides agreed to pull back troops from four forward outposts along the border.
1996	16–18 October	9th meeting	Beijing	The two sides agreed to establish two additional meeting sites along the eastern section of the border, and decided to hold a meeting along the middle section.

1997	4–5 August	10th meeting	New Delhi	The two sides exchanged the instruments of ratification of the 1996 CBMs Agreement.
1999	26–27 April	11th meeting	Beijing	The two sides claimed that there was considerable scope for developing and expanding bilateral relations in economic, commercial, and other fields, but no progress was made.
2000	28–29 April	12th meeting	New Delhi	The two sides agreed to exchange maps as a further step toward working on the identification of the LAC.
2001	31 July–1 August	13th meeting	Beijing	The two sides defined their individual perceptions of the LAC along the middle sector and recorded the differences on the maps.
2002	21–22 November	14th meeting	New Delhi	The two sides agreed to exchange the maps in the western sector in January 2003.
2005	30 March	15th meeting	Beijing	Both sides reviewed the on-going process of LAC and CBMs.

Source: Author.

also contribute to the steady development of their bilateral relations (*Xinhua* 1993a: 14).

Some Chinese scholars claimed that the early proposal to adopt the CBMs was initiated by the Chinese side in the late 1950s. They argued that, in late 1959, the Chinese had suggested both China and India should withdraw their military forces 20 km from the LAC, and not send armed personnel into the disputed areas. In November 1962, the Chinese government issued a statement proposing a ceasefire and announced that the Chinese troops would withdraw 20 km from the LAC on its own initiative, and asked that the Indian side not cross the LAC (*Renmin Chubanshe* 1962). Factually, however, it might be too simple to conclude that the Sino-Indian CBMs could be agreed upon in the early days. It was observed that Beijing began to embrace the concept and recognize the worth of CBMs only after the mid-1980s with the relaxation of the international situation, increasing economic interdependence and the launch of domestic economic reform (Foot 1996; Xia 1997). China's economic development necessitates a stable and peaceful environment; this applies in equal measure to India. Thus, Sino-Indian CBMs are due to both countries seeking a peaceful environment to focus on the paramount task of national development.

Since the early 1990s, some CBMs were proposed and followed by China and India to secure the peace along the disputed boundary areas. After Chinese Premier Li Peng's visit to India in 1991, the two sides agreed to regularize the meetings between border personnel, which would be held at Bum La in the eastern sector and in the Spanaggur Gap area in the western sector in June and October every year (*Xinhua* 1992a: 19–20). The two sides also agreed to establish telephone links to facilitate communication between border personnel. Transparency, communication, and constraint measures were on the agenda, and the discussions focused on the mutual transparency of the location of military positions, prior notification of military exercises, the prevention of air intrusion, and the redeployment of forces along the LAC (*All India Radio Network* 1993a, *Xinhua* 1993b).

The visit to China by Indian Prime Minister Narasimha Rao in September 1993, provided the setting for the codification of the work done by the JWG meetings. The two sides signed the 'Agreement on the Maintenance of Peace and Tranquillity along the LAC in the China–India Border Areas' (hereafter the 1993 CBMs Agreement).[7] The issues included in this agreement were troop-reduction, conflict-avoidance measures, notification measures, and the establishment of the Expert Group, comprising diplomatic and military representatives from both sides to assist the JWG.

Being the first CBMs agreement between China and India, the deal was described as a 'positive breakthrough' in Sino-Indian relations (*All India Radio Network* 1993b: 38). In fact, due to the ground already covered at previous JWG meetings for the CBMs, many unforeseen outcomes that might have arisen from the agreement were avoided. The 1993 CBMs Agreement was a mere formalization of the principles to which Beijing and New Delhi had already subscribed. Moreover, the agreement was declaratory in nature and failed to cover details in any depth. Instead, the task of formulating the implementation measures was assigned to the newly-established Expert Group.

A more credible explanation for the lack of implementation measures is that the two sides could not reach a consensus on detailed measures. For example, although discussions about a reduction in the number of troops continued, there was no convergence of views on the specific content of this issue. Up until 1993, it was estimated that Chinese troops in Tibet outnumbered Indian troops in the China–India border areas by two to one (*The Economist* 1993: 69). Given its numerical advantage, Beijing preferred a 'one-for-one cutback of troops' approach. Conversely, the Indian side argued that geographical factors needed to be considered. From the Indian point of view, the Chinese troops on the plateau could be quickly moved on the Chinese side of the border. For that reason, the Indian side suggested, the troop reduction along the LAC should be based on the 'adjusted ratio' approach to reflect the steep terrain and logistical difficulties on India's side (*The Economist* 1996: 82). At last, the 'mutual and equal security' principle was accepted by both sides to cut their respective troop numbers, but no details were given on how to reach the goal. The significance of the 1993 CBMs Agreement, therefore, lies not in the introduction of new measures, but in the political willingness to translate the progress made and the consensus reached by previous JWG meetings into a formal arrangement that would bind India and China more legally.

Although a final resolution on the border issue was not yet in sight, Beijing and New Delhi reiterated that the CBMs already in place were working well. At the eighth meeting of the JWG, which took place in New

Delhi in August 1995, the two sides agreed to pull back troops from four forward outposts, two on each side, located in the Wangdun area near the Sumdorong Chu Valley in the eastern sector (*Renmin Ribao* 1995: 6). The stations of the Chinese and Indian troops in this area had been located about 50–100 yards from each other, provoking the military clash of 1986–7. The decision to withdraw troops further back was calculated to prevent a recurrence of a similar incident.

After Indian Prime Minister Narasimha Rao's visit to China, the JWG and the Expert Group worked toward the 1993 CBMs Agreement's implementation. A further step in that direction was taken with the signing of the 'Agreement on the Confidence-Building Measures in the Military Field along the Line of Actual Control in the India–China Border Areas (hereafter the 1996 CBMs Agreement) during Chinese President Jiang Zemin's four-day state visit to India in November 1996, the first by a Chinese head of state since the two countries had established diplomatic relations in 1950.[8]

In this agreement, Beijing and New Delhi advanced beyond agreeing on declaratory principles and proposed more detailed implementation measures. For example, they set a ceiling on the scale of any military exercises and created a 'no-fly zone' along the border areas. However, more work was needed. Despite agreeing to limit their respective military forces to 'minimum levels compatible with the friendly and good-neighbourly relations between the two countries', Beijing and New Delhi still could not reach an accord on the method of troop reductions. Furthermore, the 1996 CBMs Agreement was held up by a discussion over provisions for communication and constraint measures, and the lack of any means to verify and monitor.[9] Like the 1993 CBMs Agreement, the 1996 CBMs Agreement functioned more as a conflict avoidance measure. However, there is no denying that the signing of the agreement was another new political initiative to help ease tensions along the Sino-Indian border.

The Chinese side attached a high degree of importance to the 1996 CBMs Agreement. For example, the Chinese President Jiang Zemin hailed the agreement as a factor that would further enhance peace and security in the border areas and create a sound climate for the eventual resolution of the boundary question. The senior Chinese specialist on Sino-Indian relations, Wang Hongwei, even considered the treaty as a 'no-war pact' between the two sides, on the grounds that the 1996 CBMs Agreement removed the only dangerous or explosive element in the bilateral relationship (Wang 1998b: 376). The reactions from the Indian side were also quite positive. Some Indian analysts deemed that the agreement had eased the security concerns of both countries (Cherian 1996: 38).

In fact, the two sides were still unable to narrow their differences on troop reductions along the border (Singh 1997: 543–59). Nevertheless, both sides expressed satisfaction with the results of the two CBMs agreements, and the border has since remained peaceful. Furthermore, both sides tried to marginalize the boundary dispute to make sure that the overall development of Sino-Indian friendship and cooperation would not be hijacked by the boundary issue.

Identifying the Line of Actual Control

India's Nuclear Tests and the Border Talks

Although the CBMs have worked well to avoid any border conflict, the absence of a mutually-accepted alignment of the LAC created problems for the CBMs. In fact, the significance of this is well-acknowledged by the 1996 CBMs Agreement, as Article X noted that the full implementation of some of the provisions of the treaty would depend on the two sides arriving at a common understanding of the LAC. However, neither side advanced the identification of LAC after acknowledging this problem.

As codified in the 1993 CBMs Agreement, China and India agreed to 'check and determine the segments of the Line of Actual Control where they [had] differing views as to its alignment'. Both sides also agreed that the Expert Group meetings would assist the JWG in the task of clarifying the LAC. Compared to the evolution of the CBMs, however, the pace of the talks on the delineation of the LAC has been slow. Issues related to the clarification of the LAC were addressed only intermittently in the early days of the JWG and Expert Group meetings. At the eighth meeting of the JWG in August 1995, the two sides identified certain parts of the LAC where there was a difference of opinion concerning the alignment, and agreed to resolve the questions one by one through consultation (*Renmin Ribao* 1995: 6). At the ninth session of the JWG meetings in October 1996, both sides reiterated their wish to resolve the differences gradually through consultation (*Xinhua* 1996b). And, at the 10th meeting of the JWG, held in August 1997, the two sides agreed to speed up the clarification of the LAC. Despite these commitments, no concrete progress was made during the early border talks when the CBMs emerged as a high-priority issue.

Although the CBMs have proved helpful in avoiding further unnecessary conflicts along the border, they do not represent a final solution to the border issue because China's and India's competing irredentist claims remain unresolved. The two sides have yet to arrive at an agreement on where the LAC actually runs.

In addition, the conclusion of the CBMs has successfully created a somewhat complacent atmosphere that sometimes hides the fact that the unsettled boundary problem remains a graver concern to India than to China. Although the CBMs contributed to maintaining the *status quo* along the border, the JWG meetings were not able to frame any possible proposal for a solution to the border dispute. The CBMs did not generate enough confidence to satisfy New Delhi. Even the Chinese side gradually ignored India's concerns and then was shocked by India's determination to justify the nuclear tests by citing the border problem as a concern. The Pokhran II nuclear tests, and the harsh Chinese reaction to them, strained relations between China and India despite the diplomatic efforts that were conducted in an attempt to avoid further conflict along the disputed border.

India's China threat accusation seemed to be an embarrassment for those who had hailed the CBMs as a symbolic achievement for enhancing mutual trust. In a low-profile gesture, the Chinese tried to play down the significance of the Sino-Indian CBMs. A comparison between China's two White Papers on national defence yields some indications of Beijing's changed perception. In the White Paper titled 'China's National Defence', which was issued in 1998, China cited the Sino-Indian CBMs as one example of its preference for CBMs. However, in a revised vision of the White Paper, 'China's National Defence in 2000', no mention of the Sino-Indian CBMs was made, while most of the other examples in the previous version remained.[10] The changes in the content of references to the Sino-Indian CBMs are worthy of attention. If nothing else, they reflected Beijing's reservation over the CBMs with India.

The boundary dispute has been seen as one of the most important issues between China and India. The progress of the border talks was viewed as an index of the normalization of China–India relations. Aware of the symbolic significance of the border talks, Beijing then used the border talks as an instrument to increase the pressure on New Delhi by suspending the JWG talks.

In fact, Beijing did not immediately sever all dialogue regarding the border problem in the wake of the Pokhran II tests, as the sixth meeting of the Expert Group went ahead as scheduled in Beijing on 8–9 June 1998. The meeting was held less than one month after India conducted the tests, and was the first contact between two countries at an institutionalized level. Amid the uneasy atmosphere created by the shock of the nuclear tests, the Chinese side tried to play down the significance of the meeting by describing the talks as routine. Moreover, the Chinese used the meeting to convey their deep dissatisfaction with India, instead of attempting further negotiations on the border question (*Agence France-Presse* [*AFP*] 1998). Since nuclear tests dominated the agenda of the meeting, not surprisingly, no headway was made with regard to the border talks. For the first time, the Chinese Foreign Ministry spokesman admitted that no progress had been made at the boundary meeting (*AFP* 1998). Still angry at India's accusation, the Chinese side then refused to fix a date for the 11th round of JWG meetings, which had been scheduled for 1998. Meanwhile, China also hardened its position towards the border dispute in the wake of the nuclear tests by re-claiming sovereignty over the disputed area.

Such a diplomatic manifestation of delaying the boundary talks reveals some messages. First, China thought the suspension of border talks would place more pressure on Delhi than on Beijing. Second, the Chinese sensed that India was more eager to solve the boundary problem than China was. As a result, Beijing adroitly made use of the border negotiations against India. This strategy further demonstrated that both sides' concerns about the border problem are asymmetrical.

Only after deciding that New Delhi had showed renewed sincerity for developing China–India relations, did Beijing take note of India's plea for the resumption of the JWG meetings. The JWG talks were then resumed in April 1999 when the 11th meeting of the JWG was held in Beijing. Among the issues discussed were security concerns and nuclear disarmament. New Delhi spent much time at the meeting assuring its counterpart that India did not regard China as a security threat. While no agreement on the border issue was made at the meeting, the two sides turned their attention to expanding further ties in other fields, claiming that there was considerable scope for developing bilateral relations in economic, commercial, and other areas (Singh 1999a).

A positive shift was seen at the seventh meeting of the Expert Group, held in November 1999. Unlike the negative assessment of the previous round of the meeting, the Chinese considered the meeting as having made progress (Fang 2002: 169). Following the trend of restoring the pre-Pokhran II relationship, at the 12th JWG meeting in April 2000, Beijing and New Delhi agreed to resume high-level military interactions, which had been suspended after India's nuclear tests in May 1998 (*The Hindu* 2000j).

The early days of the 1990s witnessed an increasing imbalance between China and India in terms of economic growth and military strength. An assessment by India concluded that India's negotiating clout with China might be weakened, as the power gap between the two countries was widening. After the nuclear tests, however, that perception has been partly reversed. As an Indian newspaper commented, a 'confident India' was ready for talks with China after the nuclear tests (*The Indian Express* 2000b). Some Indians also believed that a credible deterrent would facilitate a breakthrough on the border talks with China (*The Indian Express* 1998f).

Thus, given India's nuclear capability and rising status in the international community, some Indians came to feel that they were in a stronger negotiating position than ever and should grasp the occasion. As a result, in the current circumstances, India is keen to resolve the issue in a timely manner, while China still emphasizes that 'time' and 'patience' are necessary to solve a problem left over from history.

Exchange of Maps

In brief, the burdensome task of delineating the boundary consists of a two-step procedure. The first step is the clarification of the LAC, namely, translating a notional line into a real delineated one. After exchanging and comparing their delineations of the LAC, the two sides need to reconcile their differences over the alignment to arrive at an agreement on where the LAC really runs. The second task is to convert the *de facto* LAC into a *de jure* international border, which might involve territorial adjustments.

Thus, early delineation of the LAC emerged as an option for stabilizing the border regions and securing a working boundary that the military forces on both sides would respect (Dutta 2001). While the CBMs dominated the agenda of the early talks of the JWG, after 1999, the focus was shifted to the clarification of the LAC.

After a long period of hesitation, the task of clarifying the LAC gained fresh momentum after the Indian External Affairs Minister, Jaswant Singh, visited Beijing in June 1999, the first visit by an Indian high-ranking official since the 1998 nuclear tests. During the trip, the two countries agreed to begin formal talks on the clarification of the LAC (*The Indian Express* 1999b). At the 12th JWG meeting in April 2000, the two sides decided to conduct a 'maps exercise', i.e., exchanging and comparing their respective maps on the LAC as a way of working toward the identification of the line. The two countries also decided to choose the middle sector as the first section to be determined, because it was smaller and less controversial than the other parts of the border.

In fact, the idea of exchanging the LAC maps had been proposed some time earlier, and had been included in the 1996 CBMs Agreement, but had not materialized. After a lengthy period, China and India finally increased their efforts toward this end. At the eighth meeting of the Expert Group in November 2000, the two countries, for the first time, officially exchanged their respective maps depicting the 545-km middle sector of the LAC (*The Hindu* 2000k). At the ninth meeting of the Expert Group, held in New Delhi in June 2001, the delegations from both countries reviewed the other side's maps and exchanged views about the differences (*The Hindu* 2001j). The two sides then reviewed the work of the Expert Group on clarification of the LAC in the middle sector and recorded their individual perceptions on the maps at the 13th session of the JWG in July–August 2001. Reports said that there was a convergence of views on the LAC alignment along large portions in this sector (*The Hindu* 2001).

The Indian side made some moderate progress in keeping pressure on the Chinese to quicken the pace of the negotiations. According to Indian sources, the first-ever exchange of maps took place after Indian External Minister Jaswant Singh had written to his Chinese counterpart urging that the process of clarification and confirmation of the LAC be expedited (MEA 2001). However, this did not imply any shift in China's management of the border problem. In fact, the Indian officials involved in the maps exercise sensed that their Chinese counterparts were not interested in solving the LAC issue (Fang 2002: 175).

China and India spent more than a year completing the exchanges of the less-controversial middle sector maps. Given the tempo of the talks, however, it did not seem that the clarification of the entire LAC would be a short-term process; it was unlikely that a quick settlement about the final alignment of the entire border would be found. Moreover, China's reluctance to set a time frame to clarify and confirm the LAC would result in a delay of the border resolution.

A breakthrough seemed to have occurred during Indian External Affairs Minister Jaswant Singh's visit to China in March 2002. Singh announced that China and India had agreed to put a time frame on the exchange of maps, and added that the two sides would begin to exchange maps on the western sector in June 2002 with a view to concluding the process by the end of the year, while a similar exercise on the eastern sector would be conducted in early 2003. The Indian side was very optimistic about the development, with Jaswant Singh claiming that this step was 'something India has not been able to achieve in the last 50 years (*The Hindu* 2002g). Contrary to India's optimism, however, the Chinese media's silence on the matter reflected China's cautiousness.

To the surprise of many, the two sides failed to keep the promise to exchange their own maps of the western sector as had been announced earlier. Chinese sources revealed that the two sides had been ready to exchange maps in the boundary meeting. However, the Chinese side had suddenly found that the map of the western sector presented by the Indian side included the very western part of the disputed China–India border, covering Kashmir. The Chinese side considered this as going beyond the consensus and decided to call off the process of exchanging maps (Liu 2007a: 58).

The Indian side acknowledges that the LAC established after the 1962 war remains more or less stable, but has not been demarcated. For example, the Indian side argued that between 1956, 1960, and 1962, Chinese maps showed three distinct and advancing LACs, especially in the Ladakh sector (Dutta 2001). The Indian side might want to make use of the opportunity to clarify the differences over that section, and also make China stabilize its western part. However, the Chinese suspected that India had tried to use the exchange to gain an extra advantage during the boundary talks. As a result, the Chinese refused to continue the exchange of maps.

Again, the Chinese seemed quite unconcerned about the interruption of the border talk process. This development proved that China is not aiming for an early resolution unless it was favourable for the Chinese side. In addition, China did not think it necessary to solve the boundary dispute in a timely manner.

Gap in the Sense of Urgency

The Indian side has been aware of China's reluctance to make any further compromise to quicken the boundary process. Just as the senior Indian analyst Sujit Dutta (2001) anticipated, China has stuck to its territorial claims and refused to budge from any part of the disputed territories, while showing little interest in an early settlement of territorial issues.

On the other hand, the Chinese have defended their position by stressing that they have maintained a positive attitude in seeking solutions to the border issue, and blame India for the negligible progress in the Sino-Indian border talks. The Chinese side argued that India had been anxious to settle the boundary question on its own terms and was unwilling to settle the issue on the basis of mutual accommodation. Ye Zhengjia, a veteran Chinese diplomat specializing in Sino-Indian relations, complained that the Chinese were finding it very difficult to deal with the Indian side in the JWG meetings (Ram 1998c: 18). Chinese Assistant Foreign Minister Wang Yi also claimed that the Chinese side had been making specific proposals to India since 1996 to resolve the boundary issue, but that the Indian response had always been that it was too early to deal with issues such as the delineation of the border (*The Hindu* 2000l).

In fact, Beijing also desires an early solution for the Sino-Indian border problem, but it does not consider that there is any possibility of solving the issue completely in the near future. One basic contention embraced by the Chinese is that the border dispute is a complicated question left over from history; both sides are, therefore, required to show patience and allow ample time to solve the problem. The late Chinese leader, Deng Xiaoping, even suggested that if the Sino-Indian border dispute could not be resolved at an early date, both countries could agree to leave the issue to a later generation, while developing relations in other fields (Ranganathan and Khanna 2000: 166). Deng's position was well-explicated by Sha Zukang, China's Director General of Arms Control and Disarmament. Addressing a conference on the CBMs in the Asia-Pacific region, Sha said that some territory or border issues that could not be resolved immediately should be shelved and be negotiated only when conditions became favourable. Before the dispute could be resolved, he argued, the countries concerned should adopt security and CBMs to maintain normal relations and economic cooperation (*Renmin Ribao* 1993: 6). Concurring with this position, Cheng Ruisheng, former

Chinese Ambassador to India, said that it was unrealistic to try to resolve the border dispute overnight and suggested that the two countries should hammer out relevant agreements to ensure peace and stability along the LAC (Joseph 2002).

New Delhi once also held the position that the border dispute could not be resolved in the short term. For example, when Indian President R. Venkataraman visited China in May 1992, he admitted that 'the boundary question was complex and was far from being resolved' (*Xinhua* 1992b: 18–19). In 1995, Indian External Affairs Minister Pranab Mukherjee, noted that the border dispute was a complex problem that required time and patience (*All India Radio Network* 1995: 36). After the resumption of the JWG talks in 1999, however, the Indian side felt that progress had been too slow.

There are two plausible explanations for the change in India's stance. First, the tension between China and India following Pokhran II reminded the Indian leadership that the Sino-Indian border dispute remains a security concern for India's northern frontier. Despite the official clarification that the border has remained peaceful, there have been repeated reports that Chinese troops at some places along the LAC have been conducting aggressive patrolling (*The Pioneer* 2001: 5). Although New Delhi still identifies China as a potential enemy, the threat India faces from Pakistan is, in fact, more immediate. Moreover, the Indian side needs to allocate more resources to tackle Pakistan-related issues. For example, Indo-Tibetan Border Police Chief Gautam Kaul, revealed that he was facing a shortage of troops due to militancy in Kashmir (*The Hindu* 2000m). Amid the India–Pakistan tensions following the terrorist attack on the Indian Parliament on 13 December 2001, India moved part of its troops that faced China in the east, toward the north, in order to put pressure on Pakistan (*The Hindu* 2001l). As its security forces are stretched thin in the China–India border region, India has an added incentive to find a resolution to the Sino-Indian border dispute. Furthermore, an early resolution of the border issue could help reduce the possibility that China uses the unresolved border dispute as an excuse to take military action in order to ease India's pressure on Pakistan.

In order to address its security needs, therefore, the Indian side is more enthusiastic about clarifying the alignment of the LAC than China. Since the 12th JWG meeting, the Indian side has increased its efforts to find an early resolution. In April 2000, Indian External Affairs Minister

Jaswant Singh told the visiting Chinese delegation of the JWG that India attached importance to 'result-oriented negotiations' (*The Hindu* 2000j). Jaswant Singh's statements came just days after Chinese Foreign Minister Tang Jiaxuan's repetition that time and patience would be required from both sides in order to arrive at a reasonable settlement, underlining India's suspicion of China's real intentions with regard to the border dispute negotiations. This kind of friction surfaced again when Indian President K.R. Narayanan visited China in May 2000. Rebutting the Chinese stance that the boundary question was a remnant of history, Narayanan retorted that inherited problems needed to be resolved and 'must not be left over for history' (*The Hindu* 2000n).

It is obvious that the Chinese leadership remains loyal to the 'time and patience' principle despite the fact that they have promised to accelerate the negotiation process. For example, when Li Peng, Chairman of the Standing Committee of the National People's Congress, visited India in January 2001, he reiterated Beijing's insistence on this position of 'time and patience' (*The Hindu* 2001c).

China's approach towards the boundary problem has been more consistent than India's. The basic reason for this is that China does not consider the unresolved boundary problem as a serious security concern, and as a result, has the patience to wait for a more beneficial solution. China's strategy remains to develop relations in other fields in order to create an atmosphere more conducive to solving the dispute. On the contrary, the Indian side looks with misgivings at the disputed border and worries that China would use the unsolved border problem to bully India. In addition, India is keen to wipe out the displeasing history of the border dispute by concluding the border issue. Due to the asymmetrical concerns, an early solution to the boundary problem is more important to India.

Revisiting China's Package Proposal

China's emphasis on 'time and patience' during the Sino-Indian border talks, however, fails to explain why China has resolved other border disputes left over from history yet appears half-hearted about resolving the one with India. The underlying reason for China's apathy toward an early border resolution is that China sees no indication that India is going to accept China's package proposal.

China's official report on its foreign relations argued that it had already proposed the 'one package deal (*yi lanzi jiejue*) to solve the border dispute (Han *et al.* 1987: 252). The package proposal was later renewed as an approach of 'mutual understanding and mutual accommodation' (*hu liang hu rang*) by the Chinese. While 'mutual understanding' calls for both sides to understand the other side's position, 'mutual accommodation' means there should be a 'give-and-take' approach for settling the border dispute. Thus, 'if one side hopes to get a piece of land from the other, it should offer a proper piece of land to the other' (Liu 1994: 181). During his visit to India in January 2002, Chinese Premier Zhu Rongji still stressed that the historical issues between the two countries could be resolved gradually through mutual accommodation (Cherian 2002).

Through the package proposal, the Chinese said they were willing to make some concessions in the eastern sector in exchange for India's concessions in the western sector (Zhao 2000: 242). In the western sector, China's main aim is to secure the strategically important Aksai Chin, containing the Tibet–Xinjiang link road. As far as the eastern sector is concerned, the Chinese demand territorial adjustments in order to hold the Tawang tract. The so-called package proposal seemed to be pragmatic and a mutually beneficial resolution of the border problem. For China, it could have secured Aksai Chin in the eastern sector. For its part, India could have legalized its possession of Arunachal Pradesh in the eastern sector. However, the proposal for the mutual ceding of territory was rejected by India.

The Indians were reluctant to endorse China's mutual accommodation approach. C.V. Ranganathan, the former Indian Ambassador to China, argued that it was unclear what the Chinese had in mind regarding the 'mutual accommodation' proposal (Ranganathan and Khanna 2000: 167). That might be true, as China's claim on the western sector of the LAC has been changing; also, India was taken by surprise after China laid claims to Tawang (Liu 2007a: 49). However, while some analysts in India realize that India's flexibility over Tawang along the eastern sector is likely to mean China will accommodate India's claims along the rest of the boundary, India shows no sign of conceding Tawang, as New Delhi has invested a considerable amount in building defence and administrative architecture there (*The Hindu* 2001j).

The disagreement on the package deal has been identified as the main obstacle to the eight rounds of border talks in the 1980s (Zhang 2000:

28). The Chinese seem to be confident that the 'mutual accommodation' deal is the only possible approach to solving the border dispute. On this point, however, Beijing underestimates the pressure that a democratically-elected government has to face in dealing with any territorial 'concession'.

A study of China's negotiating behaviour has concluded that the Chinese tend to postpone indefinitely negotiations that they consider unfavourable, and show steadfast patience in maintaining their positions (Chang 2001: 13–17). Since the border dispute cannot be resolved on terms favourable to China, the Chinese have shown a tendency to freeze the issue in order to protect their own interests. As Ranganathan and Khanna have pointed out, 'Where it has not been possible to resolve an issue peacefully, China has been willing to shelve it, because the Chinese are not willing to surrender or compromise on what they consider to be their legitimate interests and entitlement' (Ranganathan and Khanna 2000: 158). Particularly, considering that the Sino-Indian border has generally remained peaceful, there is no urgency for China to resolve the problem if Beijing cannot bring New Delhi to agree to its terms.

Finding a Mutually Acceptable Solution

Special Representative Mechanism

The JWG mechanism has helped to build a CBMs regime along the disputed China–India border, and to stabilize the LAC, but the difficulty of delineating the LAC made the Indian side believe that the boundary problem should be solved from a political perspective, rather than in a historical, technical, or legal manner.

Again, it was India that proposed a new initiative to find an earlier final solution for the boundary problem. During the visit of Indian Prime Minister Vajpayee to China from 22 to 27 June 2003, a new mechanism for border talks was set up. China and India agreed to raise the level of negotiators to a higher political status by appointing their respective Special Representatives as the key negotiators to explore the framework of a boundary settlement from the political perspective of the overall bilateral relationship.

To show its emphasis on the initiative, New Delhi then appointed its National Security Advisor as the Special Representative of the China–India boundary problem. As it was New Delhi that had taken the decision to upgrade the level of talks, however, Beijing accepted the overture reluctantly. China initially desired to appoint a secretary-level official as its special envoy, but India had no intention of making the special representative a sequel to the JWG meetings, and favoured a more senior leader with sufficient political clout (Chawla 2003). Then, China's Executive Vice-Foreign Minister, Dai Bingguo, became China's special representative. Apparently, the political level of Vice-Foreign Minister is below that of National Security Advisor, but India believed the change of formalities for the boundary talks would help resolve the problem.

The first meeting of the Special Representatives took place in Delhi from 23 to 24 October 2003. By early 2013, 15 rounds of Special Representative meetings had taken place on the basis of their mandate to evolve a framework for a boundary settlement and address the problem from the political perspective of the overall bilateral relationship (see Table 3.2). That is, China and India decided to stop the process of focusing on technical problems, and prioritized the identification of common principles as the first task for solving the boundary problem.

In general, there were two stages for meetings. During the first phase, the aim of the meetings was to hammer out a methodology to resolve the boundary dispute. The second phase then focused on devising a framework agreement for resolving the dispute on the basis of the 'political parameters and guiding principles'. The special representative mechanism was compatible with China's strategy towards the boundary dispute. According to Chinese Premier Wen Jiabao, it was important that the two sides 'bear in mind the larger picture, expand exchanges and cooperation in all areas and properly settle questions left over from history' (*The Hindu* 2005a).

The two sides have maintained the confidentiality of the Special Representative discussions, and have not revealed many details of the deliberations that have taken place between the Special Representatives. A brief statement has usually been issued at the end of each round of talks. Regarding the tone and tenor of the meetings, the official statements have repeatedly said that the meetings have been held 'in a cordial, constructive and cooperative atmosphere'.[11]

After five rounds of talks, the Special Representative Meetings led to the conclusion of the 'Agreement on Political Parameters and Guiding Principles for the Settlement of the China–India Boundary Question' (hereafter the Guiding Principles Agreement), which was signed on 11 April 2005, during Chinese Premier Wen Jiabao's visit to New Delhi. The

Table 3.2 Special Representative Meetings

	Date	Event	Place	Major Developments
2003	23–24 October	1st meeting	New Delhi	The two sides formulated guiding principles.
2004	12–13 January	2nd meeting	Beijing	The two sides formulated guiding principles.
2004	26–27 July	3rd meeting	New Delhi	The two sides reviewed the guiding principles for the talks.
2004	18–19 November	4th meeting	Beijing	The two sides exchanged views on the principles that could form the framework of a possible boundary agreement.
2005	9–12 April	5th meeting	New Delhi	The two sides finalized the documents on guiding principles.
2005	26–28 September	6th meeting	Beijing	The two sides worked out an agreed-upon framework for a boundary settlement on the basis of the 'Agreement on Political Parameters and Guiding Principles for the Settlement of the India–China Boundary Question'.
2006	11–13 March	7th meeting	New Delhi and Kumarakom	The two sides devised an agreed-upon framework for the basic framework for settlement.
2006	25–27 June	8th meeting	Xi'an and Beijing on	The two sides continued their discussions on an agreed-upon framework for a boundary settlement.
2007	16–18 January	9th meeting	New Delhi	The two sides continued their discussions on an agreed-upon framework for a boundary settlement.
2007	20–22 April	10th meeting	New Delhi and Coonoor	The two sides continued their discussions on a framework for a boundary settlement.
2007	24–26 September	11th meeting	Beijing	The two sides exchanged views on the boundary issue.

(Cont'd)

Table 3.2 *(Cont'd)*

	Date	Event	Place	Major Developments
2008	19 September	12th meeting	Beijing	The two sides exchanged views on a framework to solve the boundary issue.
2009	7–8 August	13th meeting	New Delhi	The two sides exchanged views on the boundary issue.
2010	29–30 November	14th meeting	Beijing	Both sides agreed to seek a 'fair deal' as they made 'steady progress' on a framework to resolve the dispute.
2012	16–17 January	15th meeting	New Delhi	The two countries signed 'Agreement on the Establishment of a Working Mechanism for Consultation and Coordination on India–China Border Affairs'.

Source: Author.

Guiding Principles Agreement shows that the two sides have reduced the differences in perception on the approach to the boundary problem. For example, India had earlier insisted on a sector-by-sector approach for solving the border dispute while China wanted a package deal. The Chinese stated that Rajiv Gandhi in 1988 had agreed that the border problem could be solved by mutual accommodation, but the Vajpayee administration refused to make a similar commitment during his visit to China in 2003 (Tang 2005).

The Indian side has now agreed to discuss the problem on a sector-by-sector basis, but to announce the agreement only once the differences on all the sectors are sorted out. Article 3 of the Guiding Principles Agreement states,

> Both sides should, in the spirit of mutual respect and mutual understanding, make meaningful and mutually acceptable adjustments to their respective positions on the boundary question, so as to arrive at a package settlement to the boundary question. The boundary settlement must be final, covering all sectors of the China-India boundary.[12]

Undoubtedly, the conclusion of the Guiding Principles Agreement was an achievement of the Special Representative meetings. However, this positive development did not mean that all obstacles had been removed and that a mutually-acceptable solution could be reached any sooner. The conception behind the Special Representative meetings was that both sides first identified the principles and terms of reference on the basis of which the settlement of the boundary issue could be established. Then, both sides would apply such principles to construct a framework, which would be used to delineate the actual boundary on the ground. That is, the conclusion of the Agreement on Guiding Principles, in fact, marked the beginning of the second phase of negotiations under the mechanism of Special Representatives. Moreover, the task of constructing a framework to delineate the border between India and China might be more difficult than the initial assignment, as it involves devising an agreed-upon framework for the boundary settlement.

The Sikkim Issue

For India, a more symbolic achievement on the boundary talks in the post-Pokhran era was the Sikkim issue. Previously, Beijing had steadfastly questioned the legality of Sikkim's merger with India in 1975. However, in

July 1994, the Chinese Vice-Premier and Foreign Minister, Qian Qichen, stated that Beijing was dropping its opposition to Sikkim's accession to India (*All India Radio Network* 1994: 62). China's decision at the third Expert Group meeting in March 1995 to hold border personnel meetings with India at Nathu La in the Sikkim sector implied its acquiescence that Sikkim was under India's rule. Cheng Ruisheng, the former Chinese ambassador to India, also revealed that Beijing was considering recognizing India's merger with Sikkim (*The Hindu* 1999e). Despite these signals, by the early 2000s, Beijing did not formally recognize Sikkim as a state of India's Union. China's inflexibility on the Sikkim issue was because Beijing saw the Sikkim issue as a bargaining chip to be used in the boundary problem. As one Chinese scholar argued, the Sikkim issue could be settled only within the framework of a package deal (Liu 1994: 176).

During Prime Minister A.B. Vajpayee's visit to Beijing in 2003, India successfully persuaded China to change its position and to accept the reality that Sikkim had become part of India. India and China signed a bilateral agreement about opening a point in Sikkim for border trade. India had recognized China's take over of Tibet by signing the 1954 agreement, so it was expected that China would recognize Sikkim by signing the border trade agreement. In return for recognition, India agreed to China's terms on the status of Tibet as being an equivalent concession.

Although the Indian spokespersons quickly claimed China's recognition of Sikkim was a tenuous advance, India's expectations were soon struck a blow by Beijing. China rejected any suggestion that it had recognized India's sovereignty over Sikkim, without even waiting until Vajpayee and his party were in China (*The Times of India* 2003). The spokesperson of the Chinese Foreign Ministry said that the political status of Sikkim was historical baggage and would still require to be solved in a gradual manner' (*The Hindu* 2003a). China's reluctance to recognize India's annexation of Sikkim was seen as a surprise and embarrassment to the Indian side. Critics in India felt that China had decided not to reciprocate India's goodwill again following India's new statement on Tibet.

China saw the Sikkim issue as part of the broader border negotiations, and as a means to deny India the possibility of taking advantage of the Tibet issue. However, Beijing was also worried that India might withdraw its endorsement of the new discourse on Tibet if Beijing were to continue to reject India's claims over Sikkim. As a result, Beijing assured the Indian side in a low-profile way that the Sikkim issue would cease to be an irritant in Sino-Indian relations and that Beijing wanted to build a 'long-standing, stable and healthy' relationship with India amid the fast-changing global scenario.[13] The Chinese Foreign Ministry then deleted a webpage from its official website, which had showed Sikkim as a separate country in Asia, ahead of Chinese Premier Wen Jiabao's meeting with his Indian counterpart, A.B. Vajpayee, on the sidelines of the ASEAN summit in Bali, Indonesia (*PTI* 2003).

The change in China's position towards Sikkim appeared clearer as the Chinese Consul General in Kolkata, Mao Siwei later admitted. Beijing had already recognized Sikkim as part of India during Indian Prime Minister Vajpayee's visit to Beijing in 2003. However, Beijing was reluctant to openly assert that it had already recognized Sikkim as part of India. When Chinese Premier Wen Jiabao visited India in 2005, the Chinese side finally presented to India a newly-printed official map that showed Sikkim as being part of India (*The Hindu* 2005). The Joint Statement issued by the two sides clearly speaks of 'the Sikkim State of the Republic of India'. Despite China's reluctance to publicly announce its policy change, such developments had already helped eliminate China's ambiguity on Sikkim's status.

Following this positive development, in July 2006 the two sides reopened border trade across the 15,000-ft Nathu La Pass, in addition to the Shipkilah Pass, opened in 1993, and the Lipu Lake Pass, opened in 1992. Border trade between the two countries does not in fact contribute much to the overall volume of trade between the two countries, partly due to restrictions in tradable items, but in this instance, it was an indication of a broader rapprochement (Fang 2006: 47–50).

The boundary along Sikkim was considered a less difficult issue compared to other sectors. As far as India was concerned, Sikkim was a settled matter. However, the Tibet–Sikkim border was to play a further role in the boundary controversy and became a new point of contention. The Indian media from 2007 began to report Chinese intrusions into Indian territory in Sikkim. Close to 400 such incidents occurred during 2005–8 (Shukla 2008). This time, the Indians were tormented with anxiety by China's claims over the so-called 2.1 sq km 'Finger Area' in northern Sikkim. China further surprised India by threatening to demolish existing stone structures there. India strongly rebutted these claims, lodged an official protest, and barred the Chinese troops from entering the area. This was after China had protested against other troop deployments in

Sikkim resulting from the relocation of Indian troops from the western border. As a result of this diplomatic discord, road construction near the area was halted (*The Indian Express* 2008c: 1). During Indian External Affairs Minister Pranab Mukherjee's visit to Beijing in June 2008, the Chinese reportedly tried to corner India by raising the issue of the 'Finger Area' (*PTI* 2008).

The Indian side accused China of treading on India's toes in Sikkim as the increase in the number of incursions into Sikkim was a relatively new feature. China had been indulging in border patrols to strengthen its claim over the disputed areas as well as hardening its posture in the problematic border talks to delineate the LAC. In 2007 alone, India recorded well over 150 intrusions by Chinese troops in all three sectors—western (Ladakh), middle (Uttarakhand, Himachal) and eastern (Sikkim, Arunachal) (*PTI* 2008). The total number of Chinese 'incursions' into Sikkim increased to over 70 during the first half of 2008 (*The Times of India* 2008b: 20). Again, Indian officials had to respond with a clear statement. The Indian Minister of State for Defence, M.M. Pallam Raju, said that India would not 'yield an inch' of territory and would 'stand its ground' on Sikkim. India, incidentally, also launched a fresh survey of the northern plateau in Sikkim to counter territorial claims by China (*The Times of India* 2008e: 16).

In response to India's argument that the Sikkim issue was a settled one and should not re-enter the agenda of border talks, the Chinese diplomats agreed that the issue of Sikkim sovereignty was a closed chapter, but that that was not the case of the Tibet–Sikkim border. According to the Chinese Consul-General in Kolkata, Mao Siwei, the Sikkim–Tibet border had been settled in 1890 after Sikkim had been brought under British protection, but the border had been demarcated only on paper at that time; no demarcation on ground had taken place and, a result, there were differences of perception over where the border lay (*The Times of India* 2008e: 16).

The Indian side viewed China's patrols along the disputed area with misgivings. This action was considered to be part of China's overall strategy to increase psychological pressure on India, and to keep India guessing regarding its agenda during the border talks. Indian Minister of State for Defence, Raju also argued that it was China's way of putting pressure on India to resolve the boundary disputes (*The Times of India* 2008e: 16). It could also be argued that the Chinese intrusion was a type of misconduct against the diplomatic mechanism that had been set up precisely to avoid such boundary confrontations.

In fact, both India and China had been indulging in regular cross-border activities along the Sino-India border. India's Army Chief, General Deepak Kapoor, had clearly pointed out the basic reason for the incursions, saying that China had a differing perception of the LAC and that 'when we come up to their perception, we call it incursion, and likewise, they do' (*The Times of India* 2008i: 15). It was inevitable that before clearly identifying the LAC, China and India would insist on terming each other's presence in disputed areas such as Tawang, as an 'incursion'. Sometimes, troops would cross each other's territory merely for practical reasons like taking the shorter and easier route (*The Indian Express* 2008c: 1). Not surprisingly, as a result, the Chinese also charged Indian military personnel with crossing the LAC into the Chinese side (*The Hindu* 2003c). Commenting on Indian media reports alleging Chinese troop intrusion in the Demchok area of Leh District in Jammu and Kashmir, Chinese Foreign Ministry spokesman in January 2011 stressed 'China's border personnel have been respecting the two agreements made between the two countries to maintain peace and tranquillity in border areas and have never crossed the LAC'. Interestingly, India's Ministry of External Affairs has issued a clarification on the issue, and Foreign Secretary Nirupama Rao confirmed, 'there are differences in perception of the Line of Actual Control in this segment' (*The Indian Express* 2011).

In the present atmosphere, it is unlikely the LAC transgressions will develop into a major row since the two neighbours have a lot at stake, and because both sides are aware of the importance of maintaining border tranquillity and making sure there are no minor clashes in the border area. Even so, this kind of event has created a certain amount of tension. Repeated incursions into Sikkim along with other disputed areas by the Chinese have been a cause of particular concern to the Indian military establishment. From India's point of view, China's act was provocative and irritating. In some cases, the intrusions were extremely provocative. In April 2008, for example, Chinese troops came 12 km inside Maja in Arunachal Pradesh (Shukla 2008). According to an Indian report, an incursion event along the LAC in the western sector of the India–China boundary at Demchok, northeast of Ladakh, nearly led to a major confrontation between the patrol teams of the two sides, but conflict was averted by the timely intervention of senior officers from an Indian patrol team (Shukla 2008). In March 2012, Indian Minister M. Ramachandran stated in Indian Parliament that the Chinese army had transgressed the disputed China–India border over 500 times in the past two years. There were 228 cases of transgression of the Indo–China border by the Chinese side in 2010, 213 cases in 2011, and 64 cases till April 2012 (*The Times of India* 2012). In October 2012, the Indo–Tibetan Border Police (ITBP) accused China of intruding into the Indian air space at least two to three times in 2012 (*The Hindu* 2012b). The number of Chinese transgressions, as Indian Defence Minister A.K. Antony put it, have 'generally been as per established pattern' during the last five years. It was argued that China is now resorting to 'a slow but steady cartographic aggression' to keep India under pressure (*The Times of India* 2012).

On the other hand, the Chinese side did not share India's security concerns or take the border skirmish as seriously. Chinese Vice-Foreign Minister Wu Dawei suggested that not too much should be read into the intrusions taking place on the Sino-Indian border (*The Times of India* 2008j). Hu Shisheng, a researcher at the China Institute of Contemporary International Relations, also argued that it would be difficult for anyone to claim that there had been incursions when the border issue had not been settled (*The Times of India* 2008k).

China has shown its ability to make use of the ill-defined LAC to disturb India. The absence of a mutually-accepted LAC being physically demarcated on the ground and on military maps means China will continue to make use of these lacunae. In response, Indian officials were compelled to announce in public the plan to upgrade the strategically located helipads in Arunachal Pradesh, including eight of them located in the Tawang district (*The Indian Express* 2008d: 9). The Indian side also sensed the need to reinforce its positions and construct pathways in the area (*The Indian Express* 2008c: 1). With no demarcation of the border, over 3,00,000 Indian soldiers remain tied down in the disputed India–China border areas, which is a heavy drain on India's economy.

Ownership of Tawang

Despite the conclusion of the Guidance Principles Agreement, China and India still found it difficult to reconcile the contradictory claims over the disputed areas. For example, not much headway was made in the talks over China's claim to Tawang in Arunachal Pradesh. Securing Tawang forms part of China's package proposal, although Tawang is lodged well to the south of the Indian side of the LAC. It is believed that China would recognize India's sovereignty over Arunachal Pradesh but would insist on taking over Tawang. However, the Chinese proposal is strategically unacceptable to India, as Tawang is close to its northeastern states and Bhutan (*The Times of India* 2008l: 11).

According to the Chinese, Tibet had traditionally exercised administrative control over Tawang. Moreover, the region was the capital of the Monyul district, which was the birthplace of the Sixth Dalai Lama. The Chinese argue that ceding the area to foreigners would 'hurt the feelings of the Tibetans'.[14] Some analysts have also warned that China's central government would fail to conciliate Tibetans if it were not able to repossess Tawang (Liu 2007a: 48).

The other reason behind China's intention to take over Tawang is more morally high-sounding. The Chinese side still argues that the McMahon Line was a product of British imperialism and, as such, is unacceptable; China should take over Tawang as a means to negate the McMahon line. Chinese scholars argue that, since neither the Qing Dynasty nor the nationalist government recognized the McMahon Line, the present Chinese government also cannot accept the legality of McMahon Line (Liu 2007a: 47). In addition, the controversy about the McMahon Line contributed to the 1962 border war. If the Chinese agree to accept it as a *de jure* border, the question that would be raised is why Beijing could not have done so before both sides slid down the slippery slope to war in the 1960s.

China's frequent claims over the Tawang region of Arunachal Pradesh are an irritant to India. China has indicated that India should be prepared for 'substantial adjustments' on the LAC, which refers to Beijing's claim on Tawang as well as other adjustments in the disputed areas (*The Indian Express* 2007b: 3). To deal with the issue, in the Guiding Principles Agreement, India successfully secured the following significant clause: 'In reaching a boundary settlement, the two sides shall safeguard the due interests of their settled populations in the border areas'. For India, the formulation implied that the *status quo* of the disputed populated areas, like Tawang or even the whole of Arunachal Pradesh, would be maintained. In other words, the Indian side was of the view that its concerns had been addressed by these principles (*The Hindu* 2005a). In return, the Indian side gave up its long-standing objection to the 'package deal' approach.

However, to India's surprise, China showed little interest in sharing the same idea. Just days before Chinese President Hu Jintao's state visit to India in November 2006, the Chinese Ambassador to India, Sun Yuxi, publicly declared that the whole of Arunachal Pradesh, including Tawang, was part of China's territory. India felt compelled to react promptly. Indian External Affairs Minister Pranab Mukherjee asserted that 'Arunachal is an integral part of India' and it was made clear that 'there could be no discussion on the issue' (Shukla 2006).

Although Sun Yuxi tried to undo the damage later by stating that the boundary question was open to negotiation, China's subtle but firm attempts to bring back the issue of Arunachal Pradesh into public discourse ahead of Chinese President Hu Jintao's visit to India, created an uneasy atmosphere. Sun Yuxi's remark is, in fact, hardly surprising, as China had consistently refused to issue visas to the residents of Arunachal Pradesh, including the denial of a visa to an Indian Administrative Service (IAS) officer from that state, on the grounds that they did not need such documentation to visit 'their own country' (*The Times of India* 2007). As a result, although Hu was the first Chinese president to have visited India in 10 years, in the light of the controversy raised by the Chinese Ambassador, the two sides chose to skirt around the vexed border issue and focused on expanding bilateral relations in other areas, such as trade.

Again, these attempts were interpreted by India as part of China's pressure tactics to push India for concessions on the border issue. The well-known Indian strategic analyst, Brahma Chellany, argued, 'By putting forward its outrageous claim to Arunachal and more specifically to Tawang, Beijing has sought to place the onus on India for achieving progress in the border talks' (Shukla 2006). Meanwhile, it was suggested that India should raise the Tibet issue to balance China's manoeuvre of continuing to raise the issue of Arunachal. The contention was that 'with the Western community backing the Tibetan cause, the issue will help India turn the tables on China, whose aggressive territorial demands have been nurtured by India's acceptance of Tibet as a part of China' (Shukla 2006).

Some Chinese experts on Sino-Indian relations had already suggested that the Chinese side should avoid reiterating the previous tougher stand that Arunachal Pradesh was one part of China. Instead, they suggested, it was better to identify Arunachal Pradesh as a 'disputed area' rather than emphasizing it as part of China.[15] This kind of thinking indicated that some Chinese were ready to take a more moderate approach to deal with the problem. That is, although Sun Yuxi's statement on the ownership over Arunachal Pradesh did not differ from China's official position, it was still seen as a step backward in the process of solving the border problem by the Indian side.

In addition to Sun Yuxi's statement, there seemed to be a gradual hardening of China's position on Arunachal Pradesh. The Chinese Foreign Minister Yang Jiechi conveyed to his Indian counterpart, Pranab Mukherjee, in Hamburg that the 'mere presence' of populated areas would not affect Chinese claims on the boundary. Yang's remarks surprised New Delhi, as the latter considered that the Guiding Principles Agreement clearly indicated the contrary (*The Indian Express* 2007a).

China's uncooperative posture pushed India to take some counter-measures. Days after his visit to China, Indian Prime Minister Manmohan Singh paid a rare visit to Arunachal Pradesh in January–February 2008. It was the first visit to the region by an Indian Prime Minister in nearly two decades. In addition to announcing various projects to develop the state, Manmohan Singh declared that Arunachal Pradesh was 'our land of the rising sun'. The move was a clear political signal that India would not compromise on its claims in the area. Although the Prime Minister did not visit Tawang during his trip to Arunachal Pradesh, China in return protested about Manmohan Singh's visit. Beijing communicated to New Delhi that it was not proper to make such comments at a time when the two countries were engaged in talks over the boundary question. New Delhi did not comply with Beijing's demand. Indian President Pratibha Patil visited Tawang directly in April 2009 to show that Tawang is part of India's territory.

Although Arunachal Pradesh has remained a stumbling block to better ties between the two countries; the issue is in fact not so impressing or crucial. In fact, China's main target on the eastern sector is less ambitious than in the 1960s. The main goal is to secure Tawang, rather than the whole of Arunachal Pradesh. Since China has abjured from using Sikkim as a bargaining chip, it needs to accentuate the Arunachal Pradesh issue more. However, such tactics, leading to distrust, could spoil even the incremental gains of the border talks.

The Talks Ahead

China and India paid a high price for the unresolved border dispute, which significantly undermined relations between the two countries through most of the Cold War era and even sparked a war in 1962. The event has become a major source of the 'China threat' perceived by India.

Thanks to the dialogue meetings and CBMs along the border, the aim of avoiding unexpected conflicts and military clashes along the disputed areas has so far proved achievable. However, the task of clarifying the alignment of the LAC seems to be more difficult than initiating the CBMs. After Indian Prime Minister Vajpayee's visit to China in 2003, the Special Representative meetings have emerged as the most important instrument by which China and India intend to address their border dispute. In April 2011, China and India agreed to set up an extra working mechanism to monitor the 1993 and 1996 CBMs agreements, and the issue of frequent transgressions (*The Times of India* 2011e: 1).

After two decades of border talks, it could be supposed that both sides have acknowledged each other's positions and concerns. However, in practice, the two sides do not give due consideration to each other's interests and concerns. China and India have not reached a shared knowledge and understanding about the solution of the border problem. On the contrary, both sides view each others' position on the border dispute with misgivings. That is, the effect of Sino-Indian CBMs along the border is limited. The China–India CBMs has helped maintain peace and tranquillity along the border, but failed to alter the asymmetry of threat perceptions between the two countries.

As the two countries engage in talks to resolve the boundary question, the above account of the development of the Sino-Indian border talks shows that the border dispute, even if far from being resolved, can be properly managed. While normalization remains a goal to be pursued by China and India, the border dispute is not the main sticking point. Unlike during the Cold War years, the boundary problem is less explosive in China–India relations nowdays. That is, the history of enmity caused by border disputes is less influential now although it remains as a source of threat perceptions. Since China and India are still far from being friendly partners, this achievement deserves applause.

On the other hand, although the Special Representative mechanism has generated remarkable results in initiating the Guidance Principles Agreement, its achievement on the alignment of the LAC and the framework of the boundary problem is also limited. The two sides need to expend a considerable effort in narrowing the differences in their own perception of territorial adjustment. The most basic issue remains that of whether the principles can help fashion a useful framework to solve the differences such as those regarding Tawang. Until this issue is effectively addressed, a final settlement of the disputed border will not be in sight.

Despite the fact that the border has remained peaceful and tranquil, this chapter has provided an alternative perspective on the China–India border problem by demonstrating that China's and India's concerns regarding the boundary issues are quite asymmetrical. Although both China and India are committed to the Special Representative process and desire an early solution, the two countries deal with the border problem with different levels of enthusiasm.

China feels more confident even though the boundary problem is far from being solved. Remarkably, unlike India, China has not considered the boundary problem as a serious challenge to its security. Therefore, China is content to wait for India to make a concession. China is sticking to the stance enunciated by the late Premier Zhou Enlai and the late leader Deng Xiaoping. China maintains its plea for a settlement based on mutual understanding and compromise and to shelve disputes for the time being if they cannot be resolved in the short term. China actually wants the border situation stabilized, but is not eager to settle the boundary question with India if both sides cannot come to terms. Hence, Beijing had no hesitation in cancelling the JWG meeting peremptorily as a response to India's nuclear tests in 1998.

India, on the other hand, is still haunted by the miserable memory of the 1962 border war, which has ever since been a source of its 'China threat' perception. Prime Minister Vajpayee's letter to justify India's nuclear tests clearly highlighted its concerns about the unsolved boundary problem. Since the border problem has given rise to concerns about the threat posed by China, India is eager to solve the problem within a specific timetable in order to bring out an early completion to the process of clarification of the LAC. Compared to India's eagerness to reach a border settlement, Beijing's attitude is more conservative. The Chinese Assistant Foreign Minister, He Yafei, reiterated that 'it takes time and strenuous efforts to reach the final agreement' (*The Tribune* 2008). China does not anticipate any possibility of an early resolution and insists that 'time and patience' are needed to reach a mutually-acceptable resolution. There is no sign that India is ready to accept the 'mutual accommodation' approach proposed by the Chinese. Both China and India still haggle over the gains in the disputed territory and continue to be insensitive to each other's concerns. As the identification of the LAC becomes the priority of Sino-Indian border talks, the rift between China and India on the matter can hardly be ignored.

China and India will both try to avoid confrontation along the border to the maximum extent possible; however, the non-confrontationist approach is not enough to change the asymmetric threat perceptions of China and India. China could easily increase pressure on the Indian side by raising the issue of border disputes, while there are few tools left for India to use in any bargaining with China. As a result, the boundary problem has further exaggerated India's 'China threat' perception. An unsolved border problem would continue to drain India's attention and resources. Without further momentum or compulsion, maintaining the *status quo* along the border seems to be the best that can be hoped for in the foreseeable future.

Notes

1. The Chinese consider the disputed border between China and India to be 2,000 km long. The Indian side suggests that the Sino-Indian border is about 4,057 km long because it should include the Tibet–Sikkim border and the one between Xinjiang and Pakistan-controlled Kashmir as well.
2. For a discussion on the McMahon Line, see Maxwell (1970: 39–64).
3. This McMahon Line was later marked on the map attached to the Simla Treaty as part of the boundary between Tibet and the rest of China.
4. On 5 October 1962, the Defence Ministry of India announced the establishment of a new army corp under the eastern command for the sole purpose of dealing with China. On 12 October, Prime Minister Nehru declared that he had issued instructions to evacuate the Chinese frontier guards from the areas over which India had a claim. On 14 October, the then Indian Minister of Defence, Krishna Menon, called for a fight 'to the last man and the last gun against China', see 'A Brief Account on the Sino-Indian Boundary Question, Vice-Premier Chen Yi's Television Interview with Mr. Karlsson, Correspondent of the Swedish Broadcasting Corporation', 17 February 1963, in Lawrance (1975: 130).
5. See Chinese scholar Ye Zhengjia's statement in Ram (1998c: 18).
6. The Indian government sent its army to quell the agitation against the Sikkim government in 1973. Sikkim became an associate state of India in September 1974, and became India's 22nd state in April, 1975. China refused to recognize India's annexation, adding that it would support the Sikkimese people against Indian expansionism.

7. The text of the agreement is available at the official website of the PRC Foreign Ministry, at http://www.fmprc.gov.cn/eng/wjb/zzjg/yzs/gjlb/2711/2712/t15915.htm (accessed 11 August 2013).

8. The text of the agreement is available at the official website of China's Foreign Ministry, at http://www.fmprc.gov.cn/eng/wjb/zzjg/yzs/gjlb/2711/2712/t15914.htm (accessed 11 August 2013).

9. For a discussion on the monitoring measures, see Sidhu and Yuan (2001: 364–74).

10. For a comparison, see SCIO (1998a, 2000).

11. See, for example, *Renmin Ribao*, 2003, 'China-India meeting on boundary questions ends', 25 October, available online at http://english.peopledaily.com.cn/200310/25/eng20031025_126804.shtml (accessed 11 August 2013).

12. For the text, see *The Hindu*, 2005, 'Text of India-China agreement', 11 April, available online at http://www.hindu.com/thehindu/nic/0041/indiachinatxt.htm (accessed 11 August 2013).

13. The assurance on Sikkim was given by Wu Guanzheng, the member of the standing committee of the political bureau of the CPC central committee, while meeting members of the political bureau of The Communist Party of India (Marxist). See (*PTI*: 2003).

14. Interview with a senior Chinese South Asian specialist, Beijing, 26 March 2001.

15. For example, see Chinese scholar Zhang Minqiu's statement in Liu (2007b: 39).

4 Regional Competition and Cooperation

REGIONAL RIVALRY HAS BEEN a feature of bilateral relations between China and India, both of which are regional powers. Continued hostility between India and Pakistan, China's involvement in the India–Pakistan conflicts, and competition between the superpowers has turned South Asia into a significant area for rivalry between China and India. In the wake of the 1962 border war and the Sino-Soviet split, China chose to ally itself with Pakistan to counter India, as well as to retain its influence in South Asia. Beijing thus became involved in India's conflict with Pakistan. For example, in the 1965 Indo-Pakistani war, China threatened to open a second front against India by sending India a 72-hour ultimatum demanding that New Delhi demolish its military structures on China's side of the border in the Tibet–Sikkim area.

As the competition for regional leadership remains a significant element in post-Cold War Sino-Indian relations, this chapter seeks to illustrate that regional competition has contributed to a culture of rivalry between China and India. Again, China–India interaction on regional issues also reveals India and China's asymmetrical perceptions of threat. India tends to be mired in the traditional security concept that China is seeking to enclose India in a South Asian straitjacket by engaging other South Asian states. On the other hand, China appears comparatively confident about threats from India although it is mindful of India's relations with ASEAN states and Japan.

Although their bilateral relations have largely improved over the decades, China and India still have misgivings about each other's' engagement with their neighbours. New Delhi keeps a wary eye on China's ties with its South Asian neighbours, especially Pakistan. Both India and Pakistan see threats emanating from each other as being major threats to their security. China and Pakistan still see each other as reliable partners whenever Indo-Pakistani relations sour. As a result, the China–Pakistan relationship, especially the Sino-Pakistani arms nexus, has been a cause of grave concern for India.

Beijing also encouraged other smaller South Asian states such as Nepal and Bangladesh to stand up to India's aspiration to dominate South Asia. India's long-standing conflicts or tensions with other South Asian states would drain and weaken India, and thus serve China's strategic interests. From the Indian point of view, China had consistently sought to constrain Indian power and confine it essentially to the region of South Asia.

On the other hand, Beijing is greatly concerned that India is increasing its efforts to extend its influence eastward, and is acutely conscious of the ongoing deep engagement between India and other Asian states. While Beijing has quarrels with some of its marine neighbours over the South China Sea, New Delhi has embarked on a 'Look East' policy to engage the ASEAN states, Japan, South Korea, and Taiwan. In addition to the traditional antagonism in South Asia, Southeast Asia emerges as a new area of China–India competition.

In contrast to studies focusing on the competitive dimension of China–India relations, this chapter also studies the linkage between the perception of threat and cooperation. In fact, China and India have found reasons to cooperate even over regional issues. In addition to geopolitical competition, sub-regional economic cooperation and anti-terrorism campaigns have been added to the agenda of Sino-Indian relations in recent years. These developments, along with China's cautious neutrality towards the India–Pakistan conflict, have suggested that India and China are willing to scale down their enmity. Therefore, from a regional perspective, China and India are not always bound to clash in their journey from regional power to global power. They could act as both competitors and partners in regional affairs. Sino-Indian relations are a mixture of competition and cooperation, although the latter might be somewhat less noticeable.

The Pakistan Factor in China–India Relations

China's Balanced Policy towards the India–Pakistan Conflict

Despite the improvement in Sino-Indian relations, note should be taken of India's concern over the Chinese presence in other small South Asian states. Particularly, India has projected the China–Pakistan relationship as a strategic convergence against India, where Pakistan is acting as the proxy of China to counter Indian influence in the region.

The Sino-Pakistani strategic relationship has been in the making for the past several decades. China has characterized its ties with Pakistan as an 'all-weather friendship' (*Beijing Review* 1990: 10), implying that the two countries have developed a strong partnership that has indeed weathered the changes that have taken place in the domestic and international scenario. In fact, China and Pakistan do not share a common political system, history, language, culture, or religion. The two countries have even followed diametrically-opposed foreign and security policies, as they joined opposite camps during the Cold War: Pakistan was a member of the US-led Southeast Asia Treaty Organization (SEATO) in 1954 and the Central Treaty Organization (CENTO) in 1955, while China allied to the USSR. These differences did not prevent China and Pakistan from forming a close relationship during the Cold War. This bilateral strategic partnership developed from the support shown to each other's cause in the international community regarding military transfers and strategic cooperation. Since the two countries had overcome many differences to forge a close relationship, the Chinese side used to hail the Sino-Pakistani friendship as the epitome of the Five Principles of Peaceful Coexistence.

The Sino-Pakistan friendship during much of the past several decades could have best reflected the saying that 'an enemy's enemy is a friend'. That is, the Sino-Pakistan bonhomie was based upon their common bitter relationship with India. Compared to the increasingly warm Sino-Pakistani ties, Sino-Indian relations have often deteriorated due to disputes over Tibet, the boundary problem, and so on. On the other hand, India and Pakistan have fought three wars and exchanged fires across the Line of Control (LOC) since independence. Just as the Indian side has affirmed, the *raison d'être* for the Sino-Pakistan friendship was their perception of India as a common enemy (Chandy 2000: 300). Being Pakistan's close ally, China has long been involved in a triangular relationship with Pakistan and India. Given the animosity between India and Pakistan, close ties between China and Pakistan have added to tensions between China and India.

With the end of the Cold War era, the Chinese used to insist that 'while the world is moving toward détente, regional conflicts are flaring up here and there' (Ren 1997). South Asia is one such case, particularly with respect to the palpable hostility between India and Pakistan in the region. The Chinese acknowledge that the Indo-Pakistani conflict is the major source of South Asian insecurity, and management of the India–Pakistan relationship has been treated as a key question for Chinese geo-strategic analysts.

Cold War architecture in South Asia was gradually rendered obsolete by the rapidly changing environment in the wake of the Soviet withdrawal from Afghanistan. The US and the USSR did not place the same emphasis on South Asian affairs as they had earlier. Other major powers also changed their attitude towards the regional conflicts in the post-Cold War era, as they tried to distance themselves somewhat from the India–Pakistan conflict and encourage India and Pakistan to solve the disputes in a peaceful manner.

The Chinese approach towards India–Pakistan conflicts in the post-Cold War era was determined by its motivation to launch economic development at home and supported by the change in the security environment in South Asia. China favours a stable peripheral environment conducive to domestic economic development. In a shift from unequivocal support to Pakistan, China no longer thinks India–Pakistan conflicts are in its interests and is now reluctant to side with either country in any dispute between them. Under the good neighbourly policy, China has sought to establish a more balanced relationship with India and Pakistan than the complicated equation in the past. As a result, Beijing has shifted from a focus on exploiting the India–Pakistan conflict to a policy designed to help stabilize the region. The Indian side has also observed that China has shown no inclination to meddle in India–Nepal relations while developing its relations with Nepal (Noorani 2002).

The Chinese assessment of post-Cold War South Asia's situation has further increased Beijing's confidence to adopt such a balanced policy. During the Cold War, the US and the USSR played out an intense rivalry as they backed opposing forces in South Asia. China had to keep a wary eye on the super powers' activities in South Asia in terms of an encirclement of China. The Sino-Soviet rapprochement since the late 1980s and the collapse of the USSR denoted that Beijing did not need to equip Pakistan to provide support against the Soviet–Indian alliance. With the advent of the post-Cold War era, neither the US nor Russia considered South Asia as a strategically important area (Ye *et al.* 1997: 437). The major powers all preferred a stable South Asia and were all unwilling to become involved in the conflicts between the South Asian states. Therefore, the rivalry between superpowers in South Asia and the Pakistan–American partnership against the Indo-Russian alliance ceased to exist. Although the Chinese thought that India's dominance in South Asia was further strengthened after the end of Cold War, they also considered that the new setting created an ambience for the improvement of Sino-Indian relations (Yang 1996: 3).

There has been evidence of China's desire to adopt a more balanced policy towards the India–Pakistan conflict. China concluded that it had more policy choices than siding with Pakistan without reservation. For the first time, China publicly explicated its South Asia policy in the post-Cold War era when Chinese President Jiang Zemin paid a state visit to South Asia in 1996. During his stay in Pakistan, Jiang delivered a speech to the Pakistani Senate, titled 'Carrying Forward Generations of Friendly and Good-Neighbourly Relations and Working towards a Better Tomorrow for All', proposing five principles for developing 'long-term, stable and friendly ties' with South Asian states.[1] China clearly conveyed the message that it hoped that the existing disputes between neighbouring states could be solved by peaceful means (Wang *et al.* 1999: 351). China tried to make it clear that it would like to maintain and develop good neighbourly relations with all countries in South Asia and preferred to see peace and stability in the region.

Despite admitting that there was strategic cooperation between China and Pakistan during the Cold War, in an attempt to relieve India's concerns, Beijing now stressed that the Sino-Pakistani friendship had no animus against any third country. Beijing emphasized that its relationship with Pakistan was 'normal' and not directed towards India. This is a far cry from Beijing's past stance when Chinese Foreign Ministry officials said that China's military relationship with Pakistan was one of the closest China had with another country (Lee 1985: 25), or when Deng Xiaoping termed Pakistan as 'a special friend' and identified China–Pakistan relations as being 'unusual' (Wang *et al.*1999: 342).

This more balanced policy also indicated that China seemed to think it possible to develop a parallel close relationship with both India and Pakistan. In order not to irritate Pakistan, China meanwhile also stressed that the improvement of Sino-Indian relations would not be to the detriment of a third party, nor would it affect China's existing friendly relations with other countries (*Sino-Indian Joint Communiqué* 1991). The then Chinese Foreign Minister, Tang Jiaxuan, asserted that the Sino-Indian rapprochement would not come in the way of strengthening the time-tested relations with Pakistan. He argued, 'Sino-India relations are Sino-India relations and Sino-Pakistan relations are Sino-Pakistan relations. Between China and Pakistan, we enjoy a profound and traditional friendship' (*The Hindu* 2000f). It was clear that China wanted to engage with India without disturbing the friendly ties between China and Pakistan.

The subsequent high-level visits by Chinese leaders to the region indicated the continuation of Beijing's strategy of maintaining a diplomatic balance in its dealings with South Asian countries (Fang 2005: 8). China has since repeated its desire to enhance the scope of a 'constructive cooperative partnership' with India. At the same time, China has also signalled its intention of remaining engaged with Pakistan.

China's Shift on the Kashmir Dispute

Despite the South Asia policy proclamation, China's position towards the Kashmir issue probably best exemplifies the change of its stance towards the India–Pakistan conflict. Both India and Pakistan claim sovereignty over the whole of Kashmir, and have fought two major wars for the region since independence. For most of the time, Pakistan has insisted that the future of Kashmir should be decided by a plebiscite. Aware of its weakness *vis-à-vis* India, Pakistan has also endeavoured to internationalize the Kashmir issue. In contrast, India has opposed holding a plebiscite in Kashmir mostly because it worried that the Muslim-majority region might not favour staying within the Hindu-majority Indian Union. India's position has been that the Kashmir issue should be resolved in the spirit of the Simla Agreement of 1972, under which India and Pakistan agreed to resolve outstanding issues through bilateral talks (Dixit 2003: 111–12; Khanna 2005: 92–7).

China has had a role to play in the Kashmir issue because of its alliance relationship with Pakistan, and also because it secured a piece of Kashmir under the 1963 Sino-Pakistan border treaty. Being a close ally of Pakistan, China openly backed Pakistan's claim to all of Kashmir after Sino-Indian relations deteriorated. However, contrary to the traditional impression, China has not always supported Pakistan's stance over Kashmir. Even Chinese scholars have admitted that China's position over the Kashmir dispute has varied over the years (Yuan 2001: 8–9).

Ever since the late 1980s, Beijing has hoped to be able to approach the Kashmir issue on its own merits. In addition, in recent years, it has appeared to avoid taking sides in tune with increasingly warm relations with India. After the end of the Cold War, in 1994, China even pressured Pakistan to withdraw a resolution, tabled at the UN Human Rights Commission in Geneva, condemning India for human rights violations in Kashmir.

Serious nationalist unrest in Xinjiang has also contributed to alter China's attitude towards the Kashmir issue. Since 1980, China has distanced itself from its support for Pakistan's position to hold a plebiscite to decide the future of Kashmir. Beijing also declined to intervene in the Kashmir issue by emphasizing the need for New Delhi and Islamabad to resolve the problem through dialogue. China's fear was that an independent state of Kashmir would inspire Muslim separatists in Xinjiang to seek independence (Foot 1996: 67).

Regarding the Kashmir issue, China's argument is that the question is a legacy from the British Empire, and it involves conflicting territorial claims, religion, ethnicity, and other complex factors. China has echoed Pakistan's stand that the sovereignty of Kashmir has not been defined and that it is the 'core issue' in India–Pakistan relations (Zhao 2003: 85), in contrast to the Indian position that Kashmir has always been a part of India. However, Beijing has also agreed that the dispute is steeped in history and India and Pakistan should seek an effective solution to the Kashmir problem through peaceful dialogue, implying the issue should be decided by India and Pakistan bilaterally. This position is against Pakistan's hope to internationalize the Kashmir issue, and meets India's demands. The Chinese referred to the UN Resolution on Kashmir in the context of solving the problem after India's nuclear tests of 1998 (Swamy 2001: 119), but then went back to insisting that a peaceful negotiated settlement between India and Pakistan is needed.

Clearly, Beijing is determined to insulate itself from the ups and downs of Indo-Pakistanities, while improving its relations with both New Delhi and Islamabad. However, Indo-Pakistan tension became a serious concern for China's strategic analysts, who acknowledged that dealing with India–Pakistan conflicts would be a key question regarding China's western geopilitical strategy and frontier security (Ye *et al.* 1997: 442). The Kargil crisis of 1999, the worst military encounter between India and Pakistan since the third Indo-Pakistani war, put China's balanced approach to the test.[2]

Although Pakistani leaders approached Beijing for support, China appeared to have taken a position of cautious neutrality and did not give any special diplomatic favours to Pakistan (Singh 1999b; Yuan 2001: 9–10). The Chinese repeatedly stated the need for restraint by both India and Pakistan, and the importance of resolving the problem through peaceful negotiations. In the view of the Indians, although China was unwilling to identify Pakistan as the aggressor, it did not lend any significant diplomatic support to Pakistan in the Kargil crisis (Mohan 1999a). This balanced posture was due to China's mounting concern about a major military conflict between India and Pakistan. The former Chinese Ambassador to India, Cheng Ruisheng, even claimed that the Chinese 'have a traditional friendship with Pakistan, but China's policy is not to side with Pakistan on the Kashmir issue' (*AFP* 1999). That is, China refused to give Pakistan *carte blanche*. Needless to say, India appreciated the way Beijing handled the Kargil issue.

Beijing's position in the Kargil crisis confirmed the trend that Beijing was determined to follow, specifically, a calibrated balanced policy in navigating the turbulence arising from Indo-Pakistani relations. China's moderate posture towards the India–Pakistan conflict altered the traditional impression of Chinese support for Pakistan and gave New Delhi some relief in its dealings with Islamabad. In fact, it was widely thought that Beijing showed a tendency to support New Delhi when it urged India and Pakistan to respect the sanctity of the LOC in Kashmir. While cherishing the traditional China–Pakistan friendship, it seemed China had no intention of being dragged into a war in its doorstep.

India–Pakistan tension flared up again after India's Parliament was attacked by terrorists in December 2001, an action that India said Pakistan had masterminded. India urged Pakistan to take the responsibility for reining in the extreme Islamic groups that planned the transgression. Both sides then deployed hundreds of thousands of troops along the border. Despite Pakistan's claim of having secured China's support, Beijing still adopted an even-handed policy and called upon India and Pakistan to exercise restraint.

In addition to the cautious neutrality in the India–Pakistan confrontation, another significant development has been Beijing's demonstration of its desire to play a more positive role to scale down the India–Pakistan conflict, rather than keeping the India–Pakistan tension at a distance. In fact, Pakistan has long appealed to China to play an 'active role' in South Asia to maintain a regional strategic balance and to settle the Kashmir issue.[3] During Chinese Premier Zhu Rongji's visit to India in January 2002, however, Beijing assured New Delhi that China had neither any intention of mediating between India and Pakistan, nor would it play any mediatory role between them (*The Hindu* 2002a).

Nonetheless, as the tension between India and Pakistan came to a high point and the international community was concerned that the India–Pakistan conflict might escalate into a nuclear confrontation, China donned the unfamiliar mantle of peace-maker (Hutzler 2002). Along with major powers, such as the US and Russia, China pursued its own diplomacy to defuse the tension, trying to leverage its alliance with Pakistan and a burgeoning relationship with India to lessen the possibilities of a potential escalation. Chinese Foreign Minister Tang Jiaxuan held telephone conversations with both his Indian and Pakistani counterparts to express China's concerns over the tensions. Tang also urged the two countries to show restraint and resolve their disputes through dialogue in a bid to ease tensions in South Asia as quickly as possible (*Renmin Ribao* 2002a: 2, 2002b: 4). Later, Chinese President Jiang Zemin held separate meetings with Indian Prime Minister A.B. Vajpayee and Pakistani leader General Pervez Musharraf in Almaty, Kazakhstan, on the sidelines of the summit meeting of the Conference on Interaction and Confidence-Building Measures in Asia (CICA) to ease the tense stand-off (*Renmin Ribao* 2002c: 4). The Chinese Foreign Ministry spokesmen also repeatedly emphasized that China was playing a positive role to contribute to peace between India and Pakistan.

Again, China tried to defuse India–Pakistan tensions following the 2008 Mumbai terrorist attack by asking India to share the evidence and to resume its dialogue with Pakistan. China sent its Vice-Foreign Minister, He Yafei, as special envoy to Pakistan on 29 December 2008. He Yafei tried to visit New Delhi from Islamabad directly, but the offer was rejected by India although it was agreed that he could visit New Delhi later on 5 January 2009. Pakistani Foreign Minister Shah Mahmood Qureshi even publicly claimed that Pakistan had given China a 'blank cheque' to negotiate with India (*The Times of India* 2009b: 9). Pakistan's Ambassador to China, Masood Khan, called for China to play a greater role in South Asia, and to act as a catalyst to address outstanding issues between India and Pakistan (*The Hindu* 2011e).

The fresh attempts by Beijing to help India and Pakistan resolve their crisis underscore China's growing concerns that Beijing might be being drawn unwillingly into an Indo-Pakistani war although it does not want to take sides in the India–Pakistan confrontation. China has acknowledged that its security interests lie in maintaining a peaceful environment and to achieve that end it will take an active role. Just as the Chinese South Asia analyst Shen Dingli said, 'China needs to send a message: For my own security I will intervene' (Malik 2002). Chinese Assistant Foreign Minister Wang Yi has also been quoted as saying that the Kashmir problem has long been at a stalemate, and 'the only way out is the peaceful settlement with help from the international community' (Swamy 2001: 120).

China's gradual shift from neutrality in the Kashmir dispute to the encouragement of an Indo-Pakistani dialogue has met with resistance from India, mainly because the Indian side regards China as part of the problem rather than part of the solution (Sidhu and Yuan 2003: 65). Although New Delhi welcomes pressure by the international community on Islamabad to stop Pakistan abetting 'cross-border' terrorism, it has firmly ruled out any third-party mediation in Indo-Pakistani affairs, let alone mediation by China. Considering the enduring and traditional friendship between China and Pakistan, it is also difficult for India to believe that China will be an objective mediator. It is no secret that China still shows a preference for Pakistan. For example, the Chinese side interpreted India's nuclear tests of 1998 as an expansionist and hegemonic policy, but expressed sympathy for Pakistan, agreeing that it was compelled to conduct the nuclear tests and missile tests.[4] Thus, India would prefer Beijing to keep its distance from India–Pakistan tensions. In an indication of India's unhappiness with China's public involvement in the India–Pakistan conflict, India dismissed Chinese calls for restraint and termed them 'inadequate', arguing that they should be directed at Pakistan (*The Times of India* 2001b). New Delhi has reiterated that the international community should urge Pakistan to stop engaging in 'cross-border' terrorism and a proxy war in Indian-administered Kashmir, instead of asking India to hold a dialogue with Pakistan.

No matter whether Indians like it or not, China's attitude towards Kashmir is very crucial. China in 2008 started to issue stapled visas to Indian citizens from Kashmir, implying that it does not recognize India's full sovereignty over Kashmir. In July 2010, India's Northern Army

Commander Lieutenant General B.S. Jaswal was denied a normal visa to visit China because he headed troops in Jammu and Kashmir. The Indian side called off high-level military exchanges to express its unhappiness. In addition, Indian Foreign Secretary Nirupama Rao urged China to show more sensitivity on core issues' that impinge on India's sovereignty and territorial integrity (*The Hindustan Times* 2010: 11). To reduce the tension, China then issued normal pasted visas to four journalists from Kashmir, who travelled with Indian Prime Minister Manmohan Singh to Sanya in China for the Brazil–Russia–India–China–South Africa (BRICS) summit in April 2011, and agreed to review its policy of giving stapled visas to Kashmiri people. The full defence exchanges with China were resumed in June 2011.

Except for the stapled visa issue, the Chinese actually tried to maintain a careful balancing act. For example, during his visit to Pakistan in December 2010, the Chinese Premier Wen Jaibao kept silent on the Kashmir issue (*The Hindu* 2010). From the Indian perspective, any comment that falls short of actual Chinese support for Pakistan's posture, is a positive development and is to be welcomed. However, China's neutrality is not enough to please India, and will incur criticism from Pakistan. It is considered that China's efforts to adopt a more balanced position with respect to the India–Pakistan conflict are an exhibition of 'absolute flexibility' (*quan bian*) (Chandy 2000: 330–1). Contrary to China's expectations, the Indian side still distrusts China's role, considering the latter ready to intervene in any India–Pakistan conflicts. As a result, China's nuanced stance towards the India–Pakistan dispute has not resulted in any improvement in Sino-Indian relations.

Sino-Pakistani Military Ties

Although the Indian side acknowledged China's changing policy towards the India–Pakistan conflict, the Pakistan factor in the Sino-Indian interactions has not been erased completely as a result of China's even-handed approach to India–Pakistan conflicts. Thus, India is still very concerned with China's intention of forging strategic ties with Pakistan and other South Asian states. From the Indian perspective, the Sino-Pakistani arms nexus is one of the main unresolved problems between India and Pakistan. The basic question that needs to be answered is why China is risking the burgeoning Sino-Indian friendship by arming Pakistan whilst still claiming to adopt a more balanced South Asia policy.

China has been trying to further relations with Pakistan in other fields, such as more cooperation in the economic field (Zhao 2003: 340), but the military tie remains an important element of China–Pakistan relations. The military establishment in China has claimed that China's military sales to Pakistan are based on the profit motive and are not a move against India. The Chinese have even argued that China would sell military equipment to India were India to request it (*Zhongguo Shibao* 1999: 14).

In fact, even though China has offered Pakistan military assistance, India traditionally enjoys better access to conventional weaponry from Russia. The US, since the Bush administration, has also given New Delhi access to America's military transfer, which was denied for most of the Cold War (Winner and Yoshihara 2002: 71). That is, the military balance is still in favour of India.

However, whether China's military equipment could significantly exacerbate the military imbalance is irrelevant; the key factor is how the Indian side interprets China's intention. India's view is that Beijing has consciously sought to develop military links with countries in its neighbourhood so as to deny India dominance in the subcontinent. The Indian side argues that the most obvious rationale for China to arm Pakistan is to imbue Pakistan with strategic parity with India (Chandy 2000: 327). Given the tension between India and Pakistan, the Indian side naturally sees the military transfer as a serious security concern and as having a direct and negative bearing on India's national security environment. Particularly, Sino-Pakistani military cooperation in the fields of nuclear and conventional missiles has caused grave concern for India's security.

In order to address these concerns, India has continually raised the issue of missile transfers from China to Pakistan during its interactions with China. For example, Indian Prime Minister Vajpayee has expressed concern over the military nexus between China and Pakistan, arguing that 'all weapons and missiles it [Pakistan] receive[s] are aimed at India' (*The Hindu* 1998e). He added that 'wh erever our neighbour Pakistan gets its arms from, we keep telling those (supplier) nations that whatever be your intention, these weapons, experience has shown, have been used against us' (*The Hindu* 2001f). Indian External Affairs Minister Yaswant Sinha said, regarding China's military transfer to Pakistan, that India expected China to show greater sensitivity to India's security concerns (*The Hindu* 2003b). It even urged China to reconsider its support for

Pakistan's nuclear and missile programmes to reciprocate New Delhi's moves to back Beijing's position on Taiwan or Tibet.

However, it appears that Beijing did not take India's anxiety seriously. Maintaining that the military supply programme and cooperation between China and Pakistan was routine in nature and well within international norms and international treaty obligations, Beijing did not agree that its military transfer to Pakistan would break regional balances or undermine peace and tranquillity in the region. Furthermore, Beijing justified its arms transfer to Pakistan on the basis that military relations are part of the normal gamut of state–state relations and that, as far as the Chinese are concerned, every sovereign, independent country has the right to acquire those materials it deems necessary for its defence, and China as a sovereign country also has the right to sell such material. Defending Beijing's stance on China–Pakistan military cooperation, the Chairman of the Standing Committee of the National People's Congress, Li Peng, said, 'Normal military trade is undoubtedly part of the normal state-to-state relations. India enjoys similar cooperation with other countries as well'.[5] The then Chinese Foreign Minister, Tang Jiaxuan, also said that the Sino-Pakistani military cooperation was a normal military cooperation based on normal state-to-state relations, and was not directed against any third party or country (*Renmin Ribao* 2000d). Despite protests from India, China argued that 'it is inappropriate and unnecessary to exaggerate or worry about China–Pakistan military relations' (*The Hindu* 2001c). China played down the significance of China–Pakistan defence cooperation and pledged its commitment to continuing such exchanges with Pakistan.

As a result, while making efforts to improve relations with India, China did not scale down its military cooperation with Pakistan to meet India's demands. The Indian side observed, for example, that within two years of the path-breaking visit of Rajiv Gandhi to China in December 1988, China supplied short-range M-11 missiles to Pakistan. Likewise, the Chinese moved ahead with the supply of medium-range M-9 missiles and ring magnets for Pakistan's nuclear weapons programme after Indian Prime Minister Narasimha Rao's visit to China in 1993 (Parthasarathy 2001). The United States CIA reports also made the point that continued contact between China and Pakistan enabled Pakistan to build up its nuclear and missile arsenal while China was strengthening relations with India. Chinese assistance has helped Pakistan to have moved toward serial production of solid-propellant SRBMs, such as the Shaheen-I and

Haider-I, and has supported Pakistan's MRBMs (*The Hindu* 2001a). In mid-January 2002, China transferred the first 10 of 40 Chinese-made F-7 PG fighter aircraft to Pakistan during the period of the India–Pakistan military stand-off, though Beijing diplomatically conducted a balanced policy towards India and Pakistan. After Pakistan Prime Minister Yousuf Raza Gilani's visit to China in May 2011, China provided fifty JF-17 Thunder aircrafts with more sophisticated avionics to Pakistan (*The Hindustan Times* 2011b: 17). China also agreed to Pakistan's quest to take over the strategic Gwadar Port. Pakistan Defence Minister, Chaudhry Ahmad Mukhtar, announced that China immediately agreed to extend assistances in whichever section Pakistan requested during Gilan's visit and considered it as a confirmation of an 'all weather friendship between Pakistan and China' (*The News* 2011).

Apparently, despite India's concerns and dissatisfaction, China is not ready to cut its military transfer and cooperation with Pakistan to court India. While trying to improve relations with India, China is very reluctant to share India's apprehension regarding China–Pakistan relations and insists that there is nothing wrong with it, consistently providing Pakistan with wide-ranging assistance regarding arms. Chinese Defence Minister General Chi Haotian expounded, 'China and Pakistan are good neighbours, friends and partners sharing weal and woe, and the relations between the two armed forces are the manifestation of a bilateral all-weather friendship' (*Xinhua* 2001). To India, China's military tie with Pakistan is far more significant than the 'normal' military ties between other countries. Despite China's protestations of innocence, China's transfer of arms and military expertise to Pakistan has been perceived as hostile by India and perhaps has encouraged India to revise its security agenda towards China. Since it is impossible for India to accept China's claim that its military transfer to Pakistan is normal and has nothing to with regional balance, these different perceptions constitute a difficulty in Sino-Indian relations.

Renewed China–Pakistan Strategic Relations

Beijing does not treat India as an immediate enemy and it has tried to broaden the bilateral cooperation; as a result, Pakistan might lose some of its strategic value as a pawn to be used in the game of strategy against India. The nature of Sino-Pakistani relations is certainly not of the same strategic genre as it was during the Cold War. However, it would be too naive to conclude that India and China are becoming friends and that China no longer needs Pakistan. Chinese scholars still consider that China has more common interests with Pakistan than with India (Yan 1998: 235–6). Pakistan remains a loyal friend in the region to counterbalance a potential Indian challenge to Chinese preponderance in Asia. China will not neglect its traditional friendship with Islamabad while trying to improve relations with India.

In addition to military transfers, there is no difficulty finding examples to illustrate the strategic bonhomie between China and Pakistan even in recent years. For example, while India was working hard in the international community to isolate General Pervez Musharraf's military regime after he took over the reins of power following a coup on 12 October 1999, China became the first non-Islamic country to roll out the red carpet for the controversial general. Ignoring international suspicion about the legitimacy of the military regime, Beijing offered support to Islamabad on the grounds that 'the internal affairs of a country should and must be handled by its own people, which is not only the core of the Five Principles of Coexistence, but also a basic policy China has steadfastly pursued and carried out in handling relations between different countries' (*Renmin Ribao* 2000e: 1). Amid new strains between Pakistan and the US following the US raid and kill of Al-Qaeda leader Osama bin Laden near Islamabad, Chinese officials and media rejected criticism from the West and India over Islamabad's failure to crack down on terrorist groups operating within Pakistan (*The Hindu* 2011e).

It also reminded the world that Chinese Premier Li Peng visited Pakistan in November 1989, the first visit abroad by a senior Chinese leader after the 1989 Tiananmen incident. Beijing assured the Pakistan leader that 'no matter what changes occur internationally or domestically, the Chinese government will continue to foster its comprehensive partnership with Pakistan'.[6]

As China–India relations deteriorated, Pakistan soon regained its significance *vis-à-vis* India. For example, in order to deal with the new strategic situation, India used the 'China threat' discourse as justification for conducting tests on its nuclear devices. In response, some Chinese scholars bluntly suggested that China should strengthen the all-round cooperation with Pakistan in the fields of political, economic, and military affairs (Liu 1999c: 28). From the point of view of the Chinese, India is a power with hegemonic ambition while Pakistan is a reliable foothold in South Asia. Given the convergence of views between China and Pakistan regarding opposition to India's 'hegemonism', there are strong reasons on both sides for maintaining a durable and practical relationship. In other words, Sino-Pakistani relations could be a counterweight to India's supremacy in the region.

Even though China might not need the Sino-Pakistani friendship as a bulwark against India as it did in the Cold War era, Beijing can find other reasons to maintain its special relationship with Pakistan, a link that includes the transfer of arms. For example, a close relationship with Pakistan would give Beijing more diplomatic and strategic angles to bring into play in South Asia. Pakistan is also an important friend in the Islamic world for China (Zhao 2003: 340), and has influence on the Xinjiang problem (Yan 1998: 220). Relations with India cannot offer China the same benefits.

As a deliberate gesture of support, China held the first ever joint marine exercise with Pakistan, code named Dolphin 0310, on 23 October 2003, just three weeks before the first China–India marine exercise. In fact, the decision to hold the China–India joint exercise had been made much earlier, during Indian Prime Minister Vajpayee's visit to China in June 2003. The sequence of the joint exercises reflected China's desire to acknowledge friendship with Pakistan as a strategic priority instead of friendship with India, and to underscore China's strategic bonhomie with Pakistan on the South Asian scene.

Beijing also has to re-assess its strategic proximity to Pakistan in the context of the US presence in the wake of the war against terror. The war against terrorism in Afghanistan has brought US troops right to China's western doorstep. The US had requested Pakistan's agreement to establish a military base and a no-fly zone in southwestern Pakistan for a 10-year period (*Stratfor* 2002). The Chinese appeared to be uncomfortable with US military presence in the Central Asian states and Pakistan. China was reported to have threatened to pull out of the project to develop the Gwadar port as a fully-fledged military base if Islamabad allowed the US to access the airports at Jacobabad and Pasni and to set up some listening posts in the Northern Areas to monitor any nuclear or military activities in the region (*The Times of India* 2002c). As early as the late 1950s, the Chinese had feared that the US might use Pakistan as a base for operations against Tibet and Xinjiang (Norbu 1997: 1086). China definitely did not want Pakistan to become a pawn to be used against China. Feeling threatened by the emergence of closer strategic bonds between Washington and the region, China is attempting to avoid the formation of an anti-China stronghold in the region by the US and its coalition partners. It is logical that Beijing should embrace Pakistan even more tightly despite its new relationship with India. The Indian side also senses that China is making special efforts to reach out to Pakistan on account of the US presence in the region (*The Hindu* 2002b). However, for India, even though China claims the renewed Sino–Pakistan strategic relations are not directed against India, a close relationship between two unfriendly neighbours can only bring trouble.

India still feels that it is been being hemmed in by China and Pakistan. Indian Northern Army Command chief Lieutenant General K.T. Parnaik publicly warned that Chinese troops are not only stationed along the Sino-Indian border, but also present on the LOC between India and Pakistan (*The Times of India* 2011c: 13). China's ever-growing presence in Pakistan Occupied Kashmir has been of a great security concern to India, and, as Indian media revealed, have led India to harden its stand on India–Pakistan talks on the Siachen issue (*The Times of India* 2011d: 6).

For the sake of its own security, the Indian side has sensed the need to separate China and Pakistan to prevent a joint China–Pakistan attack. Contrary to China's unilateral expectations and understanding, India is still very concerned by China–Pakistan relations, and treats the issue of Sino-Pakistan military cooperation as the 'litmus test' of China's sincerity (Sidhu and Yuan 2003: 63).

China's position of neutrality towards India–Pakistan conflicts has been in evidence since the late 1980s, as it has expressed its hopes that India and Pakistan will maintain stable relations in the interests of regional security. Indeed, China's more balanced policy towards India and Pakistan and its moderate position over the Kashmir dispute has been much to India's relief. However, these two examples of non-partisanship are not enough to dispel India's concerns. The mutual distrust generated by China's special relationship with Pakistan has not ceased to be a factor just because of the dismantling of the Cold War structure or China's more balanced policy towards South Asia.

China has been self-righteous in assessing the impact of Sino-Pakistani military cooperation upon India's security. China even concludes that it has already done much to remove the Pakistan factor from the normalization of Sino-Indian relations (Sidhu and Yuan 2003: 340). However, the Chinese see India's uneasiness about Sino-Pakistan relations as India's 'haunted mind' (Zhang 2004: 334). Although Beijing does not want to see its relations with Pakistan derail the process of engaging India, it is not ready to give up an 'all weather' friendship to please India.

In order to stabilize its peripheral environment, China has been trying to contribute to the establishment of peaceful relations between India and Pakistan, but the Indian side expected China to use its influence to persuade Islamabad to abandon adventurism rather than asking both sides to show restraint. It has also been made clear that differences remain unresolved with regard to India's suspicions about China's alleged contributions to Pakistan's nuclear weapon and ballistic missile programmes. Although China has denied it transferred to Pakistan nuclear weapons technology and long-range missiles, to a large extent, the Indian side holds China responsible for the nuclear proliferation and arms race in South Asia. The balance between the desire to see a stable environment in South Asia and to maintain strategic ties with Pakistan is a delicate situation for Beijing. China tends to attribute significance to these two potentially competing goals depending on its view of the strategic situation in the region. It is likely that China will continue to transfer arms to Pakistan despite India's protests.

It also appears that China has failed to convince India of the benevolent nature of Sino-Pakistan ties and has failed to marginalize the Pakistan factor in Sino-Indian relations as it had hoped. New Delhi still perceives an encirclement due to the collaboration between China and Pakistan to confine its strategic sphere in South Asia. Although China does not take India's concerns seriously, New Delhi cannot resist putting a strong emphasis on the Sino-Pakistan relationship. China's actions may, in turn, lead India to adopt some counter-measures, such as developing 'normal' military ties with China's troublesome neighbours.

India's Look East Policy

Although India feels pressure from China's engagement with South Asian states, it is not always on the defensive regarding China; it could also able to take some balancing initiatives to counter its perceived encirclement by China. For example, it could strengthen its engagement with China's neighbouring states, such as the countries in East Asia, to put pressure on China's security environment, thus distracting China.

In fact, during the Cold War, India's conflicts with China, its connection with the USSR, its support for Vietnam's invasion of Cambodia, and its renewed hostility with Islamic Pakistan alienated it from most states in East Asia. Furthermore, 'India's stubborn insistence on an inward-looking economy' was seen as one of many diplomatic mistakes, which made it increasingly irrelevant to a dynamic Asia (Limaye 1993: 8). In the early 1990s, when India began to undertake economic reforms, there was an appraisal of India's policy towards the countries in East Asia (Fang 2001). The steady economic development of the region, especially before the financial crisis, attracted much of India's attention. Against this backdrop, the P.V. Narasimha Rao administration unveiled the 'Look East policy' to revive India's relations with East Asia, particularly ASEAN states.

During the initial phase, the Look East policy had gained favourable results on the economic and trade fronts. In 1992, India became a Sectoral Dialogue Partner of ASEAN. The two sides identified four broad sectors for cooperation—trade, investment, science and technology, and tourism—that had the aim of contributing to a closer economic link between India and ASEAN states (Dutta 1997). Japan, Korea, and ASEAN states also emerged as a lucrative export market and source of foreign investments for India.

As it embarked on the Look East policy to reach out to states in East Asia, India showed its ambition to extend its influence beyond the subcontinent. India identifies Southeast Asia as its 'extended neighbourhood' with strategic implications for India, and wishes to maintain the momentum of the Look East policy to forge a closer partnership with ASEAN states. Indian External Minister I.K. Gujral argued that geography inevitably predetermined India to have close and cooperative relations with countries of the Association of Southeast Asian Nations and the Asia Pacific region.[7] The policy could be seen as one of India's successful geo–strategies because India's relations with the countries in the region have since improved significantly. On the other hand, the Look East Policy provides a possible approach for India to challenge China's status in the region. China is closely monitoring India–ASEAN ties to prevent the formation of an anti-China collaboration in the region.

Security Dimension of the Look East Policy

The economic interactions between India and ASEAN might have later slowed down with the South-East Asian economic meltdown, but the Indian side changed its previous perceptions of ASEAN states and so tended to attribute more significance to India–ASEAN relations. As a result, India continued to show its willingness to engage ASEAN states. In October 2003, India joined the Treaty of Amity and Cooperation in Southeast Asia. In November 2004, India and ASEAN further concluded the 'India–ASEAN Partnership for Peace, Progress and Shared Prosperity'. This signified India's commitment to work with ASEAN countries in maintaining regional peace and stability. In 2005, India was allowed to take part in the East Asia Summit.

Meanwhile, the economic and trade fronts remain as important elements of the relations between India and ASEAN states. In 2003, India and ASEAN signed the Framework Agreement on Comprehensive Economic Cooperation, which aimed to establish a Free Trade area by 2011. An India–ASEAN Free Trade Agreement (FTA) in goods was signed in August 2009. In addition, India has been actively conducting bilateral FTA negotiations with the states in the region. India signed a bilateral FTA agreement with Thailand in July 2003, the Comprehensive Economic Cooperation Agreement (CECA) with Singapore in June 2005, and the CECA with Malaysia in February 2011. Furthermore, India has concluded trade-related institutional arrangements with the Philippines, Vietnam, Myanmar, and Laos.

With the conclusion of such arrangements, India is poised for greater economic integration with ASEAN states and the region. While justifying economic logic as the building block of India's Look East Policy, the expanded and intense economic engagements are symptomatic of emerging trends in the respective economies of India and ASEAN countries (Shekhar 2007).

The Look East Policy was premised on trade and economic interaction with Southeast Asian nations, but subsequently expanded to other areas of common interest. Despite the economic engagement, during India's search for an association with new friends in the region, security ties and military cooperation have been identified as being among the areas of Indo-ASEAN cooperation.

Although the motivation for the Look East policy was primarily economical, the political relations and security ties between India and the ASEAN states have also gradually progressed. On the security and political front, India joined the ARF 1996, an organization aimed at fostering dialogue and consultation on political and security issues of common interest and concern, and at making significant contributions to efforts towards confidence-building and preventative diplomacy in the Asia-Pacific region. In 1996, New Delhi was accepted as a full Dialogue Partner of ASEAN, and participated for the first time in the Post Ministerial Conference (PMC) of ASEAN in Jakarta. The climax of India's relations with Southeast Asia came in 2002 when the first India–ASEAN summit was held. India became the fourth state, after China, Japan, and South Korea, to establish the summit mechanism with ASEAN.

More remarkably, the Indian side has shown interest in strengthening military cooperation with ASEAN states by offering training slots to them and holding joint military exercises with them, which have over the years, increased in scope and content while enhancing interoperability. Conducting the exercises has been institutionalized between India and Singapore, and joint patrols continue with Indonesia and Thailand .[8]

In addition, India's military relations with Vietnam and Myanmar attract much attention. India and Vietnam have been keen to expand their military ties, which have revolved round the supply of spare parts, the training of personnel, and the repair of equipment of Soviet-origin (*The Hindu* 1999b: 14). To cite some examples, during the Indian Defence Minister's visit to Vietnam in March 2000, the two sides signed a wide-ranging agreement paving the way for greater military cooperation, which included the sale of advanced military light helicopters, assisting in the repair and overhaul of Vietnam's mainstay MiG fighters and raising the level of military contacts (*The Hindu* 1999: 13). The third Indo-Vietnam Security Dialogue was held at New Delhi during 28–29 November 2007.

Bordering China and India, Myanmar has traditionally sought to maintain a balance between its two giant neighbours. On the other hand, both China and India would like to have Myanmar as their ally against the other state. The Indian side has seen China's aid to Myanmar as China's intention to infiltrate its military strength as far as the Indian Ocean. For example, Myanmar is expanding, with Chinese support, its naval facilities in Great Coco Island, the site of a major signals intelligence facility situated near India's Andaman and Nicobar Islands. In order to counterbalance China's strategic link, India has also increased its cooperation with the

Myanmar military junta. Particularly, there has recently been a substantial increase in bilateral defence cooperation between the Indian Army and the Myanmar Army in training and other fields. Recent years have witnessed exchanges of high-level visits, such as that of the Indian Chief of the Army Staff to Myanmar and the Commander-in-Chief of the Myanmar Navy to India in 2005. Indian External Affairs Minister Pranab Mukherjee claimed that India was willing to expand the ambit of military cooperation between the two countries, including military transfers, and promised to give a 'favourable response' to the Myanmar Government's request for military equipment (Loudon 2007). In addition, in April 2007, it was reported that the Indian and Myanmar security forces were conducting joint military operations along the 1,643-km India–Myanmar border to neutralize insurgent groups (Sharma 2007). Apparently, New Delhi's impulses to continue to 'Look East' are not only dictated by economic engagements, but also are grounded in the consideration of geopolitics.

This expansion of India's profile in the defence sector is mirrored by the interest of regional powers in partnering India. In the view of the Chinese, ASEAN welcomes India's military presence in this region because it considers that India could contribute to maintain the balance of power (Zhao 2007a: 15). This is why ASEAN states did not follow the US or Japan's example in criticizing India's nuclear tests of 1998. China interpreted the mild response by ASEAN states as their acknowledgement of India as a rising political power that has near-parity with China, and can be seen as a balance against China's influence.

The burgeoning India–ASEAN military engagement reflects the success of India's Look East policy. India has gradually revealed its potential as an economic power and now it is ASEAN states that are turning to India. The region sees India as one of its growing partners in trade and as a major source for future investments. The ASEAN states will keep playing an increasingly significant role in India's foreign policy and security policy as well. The question is how China sees India's move to engage states in China's neighbourhood.

Chinese Assessment of India's Look East Policy

The Chinese are aware that India sees China as a competitor in the South Asia region, and ASEAN states also welcome such a development. For example, India began seeking the FTA agreement with ASEAN after China had proposed it. However, the Chinese side seems not to give too much significance to the India–ASEAN economic engagement. For example, the India–Singapore FTA is seen as being symbolic only. On the other hand, the Chinese side acknowledged that India has achieved some results from its military engagement with ASEAN states. Yet, India's repeated and well-broadcast military engagement with the region has cast a new layer of mistrust, rekindling doubts in Chinese minds about India's intentions. The Chinese side has questioned the real strategic motivation behind India's Look East policy by arguing that the Indian side is always vague on what kind of interests they should defend in this region (Zhao 2007a: 13–14).

In the Chinese view, there are two major drives behind India's Look East policy. First, the essence of the Look East policy is the recognition that India's aspirations for a larger global role cannot be realized while its foreign policy and national security preoccupations are limited to the subcontinent. It is a necessary step if India wishes to achieve the goal of being a world power (Zhao 2007a: 13). In addition, India has to establish closer contacts with the relevant region in order to prevent marginalization in the context of the trend towards regionalism. In other words, the Look East policy is part of India's grand strategy for securing global power status (Liu and Zhang 2006: 98–101). Soon after India conducted the nuclear tests in 1998, the then Indian President, K.R. Narayanan, said that the Indian government 'will strive for Asian solidarity and enhanced regional cooperation'.[9] The reference to the notion of 'Asian solidarity' was seen as a commitment to deepen and widen India's foreign policy interaction with the major Asian powers (Mohan 1998: 13). Meanwhile, some states in the region began to recognize that India had a role to play at a global level. For example, the Malaysian Foreign Minister, Syed Hamid Albar, said that ASEAN countries would like their relationship with India to be mutually beneficial to ASEAN with India playing its role in the international sphere (*The Hindu* 2000a: 14).

Second, the Look East policy became one of India's ploys to counter China's 'omni-directional pressure' (Zhao 2007b: 30). The presence of India's navy in the South China Sea was seen as a particular source of concern to China. The Chinese media questioned why India's navy stayed in the South China Sea even after concluding a joint military exercise with Singapore, Vietnam, and so on. Given the territorial disputes between China and some ASEAN states, the report argued that India's attempt to maintain a substantial military presence in the South China

Sea had profound and long-term implications for China's polices towards the region (*Huanqiao Shibao* 2001: 1).

The Chinese side is concerned about where the impetus for these initiatives lies. Since the PLA Navy is yet to acquire credible blue water capability, China and India have had no direct clash of national interest in the Indian Ocean. Nonetheless, the Chinese side is acutely conscious of the on-going deep engagement between India and other Southeast powers. The Chinese have concluded that one aim of the present Indian naval build-up is to ensure its capability to operate outside South Asia. India's acquisition of Russia's 40,000 tonne aircraft carrier, *Admiral Gorshkov*, along with other defence deals has attracted the attention of the PLA.[10] The Chinese concerns of an India thrust eastward in the South China Sea increased when India proclaimed its plan to build a new carrier, which would be the country's third. Professor Hu Siyuan of the Chinese Defence University argued that the regional balance of power would be changed once the Indian Navy owned three aircraft carriers. He warned that the Indian Navy would then enter the South China Sea (Shao and Xu 2000).

China has some misgivings about India's initiative in forging a close relationship with Vietnam on the security front. Both Vietnam and India were part of the Soviet plot to encircle China in the Cold War. Vietnam chose not to condemn India's nuclear tests and has now recognized New Delhi's security concerns. It is also seeking to obtain nuclear and satellite technology from India. Vietnam agrees that India should become a permanent member of an expanded UN Security Council. Vietnam is emerging as India's key strategic partner for countering piracy from the Indian waters to the South China Sea; as the Indian Defence Minister indicated, India and Vietnam are partners in safeguarding commercial sea lanes (*The Hindu* 2000b: 15). The Indian Navy's decision to hold joint military exercises with Vietnam in the South China Sea appeared certain to antagonize China. The high-profile posture was interpreted as India's signal of its ability to enter China's traditional strategic region (Sidhu and Yuan 2001: 58).

The Defence Minister George Fernandes claimed that given the high stakes involved in the uninterrupted flow of commercial shipping, India's area of interest therefore extends from north of the Arabian Sea to the South China Sea (*The Hindu* 2000b: 15). A similar proclamation was issued by Indian Foreign Minister Jaswant Singh. During his visit to

Singapore in June 2000, he suggested that India's security environment and concerns involved Southeast Asia (*Jiefanghun Bao* 2000). He also claimed, 'India is a factor for stability' in the East Asian region (*The Hindu* 2000c: 14).

The overlapping claims over the sovereignty of the oil-rich Spratlys in the South China Sea have placed additional pressure on China's security. The Chinese do not want to see states in the region working together with outside powers against China over the South China Sea issue; Beijing has a deep concern about the India's propensity to extend its areas of operation and interests eastward to the South China Sea. China, looking on the South China Sea as its special domain, does not welcome India's presence in the area. The improvement in India–ASEAN relations and the establishment of a cooperative partnership would make China's security environment more complicated, putting pressure upon China's western and southern regions, challenging China's maritime security, and increasing its difficulty in solving the boundary problem and the territorial claims in the South China Sea. Thus, Chinese scholars have bluntly asserted that it is not in China's interests to see close relations between India and ASEAN states (Liu 1999a, 1999b).

Despite China's apprehension, the Indian side has repeated that its determination to engage with ASEAN states is natural, just as China has argued that its relations with South Asian states are part of normal conduct among states. It is worth noting that 'containing China' is not India's only consideration to engage ASEAN states. In fact, neither India nor ASEAN states will want to confront China because they still need China for trade and investment. However, the flourishing partnership between India and ASEAN states and India's active involvement and presence in the region have raised concerns in China, as India's growing presence will inevitably dilute China's influence in this region. As New Delhi and Beijing vie for influence in the region, India could be an instrument to counterbalance and neutralize China's predominance.

On the other hand, the Chinese have deemed that it is unlikely India's relations with this region will change the prevailing balance of power in the region, even though India is trying to establish a free trade regime with ASEAN, because they think India's power and influence are very limited in this region (Zhao 2007a). That is, China deems that there is an asymmetrical power structure between China and India, and thus enjoys a sense of superiority against India.

Evolving Indo-Taiwanese and Indo-Japanese Relations

A significant change can be found in India's relations with Taiwan (the Republic of China). After India recognized the communist regime in Beijing, the two sides had no official contact for more than four decades. In order to promote economic ties between the two sides, New Delhi adopted a more friendly policy towards Taiwan while formally sticking to the so-called 'One China' policy. After two years of negotiations, India and Taiwan agreed to set up quasi-official liaison offices in each other's capitals.[11] Even Chinese scholars have opined that there was a 'breakthrough' in Indo-Taiwanese economic relations in the wake of India's economic reforms (Ma 1994: 49).

For China, another major concern regarding India's Look East policy is the evolving Indo-Japanese partnership. Japan had suspended all Official Development Assistance (ODA) to India after Pokhran II in May 1998, but the frequent exchanges of high-level visits signalled both sides' willingness to seek a closer relationship. Japan and India agreed to establish the 'Japan–India Global Partnership in the 21st Century' when Japanese Prime Minister Yoshiro Mori visited India in August 2000. Indian Prime Minister Vajpayee visited Japan in December 2001, and the two sides issued the 'Japan–India Joint Declaration' to promote high-level dialogue, exchanges in the information-communication technology (ICT) field, and joint counter-action against the proliferation of weapons of mass destruction (WMD) and terrorism.

It was also agreed, when the then Japanese Prime Minister Junichiro Koizumi visited India in April 2005, that the two countries would further strengthen their cooperation, pursue an all-round and comprehensive development of bilateral relations, and reinforce the strategic focus of the global partnership between the two countries. On that occasion, the two sides jointly announced the 'Japan–India Partnership in the New Asian Era: Strategic Orientation of Japan–India Global Partnership'. During Indian Prime Minister Manmohan Singh's visit to Japan in December 2006, the two Prime Ministers decided to establish a bilateral 'Strategic and Global Partnership' between the two countries and signed the 'Joint Statement towards a Japan–India Strategic and Global Partnership'. Japanese Prime Minister Shinzo Abe then visited India in August 2007, and the two sides signed the 'Joint Statement on the Roadmap for New Dimensions to the Strategic and Global Partnership between Japan and India'. Manmohan Singh visited Japan again in October 2010 and met

Japanese Prime Minister Naoto Kan, discussing regional security issues. A 'Joint Statement on Vision for India–Japan Strategic and Global Partnership in the Next Decade' was signed. In February 2011, the Comprehensive Economic Partnership Agreement (CEPA) was signed in order to promote economic exchanges.

India's defence ties with Japan have also been evolving in recent years and an exchange of high-level visits has been the highlight of India–Japan military ties. The Indian Defence Minister, George Fernandes, travelled to Tokyo in January 2000, and the two sides agreed to initiate a new dialogue on security and defence. During the visit of Indian Defence Minister, Pranab Mukherjee, to Japan in May 2006, the two countries signed a joint statement, the first such document to be signed by the defence chiefs of the two countries, vowing to aim to maintain and promote peace and stability in Asia and the world. The statement called for regular meetings of the defence chiefs, exchanges on other levels, exchanging information on international terrorism and strengthening cooperation via drills, security research, and technologies. The coast guards of the two countries conducted their seventh round of exercises in November 2006 off the Mumbai Coast. A Memorandum of Understanding (MOU) between the coast guards of the two countries was also signed in November 2006. The Indian Defence Secretary led a high-level delegation to Japan during 10–14 April 2007 for the first India–Japan Defence Policy Dialogue. The visit also coincided with the first goodwill naval exercises between the Indian and Japanese navies off the Japanese coast. In April 2007, Indian Chief of Army Staff visited Japan. Japanese Senior Vice-Minister of Defence, Takahide Kiwara, reciprocally visited India in August 2007.

The significance of the above is that, in the past, both India and Japan have fought wars with China and, currently, both India and Japan have territorial disputes with China. For both India and Japan, China remains an unarticulated threat concern. The Chinese side tends to conclude that the India–Japan partnership is built on the basis of the strategic consideration of containing China, as they argued that the impact of the Indo-Japanese partnership upon Asian politics deserves attention (Jiang 2000: 2). It has also been pointed out that the Japanese media reported a suggestion by the former Taiwan President, Lee Teng-hui, that the Japanese should work together with Taiwan and India to contain China. From the Chinese perspective, all the signs indicate that India, with its growing economic and military power, has set its sights on the Asia-Pacific region (Sheng 2000).

The report on US–India–Japan trilateral military exercises recommends a scenario about which China would have significant reservations. The Malabar exercise of April 2007 by India and the US, held in the western Pacific, first took Japan into their fold and then, in September 2007, was further expanded in scope and participation to include Australia and Singapore as well. Although bilateral military exercises are not new for the four countries, there seemed to have been a new momentum for these countries to conduct multinational naval exercises.

China did not remain unaware of the development. Beijing expressed annoyance during the India–US–Japan naval exercise off the Japanese coast in April 2007. When the four powers (India, Japan, the US, and Australia) set up an initiative (informally named the Quad) in May 2007, Beijing further issued demarches to all the four countries on the purpose of the joint exercise. Chinese President Hu Jintao also sought clarification from Indian Prime Minister Manmohan Singh on the issue at the G8 summit held in Germany in 2008. Although the Quad members reassured China that their 'strategic partnership' was aimed only at maintaining regional security, and was not targeting any particular power, Beijing was not convinced and has since seemed to be increasingly worried. Many analysts saw the manoeuvres as efforts by a democratic coalition to 'contain' rising Chinese power. China believes that the Quadrilateral Initiative is an Asian version of the North Atlantic Treaty Organization (NATO), aiming to contain a rising China (Ramachandran 2007).

China later successfully persuaded Australia to pull out of the Quadrilateral Initiative, but it should be remembered that the US–Japan–Australia–India quadrilateral dialogue was enthusiastically proposed by former Japanese Prime Minister Shinzo Abe and was embraced by Delhi. As both Japan and India have described China as a potential threat, it is likely that India and Japan see each other as a military counterbalance against China. After all, apart from the 'ASEAN plus' initiatives, there are hardly any other groupings that carry weight in the region, but the launch of the Quad suggests a pattern of alliance-building activities that China cannot ignore (Ali 2007).

Indian strategists have already proposed inviting other countries in this region, such as Indonesia, to form a new quadrilateral initiative after Australia's departure (Singh 2008a). India is keen to maintain the momentum to bring more pressure to bear on China. Given the nature of the strategic partnership with ASEAN states, and India's competition with China for strategic space in Asia and Africa, India should welcome any new regional framework in the Asia-Pacific that aims at containing China's influence. China, in its turn, will hinder the formation of any anti-China Asia-Pacific framework.

Regional Cooperation between China and India

Optimists about Sino-Indian relations take the view that common interests between China and India far outweigh their differences, so both sides could focus on expanding cooperation rather than quarrelling over differences in order to improve bilateral relations. As far as the geographic proximity is concerned, it not only generates competition between China and India, but also presents an opportunity for cooperation in some areas. As Chinese President Jiang Zemin pointed out, geographic proximity could be an advantage for China–India cooperation, along with the vast land masses, rich natural resources, large populations, and huge markets (*Xinhua* 1996). Unfortunately, in the past, border disputes had prevented both sides from exploring the possibility of benefiting more from their geographic proximity.

In order to move Sino-Indian relations away from the notion of competition and towards cooperation, both sides are also seeking opportunities to make use of the geographical advantages, rather than focusing on the disputes only. In a development likely to forge more benign interactions, China and India are working to place the issues regarding regional cooperation on their agenda, with the expectation of imparting additional momentum to improve the bilateral relations.

Anti-terrorism Cooperation

From a geographical perspective, another area of interest to China and India is their common concerns over malignant cross-border activities. As an initial step to cooperate in the fight against cross-border crimes, during Chinese President Jiang Zemin's visit to India in 1996, China and India signed an agreement on combating drug trafficking. The common willingness to combat Islamic militancy and fundamentalists emanating from Central Asia and Afghanistan is also likely to provide a fillip to the Sino-Indian relationship.

From Beijing's point of view, with the collapse of the USSR and the disintegration of the communist ideological system, the Central Asian region has witnessed the rise of Islamist forces that have appealed to religious enthusiasts, calling for the establishment of 'pure Islamic countries' (Gao 2001: 8). There is also concern that China's Xinjiang is being beleaguered by Uighur extremists who aim to split the Xinjiang Uighur Autonomous Region from China to establish the independent state of 'East Turkistan'. The Uighur separatists' activities have emerged as a serious cause of insecurity for China because some of them have resorted to terrorism to promote the cause. According to Chinese official sources, from 1990 to 2001 alone, the 'East Turkistan' terrorist forces were responsible for over 200 terrorist incidents in Xinjiang, including explosions, assassinations, arsons, poisonings, and assaults (SCIO 2002: 14–19, 22–3).

Where India is concerned, the Indian authorities have been laboriously battling the *jihadis* (Muslim religious fundamentalists) since the late 1980s. Indian official sources show that Jammu and Kashmir, the only Muslim-majority region of India, has suffered more than 45,000 terrorist incidents.[12] However, Muslim militant organizations have not only created disturbances in Kashmir, but also caused damage in other parts of India. The Indian Parliament, foreign embassies in India, the Red Fort, Indian Airlines aircraft, and the renowned Taj Hotel in Mumbai have all been targeted by Muslim terrorists in recent years.

Although both China and India have worked hard to repress these terrorist activities, the internal-external linkage has created difficulties. External sympathetic groups in Central Asian states, Afghanistan, and Pakistan have provided sanctuary, support, and training for the Muslim terrorists. Therefore, seeking international cooperation to block extremist movements inside their own territories and cut the links across the border is a fundamental aspect of China and India's policy to combat cross-border terrorism.

The changing international context and the common cause of the fight against terrorism in the wake of the September 11 terrorist attacks opened a new area of cooperation between China and India. China and India have benefitted to some extent from the US war against Osama Bin Laden's Al-Qaeda, which was believed to have been helping train 'East Turkistan' advocates, Kashmiri militant organizations and other terrorists outside Afghanistan.[13] While the campaign against international terrorism has gained great momentum, both China and India have used the occasion to justify their respective actions against the Uighur separatists in Xinjiang and the Islamist militants in Kashmir. By branding the Uighur separatists as terrorists, China could destroy them with less protest from the US and the West.

However, the war against terrorism has not gone entirely China and India's way. With more troops from the US-led coalition marching into Central and South Asia, the war against terrorism has begun to realign the balance of power in the region in ways that Beijing and New Delhi may not welcome. Beijing is carefully monitoring US moves to develop closer ties with the Central and South Asian states. American forces were stationed in Kyrgyzstan and Uzbekistan. Although Washington said it had no intention of building permanent bases in the region, its military presence could last as long as the campaign against terrorism. A Chinese scholar from the National Defence University of China expressed the worry that the US had seldom withdrawn troops from its overseas military bases, so its complete withdrawal from the region is unlikely (Ge 2002: 8–9). Given the uneasy Sino-American relations, Beijing needed to deal with the far-reaching implications of the American military presence close to its backdoor.

The growing profile of the US in Central and South Asia has persuaded China to be more inclined to engage with states in the region. In the face of the new international situation, China was not so reluctant to accept India's overture to contain international terrorism jointly than it would otherwise have been. When Chinese Premier Zhu Rongji visited New Delhi in January 2002, China and India agreed to initiate a dialogue mechanism on counter-terrorism (*Xinhua* 2002b). China also expressed its willingness to share intelligence with India on terrorism in Kashmir and unrest in India's northeast in exchange for India's intelligence on the Uighur separatists (*The Hindu* 2002c).

The development was a positive sign, with Indian External Affairs Minister Jaswant Singh pointing out that only the US and Russia's broad-based dialogue architecture is comparable to that of India and China (*The Hindu* 2002d). The first Sino-Indian counter-terrorism dialogue took place in April 2002 and the second was held in June 2003. However, the extent to which the dialogue mechanism can bring India and China closer remains debatable. The key to further cooperation on counter-terrorism will lie in whether the two countries can reconcile their differences over the definition of terrorism.

It is also worth noting that China tends to equate religious extremists and national separatists with international terrorists. According to the Chinese definition, therefore, there is no difference between Uighur and Tibetan separatists and both should be crushed without mercy. Apparently, it is difficult for New Delhi to accept this concept in view of fact that India still provides sanctuary to the Dalai Lama and his government-in-exile.

On the other hand, although Beijing has claimed that it opposes 'all forms of terrorism', 'no matter when, where or in what form terrorism strikes, and no matter against whom it is directed',[14] it also finds it difficult to assent to India's definition regarding international terrorism, particularly its accusations about Pakistan. China has dismissed the charge that Pakistan has rendered training to the Uighur terrorists,[15] and will not agree to expand the war on terrorism to include Pakistan. Chinese sensitivity to the issue was evident from the fact that the Chinese officials played down the significance of China–India dialogue mechanism on countering terrorism. Chinese Vice-Foreign Minister Wang Yi said that China had already held such a dialogue with many countries (*Renmin Ribao* 2002e: 3). A Chinese Foreign Ministry spokesman also said China fully supported the anti-terrorism measures taken by Pakistan and said that Beijing and Islamabad could set up a similar mechanism if necessary (*People's Daily* 2002).

Such differences could exacerbate divisions between Beijing and New Delhi and limit the scope of cooperation. Since both India and China insist that there should be no double standards in addressing the issue of terrorism, they have to forge a consensus on the definition of terrorism. Thus, it may be a while before India and China take concrete steps towards countering terrorism.

However, the common course of anti-terrorism has provided a platform for the two countries. The armies of the two countries conducted the first-ever China–India Joint Anti-Terrorism Training Code named 'Hand-in-Hand 2007' in December 2007, in Kunming, China's Yunnan province. It was followed by the 'Hand-in-Hand 2008' joint military training and exercise at Belgaum in Karnataka, India. It seems that the two armies will continue their exchanges and joint exercises in the name of 'counter-terrorism'; the fact that China and India are now sitting together to talk about counter-terrorism and other related security issues is a significant development in China–India relations.

SCO and SAARC

The Chinese take the view that the 'East Turkistan terrorist force' has links and collaborates with overseas terrorist groups (SCIO 2002: 18–19, 22–3). In order to curb the penetration of external extremists from the neighbouring areas, in 1996, China used a coordinated mechanism, the Shanghai Five, with Russia, Kazakhstan, Kyrgyzstan, and Tajikistan, to address the concern. In fact, the original agenda of the grouping was set up to resolve border issues and promote CBMs along China's frontiers with the former Soviet republics. From 1998 onward, due to the activism of the so-called 'three evil forces' (terrorism, separatism, and extremism) in the region, the focus of the mechanism has shifted from boosting border security and reducing troop levels, to curbing terrorism, separatism, and extremism (Gao 2001: 8–10).

Between 1998 and 2000, the leaders of the five member-states met annually in Almaty (Kazakhstan), Bishkek (Kyrgyzstan), and Dushanbe (Tajikistan) to discuss how to deepen cooperation on issues of concern. They agreed to fight jointly against national separatism, international terrorism, and religious extremism, as well as to combat the cross-border criminal activities of arms-smuggling, drug-trafficking, and illegal immigration. The five states also made a commitment not to allow any attempt to use their territories to engage in activities harmful to the sovereignty, security, and social order of the other member states. To strengthen security cooperation, they called for the formulation of a multilateral cooperation guideline, the conclusion of necessary multilateral treaties and accords, and the holding of regular meetings of officers from the law enforcement, border patrol, customs, and security departments of the five countries. Furthermore, they agreed to hold anti-terrorism and anti-violence manoeuvres within the five-nation framework if necessary, and supported Kyrgyzstan's proposal to establish a regional anti-terrorism centre in Bishkek.[16]

In June 2001, the mechanism was converted to the more institutionalized Shanghai Cooperation Organization (SCO) and incorporated Uzbekistan as the sixth member. The six states then signed the 'Shanghai Convention on Combating Terrorism, Separatism and Extremism',[17] which provided the definition of terrorism, separatism, and extremism and laid a legal foundation for jointly cracking down on the 'three forces'.[18] That is, the Chinese would like to use the SCO as one of a series of platforms to address its concerns about the cross-border terrorist activities emanating from Central Asia.

Although India does not border Central Asia, it was keen to join this regional group.[19] The main reason for India wishing to associate itself with this forum is because it has been plagued by terrorists emerging from that region, especially Taliban-held Afghanistan. To cite an example, in December 1999, an Indian Airlines aircraft (IC-814) from Nepal to Kandahar in Afghanistan, was hijacked. The Indian Government was forced to release three jailed terrorists in exchange for the freedom of the 155 hostages.

India's case for joining the grouping has been supported by Russia. General Leonid Ivashov, head of Russian Defence Ministry's International Cooperation Department, said in public that India could join the Shanghai Five forum if it wished to (*The Hindu* 2000d: 14). Russian President Vladimir Putin also said that the Shanghai Five was not 'a closed club' and was open for other countries to join (*The Hindu* 2000e: 13). Being another major sponsor of the organization, China also agreed to recruit India to the SCO, with the proviso that it would be necessary to wait for 'when conditions are ripe and on the basis of consultative consensus'.[20] Thus, it seemed possible that China and India could jointly address their concerns over terrorism through the regional framework.

However, the membership issue became more complicated and complex when Pakistan also made a formal bid to join the group. Pakistan applied for membership on the grounds that it, too, was facing a similar threat of terrorism and could make a contribution to the mechanism. Pakistan's case met with strong opposition from Russia because of its record of involvement with Islamic insurgent groups. In addition, Russia was not happy about Pakistan sponsoring the Taliban regime, and did not believe Pakistan's involvement would contribute to the curbing of terrorism. Contrary to Russia's position, China saw Pakistan's affiliation into the group as a favour in view of the close relationship between Beijing and Islamabad. Therefore, Beijing offered its approval of India's membership in exchange for Russia's acquiescence on Pakistan's accession. Since membership of the SCO should be approved unanimously by the members, China's efforts to induct Pakistan and Russia's plan to induct India in the SCO were delayed due to the lack of consensus among the member states.

The SCO then decided not to admit new members, but agreed to recruit observers. Thus, India finally joined the regional group together with Pakistan and Iran in 2005, as the group sought to enhance its security role in Central Asia. The decision to co-opt the three countries was a compromise between different interests within and outside the group. China insisted on the simultaneous admission of India and Pakistan, even though Delhi and Moscow were unhappy with this linkage (*The Hindu* 2005b).

India was disappointed about securing observer status, as it was only a spectator at plenary meetings. However, the SCO decided in 2008 that the observer nations could participate in all the organization's deliberations. The Indian Prime Minister, Manmohan Singh, then decided to attend the 2009 SCO summit, held in Yekaterinburg, Russia, to highlight India's full involvement in SCO activities. Furthermore, participation by India and Pakistan in the SCO could help reduce the leverage the US has on South Asia. On the other hand, India's presence in the SCO will allow it to deepen security and economic ties with the entire resource-rich Central Asian region as well as reinforce its ties individually with each of the countries. Indian officials are very optimistic about securing the full membership of SCO as they find affirmative responses from member countries. Even if the process of becoming a full member may take some time, India feels satisfied because observers in the SCO have a role in framing of documents (*The Hindu* 2011b). In the short term, although India is unlikely to be able to challenge China's dominant role in the SCO, it still could extend its influence, as the other members may approve of India's presence as a means of undermining the growing Chinese influence in the region.

Interestingly, soon after India gained observer status in the SCO, China was accepted in 2005 as an observer at the South Asian Association for Regional Cooperation (SAARC), a grouping established in 1985 as a vehicle for political and economic cooperation among the South Asian countries.[21] It was the first time the regional organization had accorded observer status to a country. In contrast to China's confidence in including India into the SCO, New Delhi was reluctant to see China's presence at the SAARC. Though India had been aware of China's intentions to participate in the grouping, the move to include China in SAARC as an observer came as a shock to India. It was Nepal that threatened to veto Afghanistan's membership unless China was simultaneously granted observer status.

Clearly, India had misgivings about China's formal presence at SAARC. The Indian side argued that China is not a South Asian state and has no role to play in the region. However, the observer status highlighted Chinese foreign policy imperatives and its bid to claim global power status; it also indicated the success of China's multilateral efforts (Bhattacharya 2005). Obviously, the other member states in South Asia had no reason to share India's distress. For India, this was a cause of some concern, but for the smaller countries it was a matter of satisfaction. Just like India's presence in Southeast Asia and the SCO, for the smaller countries, China was to be welcomed as a potential countervailing force within an India-dominated South Asia, though China's association was couched in the more appealing language of economics rather than politics.

Again, despite its growing concern, New Delhi was trying to downplay the potential competition with Beijing and decided not to block China's entry as an observer country to avoid creating more distrust between India and China. As a result, New Delhi could respond only by insisting that Japan should also be invited as an observer, as it would indirectly counterbalance China's role in SAARC. The US was also invited by India in 2005 to become an observer in 2006 as a possible attempt by India to balance Pakistan's request to include China (*The Hindu* 2011c).

Undoubtedly, China is determined to use its observer status to expand its clout in the South Asian region. The official *China Daily* in an editorial on the SAARC Summit noted that China's association with the grouping would help Beijing forge diplomatic ties with landlocked Bhutan, the only country in South Asia with which China does not have diplomatic relations (*China Daily* 2005: 4). Irrespective of whether or not this represented another triumph for China and Pakistan *vis-à-vis* India, SAARC has changed forever (Sridharan 2005: 29). China's formal entry to SAARC demonstrates China's rising diplomatic and economic clout in the region, and exposes the limits of India's regional influence.

The space that China has now gained within the region is likely to expand because China's formal presence in South Asia gives Beijing a say in South Asian affairs. At its debut at SAARC, China enunciated a comprehensive five-point proposal for enhanced engagement with SAARC. For example, China proposed to institutionalize the China-South Asia Business Forum so that it could serve as a platform for discussions on economic cooperation and trade. China's action plan at SAARC was seen as rather ambitious for a country that had just been admitted as an observer at the regional grouping (*IANS* 2007). The distrust between India and China also began to mar the SAARC. India is totally opposed to observer members' contribution to the development fund, in order to prevent China from using its economic clout to strengthen its position in the organization.

Apparently, China and India take very different views of each other's involvement in related regional organizations. The asymmetrical concerns explain the differences. Beijing's enthusiasm for SAARC is being watched cautiously in New Delhi. On the other hand, China sees India's joining as an expansion of SCO's influence; China has shown confidence in dealing with the rivalry between China and India.

The Kunming Initiative

The potential of both China and India's economic power has been recognized. The generally improved relations between China and India since the late 1980s and the introduction of India's economic reforms have provided a new setting for stronger economic engagement. The prospects of economic and trade cooperation between them are also vast. Various proposals involving two sub-regions, China's Southwest and India's Northeast, had also been suggested, although the continued political differences and low national priorities attached to these areas had not allowed for much progress to be made on the ground.

By focusing on economic development, the Chinese side has been keen to promote sub-regional economic cooperation. It was thought that the time was ripe for Southwest China to adopt an opening-up policy towards its neighbouring countries.[22] Back in 1991, Sichuan's officials had publicly demanded that the entire region of Southwest China should open up to India, along with Myanmar, Bangladesh, Pakistan, Thailand, and Malaysia (*Central News Agency* 1991). Similarly, Yunnan's officials said that they wanted to make the province an 'international hub' for transport through Southeast Asia and the South Asian subcontinent (*Renmin Ribao* 2000a: 4, 2000b: 12).

Like Southwest China, India's northeast region is interested in engaging with contiguous regions. This section of India, comprising the seven states of Assam, Arunachal Pradesh, Manipur, Meghalaya, Mizoram, Nagaland, and Tripura, shares borders with Bangladesh, Myanmar, Bhutan, and Tibet. Economic backwardness in Northeast India has contributed to the development of various insurgencies and other riot activities, making it one of the most volatile and sensitive regions of India (Datta 2001). The fact that this area shares less than 2 per cent of its borders with the rest of India reflects the importance of opening it up to its neighbouring countries.

It seemed natural to increase exchanges between the two land-locked sub-regions, Southwest China and Northeast India, to boost the economy. In order to transform geographic proximity into an economic advantage, some initiatives have been taken. However, since there is no common border between the two sub-regions, it was decided the engagement had to be carried out in a multilateral framework, involving a third party, such as Myanmar. The proposals centred round the theme of transportation infrastructure links and the development of a sub-regional economic integration forum. It was evident that the lack of transportation links was chiefly responsible for the sluggish growth of foreign trade between Southwest China and India. Thus, the key to increasing the exchange among the sub-regions was the construction of transport links.

Chinese scholars are interested in reviving the concept of the 'Southern Silk Route', an ancient passageway starting from China's Sichuan, and progressing to India's northeast region via Myanmar and China's Yunnan, by constructing a China–Myanmar–India railway as a land bridge to link Southwest China and Northeast India. In their opinion, the railroad could integrate with their respective domestic rail systems and facilitate the movement of goods and people from Shanghai to Mumbai (Chen 1998).

The renovation and reopening of the 'Sino-Indian Road', also known as Stilwell Road or Ledo Road, is another proposal under discussion. The 1,726-km long road, linking Ledo in Assam to Kunming in Yunnan, was an important route by which beleaguered China could obtain external supplies during World War II. Authorities in India's northeastern states have repeatedly called for reopening the old link to boost trade and the economy. For example, Assam's Chief Minister Prafulla Kumar Mahanta argued, 'This is the road that can bring drastic economic change for good to the north-eastern region' (*The Indian Express* 2001). Similar statements have been made by other officials from that region.

Both Southwest China and Northeast India are relatively backward regions where foreign trade is limited. Thus, it seems natural for both sides to become the gateway to international commerce rather than remain as an isolated corner. The proposal for the sub-regional quadrangle cooperation and the transport links has received broad support from the academic communities of China and India.

As for the sub-regional economic integration, there is a major initiative that involves China's Sichuan and Yunnan provinces, and India's northeastern states, Myanmar and Bangladesh. This track-II Kunming Initiative, named after the capital of China's Yunnan province, came out of an academic symposium called the 'Conference on Regional Cooperation and Development among China, India, Myanmar and Bangladesh'. The symposium, which took place in Kunming in August 1999, was jointly organized by the Yunnan Academy of Social Science and the Yunnan Provincial Economic and Technological Research Center. As a consequence of the conference, the 'Kunming Initiative' was discussed and signed by the leaders of the four delegations. The main thrust of the exercise was to exhort the governments concerned to establish a forum for sub-regional economic cooperation comprising China, India, Myanmar, and Bangladesh. They believed that the economies in the sub-region could be strengthened significantly through increased cooperation by the quadrangle (*Nanya Yanjiu* 1999: 94, Indiresan 2000).

Formal approval of the four governments is necessary for the success of the initiative. During his visit to China in May–June 2000, Indian President K.R. Narayanan welcomed the initiatives, saying that there was a 'real opportunity now to inject economic and technical content' into Sino-Indian relations (*The Hindu* 2000i: 1). During his visit to India in January 2002, Chinese Premier Zhu Rongji talked about the necessity to promote further regional economic cooperation (*Renmin Ribao* 2002f: 1). However, the response from New Delhi about the regional economic cooperation was still lukewarm. As a result, the implementation of the Kunming Initiative has not taken place due to a lack of official approval and participation. In particular, Indian policymakers seem to have a deep anxiety about being part of a sub-regional grouping with China.

The most frequently cited argument against India–China economic integration paints the two countries as natural competitors in labour-intensive exports where the success of one would reduce opportunities for the other (Singh 2001). There is a fear in India that the land bridge might benefit the Chinese side only, and would not bring greater prosperity to India's Northeast, because cheaper Chinese imports may dominate Indian domestic markets after gaining direct access to those markets. The Indian side was accused of placing obstacles in the way of economic engagement due to the consideration that some of the Chinese activities may damage Indian security. For example, the Indian government has been considering imposing curbs on Foreign Direct Investment (FDI) from China along with other suspicious neighbours, such as Pakistan and Bangladesh, on national security grounds (*The Economic Times* 2002). The Chinese also find it difficult to get or extend their Indian working visas.

Another reason for India's concern are the long-term consequences in the troubled Northeast after an increase in exchanges across the border (Mohan 2000a: 12). For India, there is reason to worry that the openness will increase the links between border communities, such as the Nagas, with their cousin communities living across the border, as well as strengthening rebellious elements among such tribes. Given that the Chinese have sponsored rebellion in the past, the Indian government believes that the best option is to keep the borders closed to the Chinese side to prevent any external influence over disaffected people in the region (Indiresan 2000).

Therefore, India, disapproving of the quadrangle proposal, has appeared to feel more comfortable in boosting sub-regional cooperation by bypassing and excluding China. For example, after setting up a sub-regional grouping called the Bangladesh, India, Myanmar, Sri Lanka, Thailand Economic Cooperation (BIMSTEC) in June 1997, India launched the Mekong Ganga Cooperation (MGC) project with five ASEAN and Mekong river basin countries—Myanmar, Laos, Cambodia, Thailand, and Vietnam, in November 2000.

The establishment of the forum gave rise to some speculation. The MGC was preceded by initiatives similar to the Mekong Basin Project, set up in early 1996 and involving Myanmar, Cambodia, China, Laos, Thailand, and Vietnam. The Mekong River runs through China, bearing the name *Lancang Jiang*, and China has fully engaged in the Mekong Basin projects. China also promoted the Lancang–Mekong River navigation programme with Myanmar, Laos, and Thailand in April 2000, in a bid to improve the conditions of navigation and make heavy-duty ships operational on the river. However, China has not been invited to join the new grouping, even though some commentators have already pointed out that BIMSTEC's effectiveness has been reduced by the exclusion of China (Haidar 2004).

The grouping still had no desire to expand the membership, although China informally expressed to India its interest in associating itself with the MGC (*The Hindu* 2001g: 9). The message was clear that India did not feel comfortable in engaging China in a sub-regional cooperation framework.

A development that is similarly in contrast to the enthusiasm of the Kunming Initiative was seen in the transport links project. Neither China nor India has made any coordinated efforts to build any links between the contiguous regions, choosing instead to construct links with other neighbouring countries. For its part, China is helping Myanmar build and improve roads from the China–Myanmar border. The roads are seen both as a new trade route and military corridor to the Indian Ocean (*Far Eastern Economic Review* 2000: 26–7). Meanwhile, a 1,850-km Kunming–Bangkok Road via Laos was expected to be fully operational with the sections in China having been completed already.

On the other hand, the Indian Ministry of External Affairs donated a 160-km Tamu–Kalewa–Kalemyo road, inaugurated in February 2001 and known as the India–Myanmar Friendship Road, to Myanmar. The road is an improvement of a World War II road, connecting the Indian town of Moreh in Manipur to central Myanmar (*The Hindu* 2001d: 1). A road linking India, Myanmar, and Thailand has also been under discussion (*Renmin Ribao* 2002d: 7). As China and India exercise their own options to foster sub-regional cooperation without the involvement of the other side, scepticism continues to affect Sino-Indian economic interactions. For example, the Chinese considered the construction of the India–Myanmar Friendship Road as 'conspicuous' (Qian 2001b: 3). No matter what their real intention is, both India and China will view any project engaging a third party as an attempt to undermine the other's strategic influence; this will thereby impair the bilateral relationship. On the other hand, while advances are made by China and other neighbouring countries, the Indian side still hesitates to embrace sub-regional cooperation because it fears seeing China reinforce its position in the region.

China's Confidence *versus* India's Concern

Since independence, India has regarded the South Asian subcontinent as a strategic entity and has been attempting to take advantage of its geographical advantages, large territory and rich resources to capture the leadership in South Asia (Shao 2001). However, China's relations with other South Asian states have worried New Delhi and contributed to the Indian threat perception regarding China. China's engagement with other South Asian states has been seen in New Delhi as a long-term strategy to challenge India's dominance in South Asia. On the other hand, the smaller South Asian states have used their relations with China to counterbalance India's influence (Garver 1991: 957). China, for its part, also welcomes the attempts of the South Asian states to maintain an equal distance between India and China. India's worries of being surrounded by hostile nations that are friendly with China, have grown.

As previously mentioned, in the post-Cold War era, China changed its past thinking and began a trend of not exploiting India's conflict with other South Asian states. Although China would still like to keep its influence in the region, it does not want to see its peripheral region unstable and is no longer eager for the fray as it was in the Mao era. Instead, China expresses support for regional stability and cooperation among the South Asian states. In addition to displaying cautious neutrality in the India–Pakistan conflict, Beijing is also reluctant to be dragged into any conflicts between India and other South Asian states.

However, this change in China's policy stance is not because of India's greater investment with China, but is based on China's own interests and needs. Adopting a more balanced South Asia is not a diplomatic gesture of good faith by the Chinese. Instead, it is a decision to ensure that China's own development would not be derailed by the India–Pakistan disputes. That is, China did not intentionally change its South Asian policy to please New Delhi. As a result, although Beijing has sought to minimize the adverse effect that confrontation might have on Sino-Indian relations, it is unlikely that it would limit Sino-Pakistani cooperation to meet India's demands.

There is an impression that Beijing has tended to take advantage of India's difficulties with its smaller neighbours in the subcontinent. Although China's relations with smaller neighbours have not resulted in any formal military alliance against India, India has been wary of a two-pronged attack by China and Pakistan along its northern border. Indian scholars still believe that China's indulgence with India's smaller neighbours 'does have a major influence on the South Asian threat perception that mainly moulds the South Asian security profile' (Singh 2000).

For India, one goal of its security and foreign policy is to find an effective way to successfully counter the threat from China. The threat perception about China partly explains India's focus on building military relations with ASEAN after it launched the Look East Policy. One of the attractions of close relations with India from the standpoint of ASEAN states is the belief that those relations will help mitigate the effects of Chinese pressure in the region. Thus, both India and ASEAN countries find common interests in building stronger ties. Although the Look East Policy was not originally designed as a grand strategic plan to counter China's influence in the region, India is now treating its engagements with states in the region, especially in the area of military cooperation, as a counterbalance to China's rising assertiveness.

The competitive aspect of India–China relations is alive and well, and is marked by the different views of China–Pakistan military relations and India's intention of engaging ASEAN states and Japan. However, at the moment, the Chinese do not worry too much as, according to their assessment, India lacks the ability to convert South East Asia into a 'strategic backyard'.

While there is rivalry between India and China for influence in the region, there is also a cooperative dimension of Sino–Indian relations, built on the cause against terror, expanding sub-regional economic cooperation, and joining the other dominant regional groupings. The aspect of cooperation might provide an alternative to the two sides to go beyond the consideration of geopolitical encirclement.

Despite the potential strategic ploy to contain each other, both China and India sense the need to secure and extend their influence in the regions and forge closer relations with other neighbours on their journey to becoming a world power recognized by the international community. That is, their competition in the region is not always China-specific or India-specific. However, China and India are still aware of the pressure, as their strategic space is squeezed by the extension of each other's influence. A Chinese saying pithily summarizes the situation: 'Two tigers cannot live together on the same mountain'.

Notes

1. The principles are: (i) expanding contacts and deepening traditional friendship, (ii) respecting each other and fostering friendship for generations to come, (iii) pursuing mutual benefit and promoting common development, (iv) seeking common ground and minimizing differences, and (v) seeking unity and

cooperation and working together for a better future. See *Renmin Ribao*, 1996, 'Shidai mulin youhao gongchung meihao weilai, Jiang zhixi zai Yisilanbao fabiao zhongyao yanjiang' (Carrying Forward Generations of Friendly and Good-Neighbourly Relations and Endeavouring towards a Better Tomorrow for All), 3 December, Beijing, p.1.

2. The Kargil crisis erupted in early May 1999 when the Indian Army discovered the infiltration of Islamic militants into the northern parts of India-controlled Kashmir. The fighting broke out as the Indian government was determined to evict the infiltrators by force. The Kargil conflict soon attracted international attention as both India and Pakistan had been recently equipped with nuclear weapons after the overt nuclear tests in 1998.

3. See, for example, *The Hindu*, 2001, 'China Has Role in South Asian Peace', 21 May, available online at http://hindu.com/2001/05/21/stories/03210002.htm (accessed 14 August 2013); *The Hindu*, 2001, 'China Favours Indo-Pak Talks', 22 December, available online at http://hindu.com/2001/12/22/stories/2001122201100100.htm (accessed 14 August 2013).

4. See Li Peng's statement in *Renmin Ribao*, 19 April 1999, p. 6.

5. See Li Peng's interview in *The Hindu*, 2001, 'China Will Improve Ties with India: Li Peng', 14 January, available online at http://www.hindu.com/2001/01/14/stories/0214000a.htm (accessed 15 August 2013).

6. See Chinese Premier Zhu Rongji and President Jiang Zemin's statements in *Renmin Ribao*, 18 January 2000, p.1, and 19 January 2000, p.1.

7. See, 'Continuity and Change within the Global Scenario', address by I.K. Gujral, Minister of External Affairs, Government of India, at the Council for Foreign Relations, New York, 3 October 1996, available online at https://www.indianembassy.org/policy/Foreign_Policy/global%28gujral%29.htm (accessed 15 August 2013).

8. Ministry of Defence, Government of India, *Annual Report 2006–7*, pp. 31–2.

9. See, President K.R. Narayanan's address to the first session of both Houses of Parliament after the 12th General Election to the Lok Sabha on 24 March 1998, available online at https://www.indianembassy.org/inews/apr15.pdf (accessed 15 August 2013).

10. See, for example, *Guofang Bao* (Defence Times), 12 July 2000, p. 1, *Jiefang Jun Bao* (PLA Daily), 28 August 2000, p.12.

11. Taiwan set up the Taipei Economic and Cultural Center in New Delhi and India set up the India–Taipei Association in Taipei.

12. Ministry of External Affairs, Government of India, 'War Against Terror: Background', available online at, http://meaindia.nic.in/warterror/background/background.htm (accessed 15 June 2006).

13. For further details see, See Martin I. Wayne, 2007, 'Al-Qaeda's China problem', *Asia Times*, 27 February 27, available online at http://www.atimes.com/

atimes/China/IB27Ad01.html (accessed 13 August 2013); *New York Times*, 2006, 'Al Qaeda claim of Kashmir link worries India', 13 July, available online at http://www.nytimes.com/2006/07/13/world/asia/13iht-india.2194572.html (accessed 13 August 2013).

14. See, for example, Chinese Foreign Minister Tang Jiaxuan's speech delivered at the General Debate of the 56th UN General Assembly, in *Renmin Ribao*, 2001, 'Tang Jiaxuan zai di wus hi liu jie Lianda yibanxing bianlin zhong fayan' (Foreign Minister Tang Jiaxuan Makes Statement at the General Debate of the fifty-sixth session of the United Nations General Assembly), 13 November, Beijing, p. 7.

15. See Chinese Foreign Ministry spokesman Zhu Bangzao's remarks in Foreign Ministry Press in *Renmin Ribao*, 2001, 'Unveiling the Terrorist Nature of "East Tujue" Elements', 13 November, available online at http://english.people.com.cn/200111/16/eng20011116_84659.shtml (accessed 15 August 2013).

16. For the details of the summits, see *Renmin Ribao*. 1998. 'Jiaqing Mulin Youhao, Cujin Heping Fazhan: Relie Zhuhe Jiangzemin Zhuxi Alamutu Zhixing Yuanman Chenggong' (Enhance Neighbourly Friendship, Promote Peace and Development: Warm Congratulations on President Jiang Zemin's Successful Trip to Almaty), 5 July, Beijng, p.1.

17. The full text of this convention is available online at http://english.scosummit2006.org/en_bjzl/2006-04/20/content87.htm (accessed 15 August 2013).

18. *Renmin Ribao*. 2001. 'Mulin Youhao, Guang Hui Dien Fang: Relie Zhuhe "Shanghai Hezuo Zuzhi" Xuan Gao Cheng Li' (Neighbourly Friendship, Splendid Paragon: Warm Congratulations on the Announcement of Setting up of Shanghai Cooperation Organization), *Renmin Ribao* Editorial, 16 June 2001, Beijing, p. 2.

19. See, for example, *The Hindu*, 2000, 'India may join "Shanghai Five"', 6 July, New Delhi, p. 13; M.K. Dhar, 2000, 'A Shanghai Forum with India', *The Pioneer*, 19 July, available online at http://www.ratical.org/ratville/CAH/ShanghaiCO.html#p9 (accessed 15 August 2013).

20. See Jiang Zemin's remarks at the opening of the SCO summit meeting in *Renmin Ribao*, 2001, 16 June, Beijing, p. 1.

21. The SAARC members are Afghanistan, Bangladesh, Bhutan, India, the Maldives, Nepal, Pakistan, and Sri Lanka, while China, Japan, South Korea, the United States, Australia, Iran, Mauritius, Myanmar, and the European Union are observers.

22. For more analysis, see Yu (1992), Wang (1994), Song (1994).

5 China–India Relations in the Global Context

THE FUTURE OF CHINA–INDIA interactions is widely believed to be a crucial factor in shaping the international order. China and India are big developing countries with populations of more than one billion, as well as being rising players in the international system; their interactions not only affect the two countries, but also the international community; the China–India relationship has gone beyond the bilateral context and acquired a global dimension. Just as China suggested, 'a stable, normal and friendly relationship between China and India not only conforms with the fundamental interests of the two countries, but also helps promote peace, stability and development throughout Asia and even in the world as a whole'(*Beijing Review* 1999: 15). On the contrary, if China and India work to counterbalance each other, it will serve the interests of the so-called 'hegemonists' (Ye 1999: 10).

So far, several possibilities regarding how China–India interactions could shape the international order have been discussed. Of these, the most noticeable includes an Indo-American alliance against China, a China–India–Russia strategic triangle against the US, and 'Chindia' as a dominant player in international society. These, in fact, are related to two different strategies of reducing threat perception: balancing and bandwagoning. The following sections will discuss the three scenarios which are helpful for understanding the future development of China–India relations.

Indo-American Alliance

Throughout the Cold War, India was viewed suspiciously by the US as being part of the Soviet camp. India's nonalignment orientation was described as 'immoral' by the then US Secretary of State, John Foster Dulles. On the other hand, American military cooperation with Pakistan and rapprochement with China undermined the possibility of building a close Indo-American relationship. US foreign policy towards South Asia was biased towards Pakistan. It was not surprising, then, that Indo-US collaboration had a low profile throughout most of the Cold War.

The Soviet withdrawal from Afghanistan, along with the collapse of the USSR and the economic reforms launched by India since 1991 have given rise to the prospect of an enhanced level of interaction between India and the US. During the Gulf crisis, New Delhi gave American military craft permission to refuel at Mumbai, but widespread domestic criticism forced the Indian government to recall the offer (Kuba and Vaidyanathan 2000: 182). During Chinese Premier Li Peng's visit to India in 1991, there was a brief mention of a shared opposition to 'international oligarchies', but this was also quickly dropped and was not mentioned in the joint *communiqué* (Bhattacharjea 1993). The Indian Prime Minister, P.V. Narasimha Rao, broke with precedent to visit Washington in May 1994 before making a similar visit to Moscow. The move sent a strong signal that his government wanted to enhance Indo-American relations even at the risk of piquing India's traditional ally. In fact, it is logical for India to turn its focus to American capital, markets, and technology in the post-Soviet era, as the US is the sole remaining global superpower.

On the other hand, the US also adjusted its South Asia policy, and gradually put increasing emphasis on India's potential as a rising economy and a strategic partner. At almost the same time, the US Commerce Department named India as one of the world's big emerging markets. Indo-US economic relations have expanded remarkably over the past few years, as trade and investment is now one of cornerstones of the revitalized Indo-US relationship.

India–US relations have continued to witness intensive engagement regarding a qualitative transformation over the past few years. There is strong willingness on both sides to strengthen their ties further and to develop a strategic partnership. The two countries have been involved in institutional dialogues and interactions on issues of mutual concerns and interests, from the issues of defence and combating international terrorism to trade, and science and technology. The two countries have also increased the number of military exchanges and have conducted joint exercises on a regular basis.

Evolving a Strategic Partnership

The improvement in Indo-American relations was affected by India's nuclear tests of 1998. In addition to postponing President Clinton's visit to India, Washington also put economic sanctions on India to force it to join the non-proliferation regime. However, India has since successfully repaired its relations with the US by conducting formal consultations and resuming high-level visits.

Indo-American relations first came to a climax after the 1998 tests when the US President Clinton resumed his delayed visit to India and Pakistan in March 2000. He was the fourth American President to have visited India, and the first American President to have visited India in the 22 years since President Jimmy Carter's tour in 1978. He spent five days in India, but only five hours in Pakistan. During his visit, India and the US signed a document entitled 'India–US Relations: A Vision for the 21st Century', pledging to deepen the partnership through institutionalized dialogue and engagement in regular consultations. They also agreed that US President and Indian Prime Minister should meet regularly. India and the US were referred to as 'partners in peace, with a common interest in and complementary responsibility for ensuring regional and international security'.[1] Although the two sides failed to reach an agreement on nuclear non-proliferation, an issue that President Clinton termed important to realize the full potential of the Indo-American relationship (Clinton 2000: 8), there is no denying that Indo-American relations have improved significantly.

The war against terrorism made the US restore a strategic relationship with Pakistan, but the role of India has also been well-recognized by Washington. That is, the US does not treat India on par with Pakistan, but does accept that India has much more strategic importance in the region. In an important manifestation of the qualitative change in India–US relations, the US President, George W. Bush, and the Indian Prime Minister, A.B. Vajpayee, announced 'The Next Steps in the Strategic Partnership' (NSSP) in January 2004, which covered cooperation in four areas—civilian space, civilian nuclear energy, dual-use items, and missile defence. In March 2005, the US revealed that it would 'make India a major power in the 21st century' (*PTI* 2005). Unlike its concerns over China's rise, the Bush administration considered the rise of India as adding value to its strategic plot.

US President Bush then termed India as America's 'natural partner' and visited India in March 2006 to advance the strategic partnership with India.[2] Both countries announced their desire to establish a global partnership. Some analysts even thought that Bush's visit could bear some similarities to Nixon's opening to China in 1972 (Zakaria 2006). That is, the US would like to bring India onto the world stage as a major player and make use of the Indo-American links to alter the strategic landscape.

As attitudes are changing in both capitals, New Delhi acquired more strategic clout with Washington after President Bush's visit. The Indo-American defence ties have been warming up over the last few years after a hiatus in mid-1998. As one major element of the enhanced bilateral engagement, India and the US sustained the momentum in expanding defence cooperation. Such cooperation received a significant boost, as manifested by the large number of high-level visits that took place on both sides. For example, the US Chairman of the Joint Chief of Staff visited India in February 2002. The Indian Chief of Army Staff visited the US in April 2002, the Chief of Air Staff in June 2002, and the Chief of Naval Staff in September 2002. The US Army Chief also paid a visit to India in February 2003.

The adjustment of the US policy towards India is another issue that Beijing is carefully observing. The George W. Bush administration soon waived economic sanctions upon India and Pakistan after the events of 11 September 2001, to seek the two countries' support. More significantly, the military cooperation between India and the US also gained momentum after the September 11 terrorist attacks. In April 2002, India signed a US$146 million deal with the US to purchase 8 AN/TPQ-37 Firefinder Weapon Locating Radars. This was the first major government-to-government weapons transaction in more than three decades between India and the US. A US Defence Department statement read, 'This sale will contribute to the foreign policy and national security interests of the US by helping to improve the security of a country that has been and continues to be a force for political stability and economic progress in South Asia'(*The Hindu* 2002e). Following the trend, in 2009, India purchased eight Boeing P-8I long-range maritime reconnaissance aircraft for US$ 2.1 billion from the US. In June 2011, India agreed to buy 10 C-17 Globemaster III heavy-lift transport aircraft from the US. The US$ 4.1 billion contract became the largest defence deal between the two nations (*The Hindu* 2011f).

In May 2002, the US and India conducted the first-ever large scale military exercise in Agra, India. Codenamed 'Balance Iroquois', the exercise was the first US–India joint exercise in seven years. In September 2002, India and the US resumed the Malabar series of joint naval exercises, which had been interrupted because of India's nuclear tests in 1998. The two sides also conducted another joint exercise in Alaska, the first such exercise involving Indian troops and airmen on American soil. In October 2002, the US sent its fighter jets to India for the first-ever India–US air exercise over Indian territory in almost 40 years, while the Indian Air Force was sent outside the subcontinent for the first time to hold an exercise with the US in Alaska in July 2004. The significant improvement in India–US military ties might not be directly aimed against China, but the development has cast a shadow on China's security environment. For example, the annual 'Malabar 2011' was held in April 2011 near Okinawa in Japan, off the Chinese coast.

Counterbalancing China

The rise of China is one of the major factors that influences US policy towards India. After the demise of the USSR, China has been seen as a possible challenger to the US in the future, and the US has watched China's rise in the international community along with its military modernization with some misgiving. It is thought that the US would like to contain China by establishing an anti-China alliance.

It is not fresh news that defence reports issued by India and the US have always described China as a potential threat. The US is aware of India's security concerns over China. For example, during a Congressional panel hearing, the US Assistant Secretary of State for South Asian Affairs, Karl Inderfurth, confirmed that 'Pakistan is certainly a component in India's security considerations but not the only one, indeed, not the major one'. After his 'fact-finding' visit to India in 1999, American Senator Gary Ackerman concluded that there was a consensus in the mainstream Indian political leadership that China was its main adversary in the region, although Indian leaders shied away from publicly identifying China as India's main military threat in order to maintain the charade of diplomatic politeness (*The Hindu* 1999c).

Despite the fact that India attracts less foreign investment than China does, some commentators in India believe that there are opinions in the

West in favour of India rather than of China. India's democratic system and values, political culture, and greater transparency in military matters seem to be more favourable to the West, and place India above China in the eyes of many Westerners (Sen 2000: 272). The perception of China's growing threat may make the US lean more towards India. As China's military grows more formidable, there might be a greater coincidence of interests between India and the Western powers in thinking about a more effective balance to manage Beijing (Manor and Segal 1998: 67).

In pursuit of a shared objective of dissuading China from aggressive actions, India's counterbalance against China is seen as a visible interest in broadening the ambit of US–India defence cooperation. The US would like to groom India as an effective counterbalance to China. Not surprisingly, many analysts see the Indo-American joint manoeuvres as efforts by a democratic coalition to contain the rise of China. The India–US nuclear deal is also viewed as a significant step in this direction. The Indo-American strategic nexus is likely to continue and to be reinforced further with the growing rift between China and the US or China and India.

Beijing is keenly observing the increasing closeness of Indo-American relations, especially on issues relating to military cooperation. Beijing seems to be increasingly worried about the formation of Indo-American strategic cooperation, which suggests a pattern of alliance-building activities that China cannot ignore. From the Chinese perspective, the coming together of the US and India could well serve Washington's plans to contain China's growing might in Asia.

The shared security concerns regarding China's rise can be an incentive to boost Indo-American relations. New Delhi is, however, hesitant to become a part of the US coalition to contain China, though India would like to have America's blessings and develop the facility to become a world power. Even the Chinese side does not believe that India will join the US in confronting China. At the moment, Beijing deems that 'India will not blindly follow the lead of the US'.[3]

The considerations within the Chinese leadership are whether China should maintain some relations with India or let India unite with the US on the international stage. Understanding the significance, Beijing will engage with New Delhi if it senses that India is becoming closer to the US. As some Indian analysts have pointed out, the difficulties in the relations between Beijing and Washington will then play an important role in encouraging the Chinese leadership to accelerate the process of normalizing relations with India (Mohan 1999b).

It is clear that America's global security interests take priority over India's hope to become an independent power. That is, the US wants to help India to become a power to fulfil Washington's own strategic goals, not in order to fulfil those of New Delhi. For example, the US has been opposing the Iran–India–Pakistan pipeline project, which is important for India's energy security.

In addition, Pakistan–US relations and nuclear issues also remain as obstacles in developing a closer Indo-American friendship. Washington had no intention of developing Indo-American relations while ignoring Pakistan, no matter what kind of government was in power. In 2000, the US Assistant Secretary of State for South Asian Affairs, Karl Inderfurth, did deny the concept of a tilt towards India, stressing that the US wants to maintain a good relationship with both India and Pakistan (*Renmin Ribao* 2000f: 4). During the visit of Alan Eastham, acting US Assistant Secretary of State, to South Asia in April 2001, he reiterated Islamabad's importance in the region and said that the US has no intention of abandoning Pakistan while forging a closer relationship with India (*The Hindu* 2001h). Although the US has accepted India's *de facto* nuclear status, it still encourages India to accede to the existing nuclear non-proliferation regime.

As a result, in assessing India's strategic alignment with the US, on one side are those who see the evolving Indo-American strategic partnership as a historic opportunity to secure a power status with the assistance of the world's most powerful nation. On the other side are those who feel that this partnership would constrain India's autonomy and erode its sovereign decision-making rights, because the US views India as its junior partner.

Traditionally, India, by and large, perceives the US as a nation given to hegemonic manoeuvres. It should be noted, for example, that in his speech at Peking University in 1993, Indian Prime Minister Narasimha Rao spoke out against affluent countries that were trying to 'choke off the legitimate needs of developing countries' and asked how this 'new suppressive process' could be resisted (*Frontline* 1993: 123). Some commentators tend to identify the US as a fickle partner instead of a reliable ally, and worry that the change of its foreign policy may harm India's interests (Malik 2003).

Indian analyst C. Raja Mohan argued that India has no interest in seeking a new Cold War confrontation between Washington and Beijing, because India's long-term objective is to emerge as an indispensable element in the Asian balance of power (Mohan 2000b). Indian External Affairs Minister Jaswant Singh also sought to dispel the misperception in China about an incipient alliance between New Delhi and Washington. He insisted that India's relations with the US would stand on their own merit and not be linked to American ties with a third party (*The Hindu* 2001e).

In the short term, however, New Delhi and Washington may also believe that the improvement of their bilateral relationship could generate greater foreign policy leverages for each other. The US may use India's growing economic and military power to meet its strategic needs in Asia and to limit further Chinese influence in the region. The US Secretary of State Hillary Clinton encouraged India to 'not just look East, but to engage East and act East', and asked India to 'take a more assertive role across the Asia Pacific' (*The Asian Age* 2011b). Earlier, the US President George Bush even argued that Indo-American relationship has the power to transform the world (*PTI* 2006).

No matter how the Chinese side perceives India–US military relations, India will continue to maintain good relations with the US. Meanwhile, it is not in India's interests to spoil relations with China. That is, India is not ready to behave like Japan, a reliable ally of the US in East Asia. As a result, sometimes India seems inclined to jump on the bandwagon with the US, and sometimes to act in pursuit of its own goals.

China–Russia–India Strategic Triangle

The idea of establishing a strategic triangle consisting of China, Russia, and India was first mooted by the then Russian Prime Minister, Yevgeny Primakov, when he visited New Delhi in December 1998. In replying to questions at a press conference, Primakov said that it would be good to establish a China–India–Russia strategic triangle (*The Hindu* 1998f: 1). Since then, the idea of establishing a China–India–Russia strategic triangle and its implications surface occasionally, as people are concerned with the possibility that the three countries will transform the potential for an alliance into a formal alliance. Although Moscow soon clarified that the remark was not a formal proposal, ties between the three nations have since grown dramatically, as a series of bilateral pacts have been signed to define the direction of the relationship. Close attention is being paid to the question of whether China and India are also in favour of turning their bilateral relationship with Russia into a trilateral bloc.

In fact, China has conducted so-called 'partnership diplomacy' with many countries and regions. As far as Sino-Indian relations and Sino-Russian relations are concerned, in 1994, China and Russia established a constructive partnership looking towards the twenty-first century and then a 'partnership of strategic coordination' in April 1996, while China and India set up a 'constructive cooperative partnership oriented towards the 21st century' in November 1996 and a 'strategic and cooperative partnership for peace and prosperity' in April 2005. Besides, India and Russia have also extended the special relationship founded in the former USSR era. An India–Russia strategic partnership was established in 1997, and the strategic partnership agreement was concluded in 2000. Therefore, in theory, it would be neither strange nor difficult for the three countries to transform their declared bilateral strategic partnership into a triangular format.

China, India, and Russia are among the world's seven declared nuclear nations, and the three nations combined have a third of the world's population. China and Russia have already secured permanent membership of the UN Security Council while India is widely tipped to gain a new seat on an expanded UN Security Council. The combined strength of the three countries is forecast to increase.[4] Such a group covering China, India, and Russia could act as a counterweight to the US on the international scene. A strategic triangle alliance may bring about a new world order where the US does not have such a preponderance of power. Even if the three countries do not build up a strategic partnership to counterbalance the US, they will find areas for cooperation. As cooperation among the three countries increases, so will their weight in international affairs. However, despite the intense discussions in the three countries involved and the international community, the concept has not yet become a reality due to various constraints.

From the Chinese perspective, the China–India–Russia cooperation has a rich and positive potential because the three countries all advocate a multi-polar world order and the establishment of a just and fair new international order, and object to the hegemonism and the US-dominated international order in the post-Cold War era (Yin 2003: 52–3). For

India and Russia, a multi-polar political order is also desirable, because they can share power with the other great powers in determining how the world should be governed. Not surprisingly, the similar viewpoints shared by China, Russia, and India on major international issues are thus seen as the basis for further development of their trilateral relationship (Liu 2001: 26–7; Yang 2001: 1). For example, an editorial in *The Hindu* argued, 'Among the ways of dissuading the US from arrogating to itself the role of a global policeman would be for Russia, India and China to get together in a strategic axis to pre-empt the aggressive and interventionist strides that the US is now taking across the world stage'.[5] In addition, the Russian Foreign Ministry's senior spokesman, Alexander Yakovenko, said, 'Interaction between Russia, China and India could become a useful tool for the consolidation of international and regional stability, and the counteraction to threats and challenges of the modern era' (*ITAR-TASS* 2003).

US policy provided a good setting and opportunities for China, India, and Russia to voice their joint concerns about the global order. It should be recalled that Russian Prime Minister Primakov's suggestion about the strategic triangle came at a time when the US and Britain launched the bombardment of Iraq, bypassing the UN Security Council. Interestingly, Russia had shown its approval of the idea of trilateral interactions barely a year earlier when the then Indian External Affairs Minister I.K. Gujral had asked the then Russian Foreign Minister Primakov to arrange a trilateral meeting because the Indian External Affairs Minister and his Chinese counterpart were staying in Russia at the same time (Katyal 2003). The reason Russia moved from its previous stance was on account of its increasing distress over the unilateral nature of the US operation. Meanwhile, Russia sensed the need to take countermeasures to check the US geopolitical 'offensive' in Eurasia, such as the NATO's eastward expansion right up to its borders.

In sharp contrast to the concept of an Indo-American strategic partnership to counter China's increasing power, the idea of China–India–Russia strategic triangle reflected the thinking about the need to check the growing dominance by the US. Given the three countries' common concern about US power politics, it would seem reasonable if China were to show some enthusiasm for the proposal, because if the three countries were to move closer, it would help to reduce the domination or attempts at domination by other great powers.

However, at the very beginning, Prime Minister Primakov's remarks proposing the strategic triangle were met with little enthusiasm in Beijing. Compared to India and Russia, there was surprisingly little discussion or debate in China on the idea of a 'strategic triangle'. Beijing cold-shouldered the concept on the grounds that it was pursuing an independent foreign policy and had no intention of changing the fundamental policy of not entering into any strategic alliances or military blocs. It was reported that Primakov had raised the issue with the then Chinese Premier Zhu Rongji when the latter visited Moscow in February 1999. However, Zhu Rongji ruled out Russia's proposal to develop a triangular alliance. Chinese Foreign Minister Tang Jiaxuan also asserted that China was not willing to forge a strategic triangle with India and Russia on the grounds that Beijing was pursuing an independent foreign policy of peace characterized by non-alliance (*PTI* 1999b).

China's reluctance to embrace the idea implied that there were some constraints about developing a China–India–Russia triangle. Although the three countries had the potential based on a common identity and common interests, and sensed the need to deepen the triangular cooperation in order to deal with issues of common concern, it was a very controversial move to transform the triangular cooperative mechanism into a political-military alliance, namely, a strategic triangle.

China's Reluctance

Despite the common rhetoric and expectations about a new international order and the multi-polar world, China finds it difficult to endorse the strategic triangle without reservation. The first major reason for the hesitancy is that China's relations with India and Russia are not as mature as India–Russia relations.

Roughly speaking, the China–India–Russia triangle consists of three bilateral interactions—Sino-Russian relations, Indo-Russian relations, and Sino-Indian relations. Indo-Russian relations are far better than Sino-Russian relations and Sino-Indian relations. In other words, the China–India–Russia triangle is a scalene one; Indo-Russian relations are the strongest side of the scalene triangle as they have always remained strong. Despite the momentous changes in the international environment after the end of the Cold War, India and Russia have maintained close ties. During the visit to India in 1993 by the then Russian President Boris Yeltsin, both sides signed the 'Treaty of Friendship and Cooperation' to set up a new framework for the post-Soviet era. The two countries then claimed to establish a strategic partnership in 1997. In April 1998, the leaders of Russia and India reaffirmed their commitment to establishing a strategic partnership. In October 2000, when Russian President Vladimir Putin visited India, the two countries issued the declaration of establishing a strategic partnership for developing future relations. One media comment was that 'There are few examples of a relationship between countries that has been as stable as the one between India and Russia'.[6]

Sino-Russian relations also developed smoothly in the post-Soviet era. In 1992, China and Russia asserted that they treated each other as friendly countries. The two sides then built a 'partnership of strategic coordination' in 1996, and concluded a 'Treaty of Good-Neighbourliness and Friendly Cooperation' in 2000. China and Russia also completely resolved their boundary problem in 2004. More importantly, the Sino-Soviet rivalry ceased to be a factor in China's foreign relations after the Cold War.

However, the trust between Beijing and Moscow is not as solid as the one between India and Russia. Among various fields, one noticeable area of the China–India–Russia relationship is the field of military technology, as both China and India are the Russian defence industry's largest clients. However, Russia has taken a sceptical view of China's rise, as it is especially vigilant in the transfer of technology to China. For example, Russia has granted India a licence to manufacture Su-30 fighters, whereas China acquired only the licence to produce Su-27 fighters. That is, Beijing did not win the full trust of Moscow. The Chinese are aware that some analysts in Russia also see China as a future threat. One Chinese analyst even suggested that the future Sino-Russian relationship may vary from alliance to conflict, but will not go much beyond the present status (Ding 2002: 63). Some Chinese scholars have cited the imbalance between Russian military transfers to India and China as evidence that some Russians are very suspicious of a rising China and believe in the so-called 'China threat' theory (Yu 2004: 43).

Worse, Sino-Indian relations are neither close nor strong enough to form a base for a strategic alliance. Despite a significant improvement in bilateral relations over recent years, China and India are far from being friends. The improvement in China–India relations in recent times may pave the way for the establishment of trilateral cooperation between New

Delhi, Beijing, and Moscow, but has not been significant enough for the three countries to form a strategic alliance.

In fact, both Beijing and New Delhi treated Primakov's 'strategic triangle' proposal with caution when the idea was first mooted, because Sino-Indian relations had reached a low ebb in the wake of India's nuclear tests of 1998 (Yin 2003: 50). The former Chinese ambassador to New Delhi, Cheng Ruisheng, frankly admitted that the relationship between China and India was 'not mature enough' even for a 'strategic partnership' (*AFP* 1999). In addition, the Chinese side has pointed out that economic exchange between the three countries does not meet their potential.[7] In fact, it is argued that if the major powers had stronger economic links and interdependence, the possibility of forming an alliance against a hegemony would be relatively higher (Papayoanou 1997). In the present circumstances, the relationship among the three countries cannot guarantee the success of forming a strategic triangle. Also, there is a need to find ways to overcome the distrust between China and India and between China and Russia before a trilateral alliance can be forged.

The US Factor

Another factor affecting the development of a strategic triangle is the US. As mentioned earlier, Russia's reason for proposing the strategic triangle was its discontent about the US-dominated international order; this implies a strong resistance to America's unilateralism. In fact, the initiative of establishing a strategic triangle had already been seen as a serious escalation of Russia's determination to undermine America's strategic dominance.[8] Needless to say, the formation of an alliance would inevitably cause more tension between the three countries and the US.

Despite the concerns and dissatisfaction over Washinton's power politics, China has no intention of confronting the US directly. Aside from the diplomatic gestures, Beijing has avoided giving the impression that it is at loggerheads with the US. Some Chinese scholars have even argued that their advocacy of a multi-polar world does not equal an anti-US position (Wang 1999b: 14). Instead, China is well aware of the importance of sustaining a benevolent relationship with the US, because its relations with the US involve a lot of economic and strategic stakes. Despite its military might, America is also the gateway to a huge pool of capital, technology, and trade opportunities.

China's priority is to build up its own strength to promote its influence during the globalization process. If China cannot play a bigger role in the multi-polar world, world multi-polarization is meaningless for China. That is, China will object to the US strongly only if it feels state sovereignty and territorial integrity are seriously undermined, such as the EP-3 incident of 2001.[9] It may be noted that Beijing's official statements have recently avoided using the terms 'hegemonism' and 'power politics' in referring to US actions.

In 1992, the then Chinese President Jiang Zemin, stated that the guidelines of China's US policy were 'increasing trust, reducing trouble, reinforcing cooperation and avoiding confrontation' (*Zeng jia xin ren, jian shao mo ca, jiang qiang he zuo, bi mian dui kan*). To some extent, the 16-word dictum still remains at the core of China's US policy. Chinese leader Hu Jintao and his government in Beijing continued to make every possible effort to avoid a direct confrontation with the US (Lam 2005: 3). Thus, since the concept of a China–India–Russia strategic triangle carries connotations of an anti-America posture, Beijing is unwilling to uphold the triangle proposal.

Besides its disinclination to undermine Sino-American relations, the Chinese side is not confident about the strength of the China–India–Russia strategic triangle. The Chinese side argues that, even if China, India and Russia are to come together to oppose the US, it is still an asymmetric struggle because the three countries' national strengths combined are still less than the strength of the US. Therefore, Chinese scholars warned, joining such a bloc does not serve China's interest (Yan 1999: 11).

Similarly, a Chinese survey about national strength confirmed the imbalance between the US and the China–India–Russia triangle by pointing out that US strategic resources account for 22.78 per cent of the world's strategic resources, while the figures for China, India, and Russia are only 7.78 per cent, 4.36 per cent, and 1.71 per cent, respectively (Hu and Men 2002). In other words, China not only finds it difficult to resist the allure of the US, but also believes that the China–India–Russia strategic triangle is still too weak to balance the US in any significant measure.

Since the Chinese side does not believe a China–India–Russia alliance would be strong enough to confront the US directly, Chinese officials have kept a certain distance from the triangle overture so as not to risk ruffling America's feathers. Beijing has stressed that it does not desire an alliance on the one hand, and, on the other, that the trilateral interactions among

China, India, and Russia are not against any third party. For example, the then Chinese Foreign Minister Tang Jiaxuan argued that China was pursuing an independent foreign policy of peace and wished to develop friendly relations and cooperation with all countries, India and Russia included (*PTI* 2000a). Chinese Premier Wen Jiabao stressed that the exchanges and cooperation among China, India, and Russia are not an alliance, and are not against any country (*Renmin Ribao* 2005: 1).

As a result, some may suggest, the possibility of the emergence of such a strategic triangle remains quite low, and the talk of anti-American strategic alliances need not be taken too seriously.[10] For example, the Director of the Washington-based Centre for Strategic and International Studies' South Asia programme, Teresita Schaffer argued, 'It's hard to think in any short-term time horizon that this will turn into a meaningful and durable forum for real international cooperation' (Kammerer 2004: 12). Indeed, at the moment, both China and India still favour cordial relations with Washington, and as a result, will avoid a direct covert confrontation with Washington or the construction of a formal bloc or military security arrangements against the US.

China's anxiety to secure a bigger position in a new international order will not simply disappear all of a sudden; there exists a great possibility that China will cooperate with Russia and India within an informal and loose framework on certain issues in order to balance US influence. For example, although China has not openly supported the establishment of a China–India–Russia strategic triangle, senior Chinese Foreign Ministry officials are of the opinion that there is scope for enhancing the understanding of important global issues of mutual concern (*PTI* 2000b). That is why the US intelligence authority has not ruled out the possibility of China, India, and Russia forming a *de facto* geo-strategic alliance in an attempt to counterbalance US and Western influence (NIC 2000: 81). As relations between China, India, and Russia improve, the conservatives in Washington will have cause to worry about the implications for American dominance. Some analysts have even cautioned that a new Cold War might be in the offing and at its focus will be China, India, and Russia (Kammerer 2004: 12).

The US will not sit idly by watching the China–India–Russia strategic triangle or the so-called BRICs economic bloc take a more forbidding shape.[11] The US would take countermeasures to sow discord among China–India–Russia interactions, especially to bring India into

US alliances. One Chinese scholar has argued that the US is trying to belittle the possibility of China–India–Russia trilateral cooperation, and is exaggerating the contradictions between the three countries. Another Chinese scholar has commented that US arms sales to India after the September 11 attacks is part of the US plan to cripple the trilateral relationship. In their eyes, the US is cultivating an adversary of China, and undermining Russia's dominant share in India's ammunitions market by equipping India (Yin 2003: 54).

Regularized Trilateral Meetings

Along with building bilateral ties with India and China, Russia is actively promoting trilateral cooperation with them. Conversely, at the beginning, China and India demonstrated a relatively lukewarm attitude towards the strategic triangle. Currently, although obstacles remain in moving towards a trilateral strategic partnership, unilateral tendencies on the part of the US are encouraging the three countries to move closer to each other. Some nuanced changes were seen in China's and India's attitudes towards the triangle proposal after the military action in Kosovo in 1999. The Chinese side argued that, although the three countries did not hold a formal meeting, they made similar declarations about their concerns (Yin 2003: 50–1). The Kosovo war reminded the three countries that they shared common interests in international affairs. As a result, the idea of establishing a strategic triangle was raised again and won more positive responses from India and China.

As was discussed earlier, the 'strategic triangle' dilemma facing China and the other countries is that they need a trilateral relationship with strategic significance to counterbalance US unilateralism, but they do not want to provoke the US needlessly. It seems that China and the other two countries have already found a way to deal with this dilemma. This is seen in their changed phraseology for the concept; the term 'trilateral coordination and cooperation' is now used to describe the efforts to promote the trilateral relationship, instead of the somewhat contentious 'strategic triangle' phraseology.

Under the catchphrase 'trilateral coordination and cooperation', the trilateral interaction between Russia, India, and China has vigorously developed in recent years, and an intensive political dialogue has been established. The three countries have begun to conduct an informal consultative exercise to make sure that they can create and maintain the necessary coordination in international affairs. Since 2002, the Foreign Ministers of the three countries have often held trilateral meetings on the sidelines of the UN General Assembly session in New York. Indian Ambassador to Russia, Krishnan Raghunath, observed that 'Moscow, Delhi and Beijing are moving from non-governmental contacts in a triangular format to discussing issues of common concern at a high official level' (*The Hindu* 2004a). Thus, irrespective of the terminology, a loose China–India–Russia format was clearly emerging (Fang 2004).

As a result, is not surprising that the trilateral meetings evolved into a gathering of heads of state. In July 2006, the first China–India–Russia summit was held in St. Petersburg, Russia, to formulate a common agenda and the possibilities of joint cooperative actions to deal with issues such as terrorism and other global threats, energy security, and health and related matters. The three countries then promptly held the second summit in New Delhi and issued a Joint *Communiqué* concerning their shared desire to work together on energy, terror, security, and trade.

Furthermore, some concrete suggestions on sensitive fields to promote the trilateral cooperation have been made and have prompted great media interest. For example, the Russian Ambassador to India, Alexander Kadakin, revealed in 2004 that Russia and India were considering inviting China to jointly develop the fifth generation, multi-role fighter aircraft (*Huanqiu Shibao* 2004: 16). A similar proposal was made earlier in January 2004 when the Russian Defence Minister, Sergei Ivanov, called publicly for Russia, India, and China to strengthen cooperation in the military-technical sphere and in the joint development of new advanced weapons (*The Hindu* 2004b). Although the Chinese side frankly admitted that there was a difficulty for the three countries to launch a joint programme of developing weapons operating under prevailing conditions, this kind of news continued to cause a stir.

Another interesting development is that, although Beijing flatly refuses to describe its relationship with India and Russia as an alliance partnership, it has been keen to conduct joint manoeuvres. In October 1999, Beijing and Moscow held their first joint naval exercises in the East China Sea. Such an event had not been seen even during the 1950s when China adopted a 'lean-to-one-side' policy of aligning with the USSR. Thereafter, the Sino-Indian naval exercises took place in November 2003, for the first time in the history of relations between the two countries. It seems to be only a matter of time before the three countries hold a trilateral exercise.

The Chindia Concept

The term 'Chindia', which refers to the combination of China and India, was coined by the then Indian Minister of State for Commerce, Jairam Ramesh, in 2004, and has since been used by some analysts as they hail the economic performance and impact of the two countries. The expectation is that China and India will emerge as the fastest growing economies and economic cooperation will act as the driving force and the focal point of bilateral ties.

However, 'Chindia' is not limited to the economic aspect, but is also being applied to broader political issues. The Chindia discourse reflects the optimistic expectations about the coming together of China and India. For example, the well-known expert Tan Chung translated the English term Sino-Indian Commonwealth as '*Zhong Yin da Tong*', and saw Chindia as a prelude to the emergence of a World Commonwealth.[12] Thus, despite their bitter experiences and differences over disputes, some still believe that China and India will stand together in international affairs as a powerful combination. The fact that China and India declared the year 2006 as the 'Year of China–India Friendship' was hailed by some observers as a realization of the Chindia idea and the resurrection of *Hindi Chini Bhai Bhai* (Yin 2007: 85).

Indeed, there is a possibility that both countries can enhance cooperation in the establishment of a new international order. A certain convergence of views on the international order enables them to project a distinctive developing countries' perspective on global affairs. Basically, both China and India have similar international identities and thus have similar preferences. As rising powers, both China and India are seeking great power status, and have felt concerned over the dangers of the US strategy of pre-emption. Both China and India hold the view that developing countries are in an inferior position in an America-dominated international order, and so both are seeking a higher position in the international community. They also call for the role of the UN to be strengthened to prevent unilateralism and oppose neo-interventionism under the guise of human rights issues. As a result, it is likely that India and China could work together in the international field in order to advance the establishment of an international order and a multi-polar world, in which both countries secure a higher position.

As early as in the 1950s, both countries had proposed the Five Principles of Coexistence as their vision of the international order.

The quest for a new international order remains, as it underpins Sino-Indian relations even after 1998. In a message to Indian Prime Minister Vajpayee for the 50th anniversary of the establishment of diplomatic relations between China and India, Chinese Premier Zhu Rongji stressed that India and China shoulder an important responsibility in building a new, fair, and rational international political and economic order (*The Hindu* 2000g). Chinese President Hu Jintao also listed the development of 'multilateral cooperation for creating a multi-polar world' as one of the five-pronged strategies India and China must follow in order to enhance their strategic partnership.[13] Chinese Ambassador to India, Zhang Yan, argued that China and India were bound to wield an important and positive influence on the transformation of the international order, which was moving in the direction of multi-polarity (Zhang 2008).

Both India and China are aware of their convergence on international affairs. For example, China and India adopted similar positions on the Libya issue. Both sides opposed the use of force and military actions while not upsetting existing ties with the West and major Arab countries. As a result, they abstained from the UN Security Council resolution on approving a no-fly-zone over Libya (Krishnan and Dikshit 2011).

Efforts are being made to help the two countries find common ground to speak with one voice at the negotiating table on issues of common interest. Mechanisms for a security dialogue, strategic dialogue, foreign policy consultation and an anti-terrorism dialogue have been established to exchange and coordinate their viewpoints. The potential for Sino-Indian collaboration is well-illustrated in a range of areas, such as human right issues, World Trade Organization (WTO) negotiation, climate change, energy security and so on.

On the WTO forum, India and China share many common interests in the negotiations, and support each other in the WTO for the interests of developing countries. India and China have agreed to coordinate their strategies in support of developing countries within the WTO (*The Hindu* 2003). Particularly, in the Doha Round, India and China have stood up to demands by the US and Europe on agricultural issues; they have worked together to ensure a development dimension. As a result, they have been most frequently targeted by developed countries. By such cooperation, India and China greatly strengthen each other and increase the possibility of their aims being fulfilled.

Similarly, on the issue of climate change, India and China object to any arrangements that might slow down their economic growth. As a result, India and China have become increasingly close allies in the climate change debate. Since the two countries are big, populous countries, their cooperative involvement will be the key to the success of any international climate deal.

On energy security issues, India and China have seen a steady increase in their energy consumption for many years and were previously locked in a battle to secure stakes in overseas oil fields. Both China and India recognized that rivalry between them only results in unduly large benefits to the seller of the assets. In 2006, the two countries decided to establish a framework under which their state-owned oil and gas companies could evolve and submit joint bids for the acquisition of assets in third countries (*The Hindu* 2006a).

Mutual support against Western resolutions on human rights in international fora has been another remarkable example of cooperation between India and China. In April 1999, when China won on a no-action motion, the vote was 22 for, 17 against, and 14 abstentions; India voted in favour of China's position (*Renmin Ribao* 1999c: 1). It is worth noting that at that time Sino-Indian relations were still at a low ebb due to India's nuclear tests of May 1998. In fact, India continued to vote in favour of China's human rights record against an American resolution in the following years. The message is that New Delhi does not endorse Washington's argument regarding the human rights issue. India itself has been often severely criticized by the US State Department's annual human rights reports for a whole range of issues including religious abuses. Beijing and New Delhi therefore share an understanding of opposing the use of human rights as a pretext to interfere in internal affairs and they have a common desire to cooperate on the issue.

That is one of the reasons why not everybody is pessimistic about the prospect of China–India relations. Arguing that common interests far outweigh differences, those who see future China–India relations in a positive light tend to claim that India and China have close and similar viewpoints regarding international affairs. To cite one example, the Chinese Foreign Minister, Tang Jiaxuan, said that China and India 'have more common ground than differences', and the two countries' positions are indeed very similar and close to each other (*The Times of India* 2002b). A similar positive argument also could be found on the Indian side. Subramanian Swamy claimed that there are hardly any international issues on which India and China have irresolvable fundamental conflicts of interest (Swamy 2001: 24). In 2012, the then External Affairs Minister, Salman Khurshid stated, 'the passage of time and emergence of a new economic order in the world have brought China and India far closer together'(*The Hindu* 2012a).

India's Place in a Multi-polar World

The establishment of a just and reasonable new international order along with the quest for multi-polarization of the world has long been on the long-term agenda of the foreign policies of China and India. The Chinese side has viewed developing countries as the backbone in the process of building a new international order.[14] Given that both China and India are big developing countries with military strength and economic potential, China should be able to convince India to unite to present a joint front for a multi-polar world.

Although their similar positions have sharpened the prospects for a new political convergence between Beijing and New Delhi, the differences between their roles in the new world order are also a stark reminder of the gap between the hype and the reality. China's and India's blueprints for the future multi-polar word are not the same. The two countries do not have a consensus on what a multi-polar world will look like and what kind of place they currently have in the world.

India is recognized as the biggest power of South Asia and perhaps only Pakistan has stood out as the main obstacle in the region to India's desire to dominate South Asia. However, India has also pursued a bigger role in international affairs since independence. The first Indian Prime Minister, Jawaharlal Nehru, said, 'India, constituted as she is, cannot play a secondary part in the world. She will either count for a great deal or not count at all. No middle position attracted me. Nor did I think any intermediate position feasible' (Nehru 1956: 43–4). This statement is widely quoted by the Chinese side as evidence that India has long been seeking status as a world power.[15]

However, Beijing does not welcome India's efforts to seek a higher position in the world order. Particularly, India's ambition to be a world power has received harsh criticism from the Chinese side. Some Chinese have argued that India has been 'too poor to build the country but rich enough to buy arms' (Shao 2001: 9–10). The Chinese have also often questioned Indian leaders' argument that the twenty-first century would be India's century (Qian 2002). This kind of viewpoint apparently does not meet New Delhi's expectations, as India will not accept playing second fiddle to China. Therefore, it is very doubtful that New Delhi and Beijing will be able to work together to promote world multi-polarization if India is recognized only as a regional power.

There are differences of opinion in Chinese academic circles about India's status and future role in the world. The first school of thought is that India has a very limited role at the global level because its strength is conditioned by domestic turmoil and the peripheral environment. Since its influence is confined to Asia, especially South Asia, India is a regional power rather than a global power. By this reckoning, some Chinese scholars conclude that India is unlikely to be one 'pole' of the multi-polar world in the twenty-first century (Deng 2003: 16–19, Fu 1999: 63, and Liang 1999: 27).

The second and very different view attaches greater importance to India's place in the world. It argues that India's strength is increasing and it should be viewed as a world power (Wang 1998a, Wen 2005). This school of thought espouses the view that India would be abreast with China, Japan, and the ASEAN and become a pole in a multi-polar world. In the near future, India would be a reputable power in Asia and the world as well. Some even claim that India has already become a pole after its comprehensive power was strengthened by the reform begun in the 1990s (Zhang 1998: 107).

The third school of thought, and perhaps the most popular one, is a compromise between the opposite opinions. It deems that India has the potential to rise as a world power, but there are numerous hurdles on the road to being a global power. Therefore, India's strength will increase, but it has a long way to go before it becomes a world power (Ma 2006, Sun 1999).

Beijing has acknowledged that India has a significant role to play in international affairs, but does not agree that India should occupy the same position as China. The former Chinese Ambassador in New Delhi, Cheng Ruisheng, argued that in terms of historical background, geographical location, constitution of nations, and overall national strength, China is in a higher position than India (Cheng 1998). Although China is willing to make concerted efforts with India for the establishment of a new international political and economic order, it has not viewed New Delhi as its peer in international affairs.

UN Security Council Membership

China and India's disagreement about India's place in a multi-polar world is reflected in India's bid for a permanent UN Security Council seat. Since the early 1990s, India has laid claims to this seat. New Delhi has been trying to garner support for entering the UN Security Council although it was dealt a blow in 1996 when it lost the campaign to become a non-permanent member. From the Indian standpoint, India deserves a permanent seat in the UN Security Council in terms of its population, size, and representational or ideological role in the Third World. The former Indian Prime Minister, I.K. Gujral, argued, 'We believe that we qualify for a permanent seat on the Security Council on the basis of any global, objective and non-discriminative criteria' (Ranade 1998). With its growing economy, India has acquired increasing confidence and is making its impact felt in regional and international affairs. India is seeking a greater role on the world stage, especially a seat at in the Security Council (Zhang 2008).

Beijing is not willing to make any promise regarding New Delhi's presence in an expanded Security Council. During his visit to China in 2000, Indian President K.R. Narayanan officially sought China's cooperation to bring about a democratic transformation of the UN to serve the interests and aspirations of humankind as a whole. Still, China did not make any commitment (*Renmin Ribao* 2000c: 1). During Chinese Premier Wen Jiabao's visit to India, both sides issued a joint statement, in which 'the Indian side reiterated its aspirations for permanent membership of the UN Security Council', but the Chinese side mentioned only that 'it understands and supports India's aspirations to play an active role in the UN and international affairs'.[16] A very small compromise was seen in 'A Shared Vision for the 21st Century of the People's Republic of China and the Republic of India', signed when Indian Prime Minister Manmohan Singh visited Beijing in January 2008, as the Chinese side said 'it understood and supported India's aspirations to play a greater role in the United Nations, including in the Security Council'. Apparently, China only vaguely backed India's quest, but avoided making any clear promise for New Delhi's membership of the UN Security Council.

Although the Chinese government chooses to remain ambiguous on the issue, the expressions of opinions by Chinese scholars are clearer. A senior Chinese scholar, Ma Jiali, argued that India might not be an appropriate member of the UN Security Council because it had broken up the process of nuclear non-proliferation (Ram 1998a: 15). Some have even cited India's failure in the campaign for a rotating non-permanent Security Council seat in 1996 as an example that India lacks influence in the world (Shao and Xu 2000).

Indeed, India's entry into the UN Security Council will be a valuable factor to advance the interest of the developing country bloc and against the drive by the developed world to set its own agenda. Even as India pursues its own interests, it could, on the whole, prove an ally in the establishment of a new international political and economic order.

However, Beijing's concern is not about maximizing the legitimate rights of developing countries, but to preserve its own interest as the sole representative of developing countries and of Asian states. This position gives Beijing a bigger say in international affairs. In order to magnify its influence, China emphasizes the need to resolutely defend the purposes and principles of the UN Charter and the dominant role of the UN in world affairs.[17] Although China is not a full world power yet, its membership of the UN Security Council has become a useful leverage against America's management of regional disputes. China also uses its position at the UN to support its allies, and punish uncooperative countries.

Given the overlapping constituency, Beijing's influence will soon be diluted if India secures a UN Security Council seat. Thus, it is natural that Beijing would not wish to see an emerging India with a standing in the Third World or Asia, which would impinge on its authority. As a result, Beijing and New Delhi have been unable to use the enlargement of the UN Security Council to affirm multi-polarity as a creed. Given that India repeatedly proposed receiving the Beijing regime as a member of the UN when communist China was rejected by the UN, China's grudging support for India on the issue only makes New Delhi feel uncomfortable. In contrast, the Chinese side maintains that India has overvalued its role regarding helping China secure a position in the international community in the 1950s (Sui 2007: 231).

Therefore, despite the common rhetoric and enthusiasm about the new international order and the multi-polar world, China and India find it difficult to structure a global condominium as the two sides are rivals regarding their influence in the world or among developing countries. China's friendly gesture to developing countries is only an attempt to increase its own status in the global order.

The Parallel Rise of China and India

While optimists from China and India, such as Tan Chung or Jairam Ramesh, look forward with positive anticipation to the future and the role India and China are destined to play in the world, there is no denying that there is also increasing competition between China and India for influence. Although China is willing to make concerted efforts with India for the establishment of a new international political and economic order, this does not mean that Beijing has come to view New Delhi as its peer. Despite recognizing India as a populous nation with an ancient civilization, China merely treats India as a 'younger brother' or junior, and is not willing to see India emerge as a major power.

India, aware of China's unwillingness, introduced the 'parallel rise' discourse to assure Beijing that both countries could simultaneously rise as global powers. That is, India's emergence would not thwart China's ambition to become a world power, and as a result, China would have no need to prevent India from rising on the global scene. At the banquet in honour of the visiting Chinese President, Hu Jintao, Indian President A.P.J. Abdul Kalam said, 'The rise of India and China is a stabilising factor in today's international economic order since both countries seek a peaceful environment to focus on the paramount task of national development' (*The Hindu* 2006c).

Not surprisingly, the 'parallel rise' idea has received wider appreciation in India than in China, as the Indian media lost no time in claiming that the parallel rise of China and India is one of the most significant developments in international affairs (*The Hindu* 2006b). Indian Prime Minister Manmohan Singh later developed the idea by arguing that 'there is enough space for both India and China to grow and prosper while strengthening our cooperative engagement' (Singh 2008). Further, Indian External Affairs Minister S.M. Krishna held the view that 'India and China may be competitive in economic and trade areas, but they are not rivals. There is enough space for both India and China to grow' (*IANS* 2009b). A similar statement was repeated by former UN Under Secretary General, Shashi Tharoor, as he said the world was big enough for China and India together and separately for realizing their development aspirations (*The Hindu* 2011d).

In fact, the 'parallel rise' or 'co-emergence' of India and China has remained an attractive proposition for China. China's Ambassador to India, Zhang Yan, also argued that China takes a positive view of India's rise, believing that the 'Dragon' and the 'Elephant' can 'dance together' to cooperate and prosper together (Zhang 2008). China's Consulate General in Kolkata, Mao Siwei, said his definition of Chindia is the joint rise of China and India, and argued that the process of rising would be a joint one with joint efforts by the peoples of two countries rather than two separate developments (*The Hindu* 2008c). It was seen as a possible development to change the so-called unjust and unfair old international order dominated by the West (Wang 2007).

Although there is no denying that the rise of China and India would affect the international system, the kind of impact it would have is not clear. More importantly, how the two rising powers get along with each other is a question of great significance. One Chinese scholar emphasized that 'parallel rise' does not mean that the two countries would reach the same level of development. The country in an inferior position may consider the other as an obstacle on its way to becoming a world power (Zhao 2006). It is unlikely that they will always go beyond their differences to take concerted steps. In fact, it will be some time before China and India really can change the existing international order with their combined strength; the depth and strength of the Chindia relationship may be exaggerated as an optimistic prediction of China–India relations.

Global Significance of Sino-Indian Interactions

Given the asymmetrical perception of threat between the two sides, the formation of an India–US alliance could help India counter its perceived 'China threat'. In contrast, Beijing is keenly observing the warming of Indo-American relations, especially on issues relating to military cooperation. Just as Shashi Tharoor observed, 'The emergence of a stronger US–India relations appears to have convinced China to place New Delhi much more in the category of a potential adversary, even as an instrument in the containment of China' (*The Hindu* 2011d).

However, India is not willing to be a pawn in the US's strategy, because it will be more controversial if it surrenders its strategic autonomy to the US. Beijing and New Delhi are in favour of the so-called 'anti-hegemonism' struggle against power politics, and the China–India–Russia strategic triangle or Chindia concept are seen as instruments to promote the new international order and the multi-polar world. Those are also part of a bandwagoning strategy to reduce threat perception. On the other hand, however, while neither the Chinese nor the Indians are very trustful of the Sino-Indian relationship, nor are they willing to put their relations at risk by joining an anti-America alliance.

In order to balance their opposite needs, interests, and considerations of risk, China and India will nevertheless continue to look for opportunities to strengthen cooperation on issues of common concerns. China, India, and Russia are in the process of working out a trilateral dialogue to share their common concerns and protect their common interests. Aware of the overwhelming power of the US, the three countries may maintain a safe distance from the term 'strategic triangle' and use a less-loaded phrase, such as 'trilateral coordination and cooperation' to deepen the trilateral interactions. The existing strategic partnership of cooperation among China, India, and Russia will continue to play a significant role in reshaping a new international order.

Notes

1. For the text, see *The Hindu*, 2000, 'Text of "Vision" Statement', 22 March, New Delhi, available online at http://hindu.com/2000/03/22/stories/02220007.htm (accessed 15 August 2013).

2. See President George W. Bush's address at Asia Society on 22 February 2006. The text is available online at http://www.asiasociety.org/policy-politics/president-addresses-asia-society-discusses-india-and-pakistan (accessed 15 August 2013).

3. See, for example, Zhang *et al.* (2005: 7).

4. See, for example, the US National Intelligence Council, *Mapping the Global Future: Report of the National Intelligence Council's 2020 Project*, Washington DC, December 2004, available online at http://www.dni.gov/files/documents/Global%20Trends_Mapping%20the%20Global%20Future%202020%20Project.pdf (accessed 16 August 2013).

5. For more on this, see, *The Hindu*. 1998. 'Strategic Triangle' (Primakov's Statement), *The Hindu* Editorial, 23 December, New Delhi, p. 12.

6. For further details, see, *The Statesman*. 2004. 'Indo–Russian Ties–I: Continued Convergence of Interests', *The Statesman*, 20 December, available online at http://www.accessmylibrary.com/coms2/summary_0286-18272640_ITM (accessed 10 August 2013).

7. This point is widely shared among Chinese scholars. See, for instance, Liu (1996: 27); Yang (2001: 3); Yu (2004: 43).

8. See, for example, Sieff (1998: A10).

9. On 1 April 2001, a United States Navy EP-3 surveillance plane collided with a Chinese F-8 fighter jet about 110 km away from China's Hainan. The mid-

air collision caused the death of a Chinese pilot. The Chinese then detained 24 crew members of the EP-3 until the US Government issued a letter of apology for the incident.

10. See, for example, *The Boston Globe*. 1999.'The Russia–India–China Axis', *The Boston Globe* Editorial, 3 October, Boston, p. E6.

11. A research paper by Goldman Sachs gave the term 'BRICs' to signify Brazil, Russia, India, and China and anticipated that the BRICs' economies would become a much larger force over the next fifty years. For details see O'Neill (2001); Wilson and Purushothaman (2003).

12. For further discussion on this, see Tan (2007).

13. See, *The Hindu*. 2006. 'Not Rivals but Partners', *The Hindu* (Editorial), 23 November, available online at http://www.hindu.com/2006/11/23/stories/2006112303770800.htm (accessed 15 August 2013).

14. See, for example, Zhan (1999: 3).

15. See, for example, Song Haixiao. 2011.'Yindu dui wai zhengce juece mushi yanjiu' (A Study on the pattern of decision-making of India's foreign policy), *Nanyan Yanjiu* (*South Asian Studies*), no. 2, pp. 1–25.

16. See, 'Joint statement of the Republic of India and the People's Republic of China', available online at http://www.hindu.com/thehindu/nic/0041/jointstatement.htm (accessed 15 August 2013; and 'A shared vision for the 21st Century of the Republic of India and the People's Republic of China', available online at http://www.hindu.com/nic/rd1.pdf (accessed 15 August 2013).

17. See, for example, Jiang Zemin's report to the 15th CPC National Congress, titled 'Hold High the Great Banner of Deng Xiaoping: Theory for an All-Round Advancement of the Cause of Building Socialism with Chinese Characteristics into the 21st Century', 12 September 1997, available online at http://www.bjreview.com.cn/document/txt/2011-03/25/content_363499.htm (accessed 15 August 2013).

Concluding Remarks

Future of India–China Relations

THIS BOOK TESTS the argument that the asymmetry in perceptions of threat between related states will encourage the state with a higher perception of threat to take initiatives to change the intensity of threat perception. This book has thus examined the major issues of China–India relations, including the nuclear issue, the boundary problem, the Tibet issue, regional competition and cooperation, and China–India relations in the global context, in order to identify an asymmetrical perception of threat as the dynamics and the constraints in Sino-Indian relations with a focus on the post-1998 period.

The case of China–India relations suggests at least four significant theoretical conclusions. First, regarding the sources of the perceptions of threat, historical enmity will not naturally disappear easily with the passing of time, and will continue to amplify present perceptions of threat for the affected state. However, historical enmity could be treated as a fixed source of perceived threat, because the degree of enmity derived from the same historical event will almost certainly remain the same over time. In the case of China–India relations, the 1962 border war has been the main source of India's perceived threat from China. Although the degree of enmity will not be easily diluted, neither will it be increased. Also, while historical enmity will increase the perceived threat, historical goodwill is not able to reduce the perception of threat. Worse still, the historical goodwill may create some overly optimistic expectations. The attempt to mention the history of 'Hindi Chini bhai bhai' has proved futile in improving Sino-Indian relations.

Second, the impact of the state identity is complex while the states are trying to reduce perceptions of threat between them. This book disproves the traditional axiom that constructing a shared identity between states will necessarily help reduce the perceptions of threat. On the contrary, interactions between China and India show that a sense of shared identity will sometimes seek to intensify the perceived threat. China and India have a shared identity as rising powers. As a result, China and India are looking for global power status and vie for influence in international and regional affairs. Particularly, the process of seeking shared identity is not welcomed by the state with a lower perception of threat. That is, China is the comparatively more reluctant of the two parties to recognize India's status as a nuclear state.

Third, this book finds that soft-balancing appears as a preferred option in the process of reducing the perceptions of threat. Although hard-balancing measures, such as developing nuclear weapons, might have a more immediate impact on the balance of threat, the state with a more intensified threat perception is very cautious in taking hard-balancing initiatives against its perceived threat, as it tends to conclude that the cost of openly opposing the perceived threat exceeds the benefits. For example, in the case of China–India relations, India is reluctant to play the so-called 'Tibet card' against China, although it dislikes China's takeover of Tibet. India is also cautious of forming an anti-China alliance.

Fourth, this study indicates that asymmetry in perception of threat between related states is a destabilizing factor. The state with a more intensified perception of threat tends to challenge the *status quo* as it feels insecure. Thus, the counterpart state should not feel satisfied with asymmetry and ignore the other country's concerns. If it does, it may be 'surprised' by the opposing state's challenge.

In addition to the above-mentioned findings, this book draws on evidence from interactions between India and China over the past few years to make an empirical case for the existence and impact of asymmetrical perceptions of threat between the two countries. India tends to be deeply apprehensive of threats from China, while China appears comparatively unconcerned about threats from India, and finds it difficult to understand why India might perceive China as a threat.

In general, India remains caught in the web of the 'China threat' perception, and has thus avoided annoying China while trying to redress the imbalance between the two sides. Thus, the Indian side tried to secure the nuclear deterrent against China. On the Tibet issue, it adopts an ambiguous position rather than seeking a definitive solution in order to keep the Tibet card in its hand. As regards the boundary problem, on the other hand, it is keen to find an early solution that can reduce its perceived security concerns. On regional issues, India is still disturbed by China–Pakistan relations, but is developing a Look East policy to increase the pressure on China's security environment. In the global arena, India is working to secure a global power position. However, since the Indian side is cautious about the 'China threat', for most of the time New Delhi's China policy has been a reactive one and allows Beijing to set the agenda and tone for talks (*The Times of India* 2008a: 18).

The Chinese perception of India's security environment is that it is evolving favourably. Under the circumstances, the Chinese find it difficult to understand how they pose a threat to India. Targeting China as a threat in order to rationalize India's nuclear tests programme is deeply resented by people in China, who do not share India's concern about a 'deteriorating security environment'. They stress that the post-Cold War Sino-Pakistani relationship is a normal one. China is not willing to use the relationship to challenge India, nor does China want to be involved in India–Pakistan disputes, but India's recent military build-up has raised fears in China of India's 'eastward progression' in its desire to contain China. Particularly, Beijing does not want to see India forge close relations with the ASEAN states and Japan. Since China has secured the upper hand against a challenge from India, there is a sense of confidence in China that it will be able to deal with the relationship in ways that meet these objectives.

Despite India's perception of China's threat, however, Beijing does not want to see the two countries in a confrontational relationship. For China, the era of 'teaching India a lesson' was a costly experience. So, China has no intention of adopting a confrontational attitude towards India. It is also not in Beijing's interest to push India away from China or put it on the side of an anti-China alliance. Even if it has a distrust of the Indian government, Beijing is working to engage India. It is unlikely that China will make it a policy to be hostile towards India. The issue-by-issue cooperation that has been established between the two sides and the building of common campaign platforms on matters such as climate change will continue.

The most important common interest for both countries is to have a peaceful environment so that they can concentrate on economic and social development. The two sides have reached an agreement not to let disputed issues get in the way of developing the overall relationship. However, there is little evidence that China will treat India as a strategic partner. Although China and India are close geographically, the psychological distance between the two countries is relatively great. China lacks due understanding of Indian security concerns and should seriously face the fact that the Indian strategic community is still haunted by the very widespread perception that China is a security threat. For example, China's behaviour is easily interpreted as part of a larger design to keep India off balance even as Beijing and New Delhi engaged in formal talks to resolve border disputes and generally improve relations (*The Times of India* 2008b: 20). While the two countries have worked closely to avoid potential points of conflict, it is short-sighted to ignore their differences. Being rising powers, China and India do not share the same understanding of security concerns and both sides are eager to expand their own influence. The prospect of forging closer political links hinges on the convergence of the security perceptions of both sides.

Bibliography

Books and Newspaper Articles

Acharya, Alka. 2008. *China and India: Politics of Incremental Engagement*. New Delhi: Har-Anand Publications.

Adams, Jad, and Phillip Whitehead. 1997. *The Dynasty: The Nehru–Gandhi Story*, London: Penguin Group and BBC Worldwide Ltd.

Agence France-Presse. 1998. 'Chn: "No Progress" in China-India Border Talks', *Agence France-Presse*, 11 June, Beijing.

———. 1999. 'China Will Not Take Sides on Kashmir', *Agence France-Presse*, 16 June, Beijing.

Ali, Mahmud. 2007. 'New "Strategic Partnership" Against China', *BBC News*, 3 September, available online at http://news.bbc.co.uk/2/hi/south_asia/6968412.stm (accessed 18 August 2013).

Ali, Salamat. 1988. 'India Plays It Cool', *Far Eastern Economic Review*, 2 October, 138(43): 13–14.

All India Radio Network. 1993a. 'Foreign Secretary on Outcome of PRC Border Talks', 28 June 1993, in Foreign Broadcast Information Service (*FBIS*), *Daily Report: Near East and South Asia*, 29 June: 58.

———. 1993b. 'Rao Views Accord with China as Positive Breakthrough', 14 September 1993, in *FBIS*, *Daily Report: Near East and South Asia*, 15 September: 38.

———. 1994. 'Comments on Bilateral Issues', *FBIS*, *Daily Report: Near East and South Asia*, 19 July: 62.

———. 1995. 'China's Qiao Shi Meets Leaders, Discusses Ties', *FBIS*, *Daily Report: Near East and South Asia*, 17 November: 36.

Associated Press (AP). 1998. 'India Not Worried by Pakistan's Missile, Defense Minister Says', April 9, New Delhi.

———. 2000. 'Tibetan Spiritual Leader Defects from China, Says Dalai Lama's Group', *AP*, 7 January, New Delhi.

Associated Press (AP). 2008. 'Dalai Lama Urges Vision of Hope in Seattle Speech but Again Avoids Mention of Tibet Crisis', *AP*, 13 April, Seattle.

Australian Associated Press. 1998. 'India Proposes Moratorium on Nuclear Tests', *Australian Associated Press*, 22 May, New Delhi.

Bajpai, Kanti, and Amitabh Mattoo (eds). 2000. *The Peacock and the Dragon: India–China Relations in the 21st Century*. New Delhi: Har-Anand Publications.

Baldwin, David A. 1971. 'Thinking about Threat', *The Journal of Conflict Resolution*, XV(1): 71–8.

Banerjee, D.K. 1985. *China–India Border Dispute Contents*. New Delhi: Intellectual Publishing House.

Baweja, Harinder and Zahid Hussain. 1998. 'Ghauri: Fire in the Sky', *India Today* (international edition), 20 April: 38.

BBC News. 2011. 'China "Will Not Talk" to New Tibetan Leader', 13 May, available online at http://www.bbc.co.uk/news/world-asia-pacific-13390842 (accessed 12 August 2013).

Beijing Review. 1990. 'Sino–Pak Friendship Flourishes in All Weather', *Beijing Review*, 1–7 October, Beijing, p. 10.

———. 1999. 'Foreign Ministry News Briefings', *Beijing Review*, 5 July, Beijing, p. 15.

Bernstein, Richard and Ross H. Munro. 1997. 'China I: The Coming Conflict with America', *Foreign Affairs*, 76(2):18–32.

Biema, David Van. 2008. 'The World's Next Top Lama', *Time*, 15 May, available online at http://www.time.com/time/world/article/0,8599,1807103,00.html (accessed 10 August 2013).

Bhat, Sudhakar. 1967. *India and China*. New Delhi: Popular Book Service.

Bhattacharjea, Mira Sinha. 1993. 'New Directions: Ending the Past, Opening up the Future', *Frontline*, p. 125.

Bhattacharya, Abanti. 2005. 'China's "Observer" Status: Implications for SAARC', *Institute of Peace and Conflict Studies*, Article no. 1891, 21 November, available online at http://www.ipcs.org/article/south-asia/chinas-observer-status-implications-for-saarc-1891.html (accessed 18 August 2013).

Biema, David Van. 2008. 'The World's Next Top Lama', *Time*, 15 May, available online at http://www.time.com/time/world/article/0,8599,1807103,00.html (accessed 10 August 2013).

Brooks, Stephen G. and William C. Wohlforth. 2005. 'Hard Times for Soft Balancing', *International Security*, 30(1): 72–108.

Buzan, Barry, Ole Wæver, and Jaap De Wilde. 1998. *Security: A New Framework for Analysis*. Boulder: Lynne Rienner Publications.

Central News Agency. 1991. 'Zhonggong guchui xinan wu sheng lianhe dui wai kaifang' (China Encourages Five Southwestern Provinces to Jointly Open Up), *Central News Agency*, 10 July, Taipei.

Chakravarti, P.C. 1961. *India–China Relations*. Calcutta: Firma K.L. Mukhopadhyar.

Chandy, Anil Joseph. 2000. 'India, China and Pakistan', in Kanti Bajpai and Amitabh Mattoo (eds) *The Peacock and the Dragon: India–China Relations in the 21st Century*, pp. 316–31. New Delhi: Har-Anand Publications.

Chang, Jaw–Ling Joanne. 2001. 'Zhonggong Guoji Tanpan Celue Fenxi' ('Analysis of China's International Negotiating Style'), *Zhongguo Dalu Yanjiu (Mainland China Studies)*, 44(6): 1–23.

Chawla, Prabhu. 2003. 'Dancing with the Dragon', *India Today*, 7 July, available online at http://indiatoday.intoday.in/story/historic-visit-to-china-by-prime-minister-vajpayee-brings-beijing-and-delhi-closer/1/206119.html (accessed 10 August 2013).

Chen, Fengjun. 1999a. 'Lun Yindu Zai Shijie de Diwei' ('India's Place in Contemporary World'), *Nanya Yanjiu Jikan (South Asian Studies Quarterly)*, 1: 6–7.

Chen, Jidong. 1998. 'Zhongguo-Miandain-Yindu Lu Shang Maoyi Tongdao Jianshe Chutan' (An Initial Study of Building of a Land Passage of Trade from China via Burma to India), *Nanya Yanjiu Jikan*, 2: 1–7.

Chen, Vincent Wen-Hsien. 1999b. 'Guoji Huanjing Dui Zhonggong he Wu Zhengce Fazhan de Yingxiang' (The Impact of the International Situation on the Evolution of China's Nuclear Force Policies), *Wenti Yu Yanjiu (Issues and Studies)*, 38(2): 1–19.

Cheng, Ruisheng. 1998. 'Zhong Yin Guoji Diwei de Bijiao' (A Comparative Study of the International Status of China and India), *Nanya Yanjiu*, 2: 3–7.

Cherian, John. 1996. 'Strengthening Relations: India and China after Jiang Zemin's visit', *Frontline*, 27 December: 38–40.

———. 1998. 'Wrong Signals', *Frontline*, 7 November, available online at http://www.frontline.in/navigation/?type=static&page=archive (accessed 18 August 2013).

———. 2002. 'Some Positive Movement', *Frontline*, 13–26 April, available online at http://www.frontline.in/static/html/fl1908/19080480.htm (accessed 11 August 2013).

China Daily. 2005. 'South Asian Progress an Achievable Goal', *China Daily* Editorial, 15 November, Beijing, p. 4.

Clinton, Bill. 2000. 'What I Hope to Accomplish on My Trip to South Asia', *International Herald Tribune*, 19 March, New York, p. 8.

Cohen, Raymond. 1978. 'Threat Perception in International Crisis', *Political Quarterly*, 93(1): 93–108.

Commentator. 1998a. 'Chengba Nanya de Tumo' (Plot to Achieve Hegemony Over South Asia), *Renmin Ribao (People's Daily)*, 15 May, Beijing, p. 4.

———. 1998b. 'Jiujing Shi Shei Zai Gao Weixie' (Who is Posing Threat Actually?), *Renmin Ribao*, 18 May, Beijing, p. 4.

Commentator. 1998c. 'Lishi Bu Rong Fouren, Shishi Sheng yu Xiongbian' (History Shall Not be Denied, Facts Speak Louder Than Words), *Renmin Ribao*, 19 May, Beijing, p. 4.

CPC Tibet Autonomous Regional Party Committee and People's Government of the Tibet Autonomous Region. 2001. 'Lishi Jinbu de Huihong Huajuan—Jinian Xizang Heping Jiefang Wushi Zhounian' (A Splendid Picture Scroll of Historical Progress—Commemorating the Fiftieth Anniversary of Liberating Tibet), *Renmin Ribao*, 23 May, Beijing, p. 6.

Datta, Sreeradha. 2001. 'What Ails the Northeast: An Enquiry into the Economic Factors', *Strategic Analysis*, 25(1): 73–87.

Dawn. 2002. 'Pakistan, India Still Acquiring N-tech: CIA Report to Congress', February 2, available online at http://archives.dawn.com/2002/02/02/top5.htm (accessed 12 August 2013).

———. 2004. 'No N-status for Pakistan and India, Says China', available online at http://archives.dawn.com/2004/06/30/top6.htm (accessed 30 July 2013).

Deepak, B.R. 2005. *India and China 1904–2004: A Century of Peace and Conflict*. New Delhi: Manak Publications.

Delfs, Robert. 1987. 'Tibet's Turbulent Monks', *Far Eastern Economic Review*, pp. 8–10.

Deng, Changchun. 2003. 'Yaoyuan de Daguo Meng: Yindu Jueqi de Qianjing' ('A Distant Dream of Great Power: Prospects of India s Rise'), *Nanya Yanjiu Jikan*, 2: 16–19.

Deng, Xiaoping. 1988. 'China Must Take its Place in the Field of High Technology', in *Selected Works of Deng Xiaoping, Volume III (1982–1992)*, available online at http://english.peopledaily.com.cn/dengxp/vol3/text/c1920.html (accessed 18 August 2013).

Deshpande, G.P. and Alka Acharya. 2000. *Crossing A Bridge of Dreams: 50 Years of India China*. New Delhi: Tulika.

Dhar, M.K. 2000. 'A Shanghai Forum with India?' *The Pioneer*, 19 July, available online at http://www.ratical.org/ratville/CAH/ShanghaiCO.html#p9 (accessed 15 August 2013).

Ding, Xiaoxing. 2002. 'Zhongguo, Yindu Zai Eluosi Waijiao Zhong de Dingwei—Dangdai Quanqiuhua Jincheng Zhong de E Zhong Yin Jie Ping' ('China and India in Russia's Diplomacy: A Review of Russia, China and India in the Current Globalisation Process'), *Xiandai Guoji Guanxi (Contemporary International Relations)*, 6: 62–3.

Dittmer, Lowell. 2001. 'South Asia's Security Dilemma', *Asian Survey*, 41(6): 897–906.

Dixit, J.N. 2003. *India's Foreign Policy: 1947–2003*. New Delhi: Picus Books.

Dubey, Muchkund. 1998. 'The World Nuclear Order and India', *The Hindu*, 27 May, New Delhi, p. 12.

Dutta, Sujit. 1997. 'India and ASEAN: A Framework for Comprehensive Engagement', *Strategic Analysis*, XX(3): 357–72.

Dutta, Sujit. 2001. 'Much Hype, Small Gains', *Rediff News*, 3 July, available online at http://www.rediff.com/news/2001/jul/03spec.htm (accessed 18 August 2013).

———. 2008. 'India's latest Strategic Weapon', *The Hindu* Editorial, 9 May 2008, p.12.

Fang, Tien–Sze. 2001. 'Yindu Shishi Jingji Gaige Yilai de Waijiao Zou Xiang' (India's Foreign Policy since Economic Reform), *Wenti Yu Yanjiu*, 40(4): 81–96.

———. 2002. 'The Sino–Indian Border Talks under the Joint Working Group', *Issues and Studies*, 38(3): 150–83.

———. 2004. 'Zhong E Yin Zhubu Mai Xiang Zhanlue Sanjiao' (China, Russia and India Move to Strategic Triangle Gradually), *Pingguo Ribao* (*Apple Daily*), 20 July, Taipei, p. A15.

———. 2005. 'China Aims to Balance Relations in South Asia', *Taipei Times*, 27 April, Taipei, p. 8.

———. 2006. 'Zhong Yin Kaifang Naidui La Shankou Bian Jing Maoyi Zhi Pingshi' (An Analysis on China and India Open the Border Trade Across Nathu La Pass), *Zhanglue Anquan Yanxi* (*Strategic and Security Analysis*), 16: 47–50.

———. 2011. 'Hou Dalai Lama Shidai Tiqian Lailin' (The Post-Dalai Lama Era Arrives Earlier), *Zhongguo Shibao* (*China Times*), 22 March, Beijing.

Far Eastern Economic Review. 1993. 'Han Habitat', *Far Eastern Economic Review*, p. 14.

———. 2000. 'Danger: Road Works Ahead', *Far Eastern Economic Review*, pp. 26–7.

Foot, Rosemary. 1996. 'Chinese–Indian Relations and the Process of Building Confidence Implications for the Asia–Pacific', *The Pacific Review*, 9(1): 58–76.

Frontline. 1993. 'Beyond Borders: Sino–Indian Ties After Narasimha Rao Visit', *Frontline*, New Delhi, p. 123.

———. 1998. 'Indians were Very Friendly towards China', available at http://www.frontline.in/static/html/fl1519/1519020b.htm (accessed 12 August 2013).

Fu, Xiaoqiang. 1999. 'Nanya: Zai Jinzhang Yu Tingzhi Zhong Zou Xiang Xin Shiji' ('South Asia: Stepping Into the New Century and Intensification and Stagnation'), *Xiandai Guoji Guanxi*, 1–2: 60–3.

Gao, Qiufu. 2001. 'Combating the Three Evil Forces', *Beijing Review*, Beijing, pp. 8–10.

Garver, John W. 1991. 'China–India Rivalry in Nepal: The Clash Over Chinese Arms Sales', *Asian Survey*, 31 (1): 956–75.

———. 2001. *Protracted Contest: Sino–Indian Rivalry in the Twentieth Century*. Seattle and London: University of Washington Press.

———. 2002a. 'The Security Dilemma in Sino–Indian Relations', *India Review*, 1(4): 1–38.

———. 2002b. 'Asymmetrical Indian and Chinese Threat Perceptions', *Journal of Strategic Studies*, 25 (4): 109–34.

Ge, Lide. 2002. 'Will the United States Withdraw From the Central and South Asia', *Beijing Review*, Beijing, pp. 8–9.

Ghose, Arundhati. 2007. 'Disarmament and India's Nuclear Diplomacy: Evolution of a Reluctant Nuclear Weapon State', in Atish Sinha and Madhup Mehta (eds), *Indian Foreign Policy: Challenges and Opportunities*. pp. 979–1007. New Delhi: Academic Foundation.

Ginsburgs, George, and Michael Mathos. 1964. *Communist China and Tibet: The First Dozen Years*. The Hague: M. Nijhoff.

Gonsalves, Eric. 1998. 'Positive Agenda for Positive Action: Better India–China Understanding', in Tan Chung (ed.). *Across the Himalayan Gap: An Indian Quest for Understanding China*. New Delhi: Gyan Publishing House.

Gopal, S. (ed.), 1993. *Selected Works of Jawaharlal Nehru, Second Series, Volume Fifteen, Part II*. New Delhi: Jawaharlal Nehru Memorial Fund.

Gu, Ping. 1999. 'Yao Zhengzhi Duihua, Buyao Junbei Jingsai' (Political Dialogue–Yes; Arms Race–No), *Renmin Ribao*, 15 April, Beijing, p. 6.

Gujral, I.K. 'Continuity and Change Within the Global Scenario'. Address at the Council for Foreign Relations, New York, 3 October, available online at https://www.indianembassy.org/policy/Foreign_Policy/global%28gujral%29.htm (accessed 15 August 2013).

Gupta, Shishir. 2002. 'Tibet: Chinese Checkers', *India Today*, 7 October, available online at http://indiatoday.intoday.in/story/us-pressures-china-to-negotiate-with-dalai-lama/1/218515.html (accessed 18 August 2013).

Gyari, Lodi Gyaltsen. 2000. 'Don't Shut Out the Dalai Lama', *Far Eastern Economic Review*, p. 28.

Haidar, Salman. 2004. 'Sub-Regional Initiatives', *The Statesman*, 10 August, available online at http://www.accessmylibrary.com/coms2/summary_0286-12909276_ITM (accessed 18 August 2013).

Han, Nianlong *et al.* (eds). 1987. *Dangdai Zhongguo Waijiao (Contemporary Chinese Foreign Affairs)*. Beijing: Zhongguo Shehui Kexue Chubanshe.

Harding, Harry, and Francine R. Frankel. 2004. *The India–China Relationship: Rivalry and Engagement*. New Delhi: Oxford University Press.

Hsu, Kuei-hsiang Hsu. 2008. 'An Analysis of the Seventh Round of Negotiations between Mainland China and the Dalai Lama's Delegation 21', *Meng Zang xian juang shung yue bao (Bi-monthly journal on Mongolian and Tibetan current situation)*, 17(5): 21–34.

Hoffman, Steven A. 1990. *India and the China Crisis*. Berkeley: University of California Press.

Holslag, Jonathan. 2009. 'The Persistent Military Security Dilemma between China and India', *Journal of Strategic Studies*, 32(6): 811–40.

Hu, Angang and Men Honghua. 2002. 'Zhong Mei Ri E Yin Youxing Zhanlue Ziyuabijiao: Jian Lun Zhi Zai "Fu Min Qiang Guo" de Zhongguo da Zhanlue' (Comparisons of the Tangible Strategic Resources Between China, the United States, Japan, Russia, and India: And an Assessment on China's Grand Strategy of Making the People Rich and the Country Strong), *Zhanlue Yu Guanli (Strategy and Management)*, 2: 26–41.

Huanqiao Shibao (Global Times). 2001. 'Yin jun dai zai Nanhai bu xiang zou' (Indian Navy Stays in South China Sea and is Not Willing to Leav), *Huanqiao Shibao*, 13 March, Beijing, p. 1.

———. 2004. 'Eluosi xiang yao Zhongguo zao di wu dai zhanji' (Russia wants to invite China to Jointly Produce the Fifth Generation Flightier), *Huanqiao Shibao*, 2 July, Beijing, p. 16.

Hughes, Christopher R. 2006. *Chinese Nationalism in the Global Era*. London: Routledge/Curzon.

Hutzler, Charles. 2002. 'In Kashmir, China Tries its Hand at Peacemaking', *Wall Street Journal* (Eastern edition), 7 June: A8.

Indiresan, P.V. 2000. 'The Kunming Initiative', *Frontline*, New Delhi, pp. 98–100.

Indo-Asian News Service (IANS). 2007. 'China on a SAARC Charm Offensive, India Cautious', *Indo-Asian News Service*, 4 April, New Delhi.

———. 2009a. 'I Call Myself a Son of India, Says Dalai Lama', *Indo-Asian News Service*, 31 March, New Delhi.

———. 2009b. 'India, China Not Rivals but Partners: Krishna', *IANS*, 22nd July, New Delhi.

Itar-Tass. 2003. 'Dialogue Important to Russia, China—Spokesman', 26 May, Moscow.

International Campaign for Tibet. 2012. 'Self-Immolations in Tibet', 13 December, available online at http://www.savetibet.org/resource-center/maps-data-fact-sheets/self-immolation-fact-sheet (accessed 15 August 2013).

Jain, Girlal. 1960. *Panchsheela and After*. London: Asia Publishing House.

Jervis, Robert. 1976. *Perception and Misperception in International Politics*. Princeton: Princeton University Press.

Jetly, Nancy. 1979. *India–China Relations, 1947–1977: A Study of Parliament's Role in the Making of Foreign Policy*. Atlantic Highlands, N.J: Humanities Press.

Jha, Prem Shankar. 2010. *India and China: The Battle between Soft and Hard Power*. New Delhi: Viking.

Jiang, Ke. 2000.'Riben Yindu taojin hu?' (Japan and India come closer?), *Huanqiao Shibao* (*Global Times*), 1 September, Beijing, p. 2.

Jiang, Xiyuan, and Xia Liping. 2004. *Zhongguo HepingJjueqi* (*Peaceful Rise of China*). Beijing: Zhongguo Shehui eKxue Chubanshe.

Jiang, Zemin. 1997.'Hold High the Great Banner of Deng Xiaoping's Theory for An All–Round Advancement of the Aause of Building Socialism with Chinese Characteristics into the 21st Century.' Report to the 15th CPC National Congress, 12 September, available online at http://www.bjreview.com.cn/document/txt/2011-03/25/content_363499.htm (accessed 15 August 2013).

Jiefanghun Bao (PLA Daily). 2000. 'Yin anquan muquag miaoxiang zhengge yazhou' (India's Set Security Eyes on Whole Asia), 12 July, available online at http://www.pladaily.com.cn/pladaily/20000712/big5/20000712001075_todaynews.html (accessed 15 August 2013).

Joeck, Neil. 1997. *Maintaining Nuclear Stability in South Asia*. Adelphi Paper, London: International Institute for Strategic Studies.

Joseph, Anil K. 2002.'Jaswant Singh's Visit to Rejuvenate Sino–Indian Relations', *Press Trust of India*, 27 March, available online at http://www.rediff.com/news/2002/mar/28china.htm (accessed 18 August 2013).

Joshi, Manoj. 1998.'George in the China Shop', *India Today*, 18 May, available online at http://indiatoday.intoday.in/story/china-is-the-potential-threat-no.-1-says-george-fernandes/1/264241.html (accessed 11 August 2013).

Kamath, P. M. 2011.'Sino–Indian Doctrine of Peace: No First Use of Nuclear Weapons', in P.M. Kamath (ed.). *India–China Relations: Agenda for the Asian Century*, pp. 65–77. New Delhi: Gyan Publishing House.

Kammerer, Peter. 2004.'Right Wing Wary of a New Order', *South China Morning Post*, 26 December, Hong Kong, p. 12.

Kanwal, Gurmeet. 2000. 'India's National Security Strategy in a Nuclear Environment', *Strategic Analysis*, XXIV(9): 1591–628.

Kapila, Subhash. 2001. 'China's Infrastructure Development in the Western Regions: Strategic Implications', *South Asia Analysis Group*, paper no. 210, 15 March, available online at http://www.southasiaanalysis.org/%5Cpapers3%5Cpaper210.htm (accessed 10 August 2013).

Katyal, K.K. 2003. 'Beijing–Moscow–New Delhi Trialogue', *The Hindu*, 22 September, available online at http://www.hindu.com/2003/09/22/stories/2003092201151000.htm (accessed15 August 2013).

Kaul, T. N. 1998.'Pokhran, China and Pakistan', *The Hindu*, 30 May, New Delhi, p. 10.

Kaye, Lincoln. 1993. 'Bordering on Peace: China and India Ease Tensions Along Frontier', *Far Eastern Economic Review*, p. 13.

Khanna, V.N. 2005. *Foreign Policy of India* (Fifth ed). New Delhi: Vikas Publishing House.

Krepon, Michael (ed.). 1998. *A Handbook of Confidence–Building Measures for Regional Security* (3rd ed.), Washington DC: The Henry L. Stimson Center.

Krishnan, Ananth and Sandeep Dikshit. 2011. 'India and China Had Similar Considerations on Libya', *The Hindu*, 26 March, available online at http://www.thehindu.com/news/national/india-and-china-had-similar-considerations-on-libya/article1571829.ece (accessed 15 August 2013).

Kuba, Daniel Joseph and G.V. Vaidyanathan. 2000. 'A Chronology of India–US Relations, 1941–2000', in Kanti Bajpai and Amitabh Mattoo (eds). *Engaged Democracies: India–U.S. Relations in the 21st Century*, pp. 159–204. New Delhi: Har-Anand Publications.

Kumar, Yukteshwar and Ramananda Sengupta. 2000. 'Hindi–Chini Bye Bye?', *Outlook*, 3 April, available online at http://www.outlookindia.com/article.aspx?209155 (accessed18 August 2013).

Lall, J. 1989. *Aksaichin and the Sino–Indian Conflict*. Ahmedabad: Allied Publishers.

Lam, Willy. 2005. 'Beijing's Alarm Over New "US Encirclement Conspiracy"', *China Brief*, 5 (8), available online at http://www.jamestown.org/single/?no_cache=1&tx_ttnews%5Btt_news%5D=30247 (accessed 18 August 2013).

Lamb, Alastair. 1964. *The China–India Border: The Origins of the Disputed Boundaries*. London: Oxford University Press.

Lawrance, Alan. (ed.). 1975. *China's Foreign Relations Since 1949*. London: Routledge and Kegan Paul.

Lee, Mary. 1985. 'Two-Way Street for Arms: Pakistan Buys From China But Also Sells What China Cannot Get', *Far Eastern Economic Review*, 12 December, p. 25.

Lei, Yinfeng. 1997. *Zai Zuigao Tongshuai Shenbian Dang Canmou: Lei Yinfeng JiangjunHhuiyilu (Being the Staff Officer to the Highest Command: Memoir of General Lei Yinfeng)*. Nanchang: Baihuazhou Wenyi.

Liang Jiejun. 1999. 'Kua Shiji de Yindu Guojia Anquan Zhanlue' ('India's Trans-Century National Security Strategy'), *Xiandai Guoji Guanxi*, 5: 23–7.

Limaye, Satu P. 1993. 'Message to India: Come Back to Asia', *The Asian Wall Street Journal*, (European edition), 20 December, p. 8.

Lin, Chao–Chen. 2000. *Zuihou de Dalai Lama* (*The Last Dalai Lama*). Taipei: Shibao Chubanshe.

Liu, Huaqiu and Zheng Hua. 1997. 'Confidence-Building Measures in Asia', in Michael Krepon (ed.), *Chinese Perspectives on Confidence-Building Measures*, pp. 1–14. Report No. 23: The Henry L. Stimson Center.

Liu, Shanguo. 1999a. "Yindu yu Dongmeng Jiangli Huoban Guanxi Dui Wo Guo Anquan de Yinxiang' (Prospects for India's Partnership with ASEAN and its Influence Upon China's Security), *Nanya Yanjiu*, 2: 30–4.

———. 1999b. 'Yindu Yu Dongmeng Jianli Huoban Guanxi de Fazhan Qianjing Ji Qi Dui Wo Guo Anquan de Yiing Xiang' ('Prospects of the Efforts to Establish Partnership Between India and ASEAN and its Influence on Security of China'), *Nanya Yanjiu Jikan*, 3: 43–51.

Liu, Xiaojuan and Zhang Jian. 2006. 'Yindu "Dong Xiang Zhengce" Xingcheng Zhong de Fei–Jingji Yinsu' (An Analysis of Non Economic Factors of India's Look East Policy), *Nanya Yanjiu Jikan*, 4: 98–101.

Liu, Xuecheng. 1994. *The Sino-Indian Border Dispute and Sino-Indian Relations*. Lanham: University Press of America.

———. 1996. 'Leng Zhan Hou Meiguo Anquan Zhanlue Zhong de Nanya' (South Asia on the U.S. Strategic Chessboard in Post-Cold War Era), *Nanya Yanjiu Jikan*, 1: 4–12.

———. 1999. 'Shiji Zhi Jiao de da Guo Nanya Zhengce' (Great Nations' Policies Towards South Asia at the Turn of Centuries), *Nanya Yanjiu* , 2: 23–9.

———. 2001. 'Zhong E Yin San Guo Guanxi Zhong de Xietiao Yu Hezuo' (Coordination and Cooperation in China–Russia–India Relations), *Dangdai Yatai* (*Contemporary Asia–Pacific Studies*), 12: 21–8.

———. 2006. 'Mei Yin Minyong He Hezuo de Zhanlue Hanyi' (The Strategic Implication of Indo–American Nuclear Deal), *Ya Fei Zongheng* (*Asia and Africa Review*), 6: 15–19.

Liu, Zhaohua. 2007a. 'Zhong Yin Bian Jie wenti Zuotanhui Jishi (Shang)' (Proceedings of Forum on China–India Border Issue (I)), *Nanya Yanjiu*, 1: 43–51, 58.

———. 2007b. 'Zhong Yin Bian Jie Wenti Zuotanhui Jishi (Xia)' (Proceedings of Forum on China–India Border Issue (II)), *Nanya Yanjiu*, 2: 33–40.

Lok Sabha Debates. 1998. 'Recent Nuclear Test in Pokhran', Twelfth Series 2 (3): Column 394.

Loudon, Bruce. 2007. 'India to Snub U.S. on Burma Arms Embargo', *The Australian*, 23 January, available online at http://www.poe-news.com/forums/sp.php?pi=1001381320 (accessed 13 August 2013).

Lu, Chih H. 1986. *The Sino–Indian Border Dispute: A Legal Study*. New York: Greenwood.

Luce, Edward. 2006. *In Spite of the Gods: The Strange Rise of Modern India*. London: Little, Brown Book Group.

Ma, Jiali. 1994. 'Hou Lengzhan Shidai Yindu de Waijiao Zhengce' (India's Foreign Policy in Post-Cold War Times), *Nanya Yanjiu*, 4: 43–9.

Ma, Jiali. 2006. 'Yindu de Jueqi Taishi' (The Posture of India's Rise), *Xiandai Guoji Guanxi*, 6: 51–5.

Malik, J. Mohan. 1995. 'China–India Relations in the Post–Soviet Era: The Continuing Rivalry', *The China Quarterly*, 142: 317–55.

———. 2002. 'Dragon's Shadow', *The Pioneer*, 23 July, available online at http://teleradproviders.com/nbn/editorialstory.php?id=NjA2MQ== (accessed 18 August 2013).

———. 2003. 'High Hopes: India's Response to US Security Policies', *Asian Affairs—An American Review*, 30 (2): 104–12.

———. 2012. *China and India: Great Power Rivals*. New Delhi: Viva Books.

Manor, James, and Gerald Segal 1998. 'Taking India Seriously', *Survival*, 40 (2): 67.

Mao, Siwei. 2008. 'Five Questions on the Tibetan Issue', *The Hindu*, 4 June, New Delhi, p. 13.

Maoz, Zeev. 1990. *National Choices and International Processes*. Cambridge: Cambridge University Press.

Mattoo, Amitabh. 2000. 'Imagining China', in Kanti Bajpai and Amitabh Mattoo (eds). *The Peacock and the Dragon: India–China Relations in the 21st Century*, pp. 14–17. New Delhi: Har-Anand Publications.

Maxwell, Neville. 1970. *India's China War*. London: Jonathan Cape.

Menon, V.K. Krishna. 1963. *India and the Chinese Invasion*. Bombay: Contemporary Publishers.

Mohan, C. Raja. 1998. 'BJP, China and "Asian Solidarity"', *The Hindu*, 27 March, New Delhi, p. 13.

———. 1999a. 'China Sticking to Cautious Neutrality?' *The Hindu*, 1 July, New Delhi, p. 11.

———. 1999b. 'Third Parties in Sino–Indian Ties', *The Hindu*, 15 June, New Delhi, p. 11.

———. 2000a. 'India and its Extended Neighbourhood', *The Hindu*, 8 June, New Delhi, p. 12.

———. 2000b. 'India, China and the United States', in Kanti Bajpai and Amitabh Mattoo (eds), *Engaged Democracies: India–US Relations in the 21st Century*, p. 31. New Delhi: Har-Anand Publications.

———. 2003. 'Tibet Static in China', *The Hindu*, 23 June, available online at http://www.hindu.com/2003/06/23/stories/2003062304041100.htm (accessed 18 August 2013).

———. 2007. 'The Evolution of India's Nuclear Doctrine', in Atish Sinha and Madhup Mehta (eds), *Indian Foreign Policy: Challenges and Opportunities*, pp. 1019–38. New Delhi: Academic Foundation.

Mohan, C. Raja. 2008. 'India's Tibet Ambiguity', *Indian Express*, 27 November, available online at http://www.indianexpress.com/news/india-s-tibet-ambiguity/391206/ (accessed 18 August 2013).

Monterey Institute of International Studies. 1999. 'China's Nuclear Exports and Assistance to Pakistan', available at http://cns.miis.edu/archive/country_india/china/npakchr.htm (accessed 12 August 2013).

———. 2000. 'China's Missile Exports and Assistance to Pakistan', available at http://cns.miis.edu/archive/country_india/china/mpakchr.htm (accessed 12 August 2013).

Mukherjee, Pranab. 1998. 'Should India Sign the CTBT?' *The Hindu*, 26 May, New Delhi, p. 10.

Mullik, B.N. 1971. *The Chinese Betrayal: My Years with Nehru*. Bombay: Allied Publisher.

Nanya Yanjiu. 1999. 'Kunming Changyi' (Kunming Initiative), *Nanya Yanjiu*, 2: 94.

Nehru, Jawaharlal. 1956. *The Discovery of India*. London: Meridian Books Limited.

Noorani, A.G. 1967. 'India's Quest for a Nuclear Guarantee', *Asian Survey*, 7(7): 490–502.

———. 2002. 'On Sino–Indian Relations', *Frontline*, 5 January, available online at http://www.frontline.in/navigation/?type=static&page=flonnet&rdurl=fl1901/19010770.htm (accessed 18 August 2013).

Norbu, Dawa. 2000. 'India, China and Tibet', in Kanti Bajpai and Amitabh Mattoo (eds), *The Peacock and the Dragon: India–China Relations in the 21st Century*, pp. 275–97. New Delhi: Har-Anand Publications.

———. 1997 'Tibet in Sino–Indian Relations: The Centrality of Marginality', *Asian Survey*, 37 (11): 1078–95.

O'Neill, Jim. 2001. *Building Better Global Economic BRICs*, Goldman Sachs Global Economics Paper No. 66, 30 November, available online at http://www.goldmansachs.com/our-thinking/archive/archive-pdfs/build-better-brics.pdf (accessed 18 August 2013).

Panikkar, K.M. 1967. *India and China: A Study of Cultural Relations*. Bombay: Asia Publishing House.

Pant, Harsh V. 2010. *The China Syndrome: Grappling with an Uneasy Relationship*. New Delhi: Harper Collins Publishers.

Papayoanou, Paul A. 1997. 'Economic Interdependence and the Balance of Power', *International Studies Quarterly* 41(1): 113–40.

Paranjpe, V.V. 1998. 'Wanted: A China Policy', *The Hindu*, 12 June, New Delhi, p. 12.

Parthasarathy, G. 2001. 'The Growing Sino–Pakistan Nexus', 24 May, available online at http://www.tribuneindia.com/2001/20010523/edit.htm#4 (accessed 15 August 2013).

Paul, T.V. 2005. 'Soft Balancing in the Age of US Primacy', *International Security* 30 (1): 46–71.

Peking Review. 1963. 'New Delhi Returns Evil For Good', *Peking Review*, 25 January: 10–11.

People's Daily. 2002. 'FM Spokesman: China-Pakistan Anti-Terrorism Mechanism Possible', 28 April, available online at http://english.peopledaily.com.cn/200204/25/eng20020425_94735.shtml (accessed 15 August 2013).

Perkovich, George. 1999. *India's Nuclear Bomb: The Impact on Global Proliferation*. Berkeley: University of California Press.

Press Trust of India (PTI). 1998. 'China is Potential Threat Number One', *PTI*, 3 May, New Delhi.

———. 1999a. 'Chinese Ambassador Notes Recent Positive Steps In Bilateral Relations', *PTI*, 9 March, New Delhi.

———. 1999b. 'China Rejects Move-on Strategic Tie-up', *PTI*, 8 March, Beijing.

———. 2000a. 'Beijing Not Keen on India-China-Russia triangle', *PTI*, 9 April, Beijing.

———. 2000b. 'China Hopes Putin Visit Will Bolster Peace', *PTI*, 2 October, Beijing.

———. 2000c. 'China Urges India to Renounce Nuke Plan', *PTI*, 7 March, Beijing.

———. 2002. 'China Not to Mediate on Kashmir Issue', *PTI*, 9 January, Beijing.

———. 2003a. 'Sikkim will Cease to be an Issue with China: PM', 23 July, available online at http://expressindia.indianexpress.com/news/fullstory.php?newsid=23273 (accessed 10 August 2013).

———. 2003b. 'Sikkim Question to be Resolved Gradually', *PTI*, 4 October, Beijing.

———. 2004a. 'China Asks Western Countries Not to Intervene in "Tibet Issue"', *PTI*, Beijing, 27 July.

———. 2004b. 'Dalai Lama Suggests Turning Tibet into Zone of Ahimsa', *PTI*, 21 January, New Delhi.

———. 2005. 'Pitroda Moots Plan to Make India Superpower', 7 January, available online at http://www.hindustantimes.com/Indians-Abroad/IndiansAbroadnews/Pitroda-moots-plan-to-make-India-superpower/Article1-27054.aspx (accessed 15 August 2013)..

———. 2006. 'India, US Relations Can Change the World: Bush', *PTI*, 3 March, New Delhi.

———. 2007. 'Hindi-Chini Bhai Bhai: Dalai Lama', *PTI*, 3 November, New Delhi.

———. 2008. 'India Wants No Confrontation with China: Antony', *PTI*, 10 June, New Delhi.

Press Trust of India (PTI). 2009. 'Separatists in Tibet and Xinjiang Major Threats: China', 20 January, available online at http://www.hindustantimes.com/world-news/RestOfAsia/Separatists-in-Tibet-and-Xinjiang-major-threats-China/Article1-368821.aspx (accessed 10 August 2013).

Qian, Feng. 2001a. 'Yindu, Shei Dui Zhongguo Zui Qiang Ying' (Who Are the Most Hard-Line Figures towards China in India?), *Renmin Wan* (People's Website), 5 April, available online at http://www.people.com.cn/GB/junshi/60/20010405/433542.html (accessed 18 August 2013).

———. 2001b. 'Yin Mian Gong Zhu Hezuo Lu' (India and Myanmar Cooperate to Construct Road), *Renmin Ribao*, 20 February, Beijing, p. 3.

———. 2002. '21 Shiji Shuyu Yindu?' (21st Century Belong to India?), *Huanqiu Shibao*, Beijing, 10 October: 3.

Radio Peace and Progress. 1979. 'China "Encourages Spread of Nuclear Weapons" in Asia', 27 April, in *BBC Summary of World Broadcasts*, 1 May.

Ram, Mohan. 1973. *Politics of Sino–Indian Confrontation*. Delhi: Vikas Publishing House.

Ram, N. 1998a. 'The CTBT Will Make a Real Difference', *Frontline*, p. 15.

———. 1998b. 'Sino–Indian Relations: What Lies Ahead?' *Frontline*, 12–25 September, available online at http://www.frontline.in/static/html/fl1519/15190040.htm (accessed 15 August 2013).

———. 1998c. 'Clarifying the Facts About 1962 is a Precondition', *Frontline*, p. 18.

Ramachandran, Sudha. 2007. 'India Promotes "Goodwill" Naval Exercises', *Asia Times*, 14 August, available online at http://www.atimes.com/atimes/South_Asia/IH14Df01.html (accessed 18 August 2013).

Ramesh, Jairam. 2005. *Making Sense of Chindia: Reflections on China and India*. New Delhi: India Research Press.

Ranade, Sudhanshu. 1998. 'India's Place in World Politics', *The Hindu*, 29 April, New Delhi, p. 12.

Ranganathan, C.V. and Vinod C. Khanna. 2000. *India and China: The Way Ahead After "Mao's India's War"*, New Delhi: Har-Anand Publications.

Rao, Gondker Narayana. 1968. *The India–China Border: A Reappraisal*. Bombay: Asia Publishing House.

Ren, Xin. 1996. '"China Threat" Theory Untenable', *Beijing Review*, 5–11 February, Beijing, pp. 10–11.

———. 1997. 'A Year of Diplomatic Feats for China', *Beijing Review*, 6–12 January, Beijing, pp. 9–13.

Renmin Chubanshe (ed.). 1962. *Zhong Yin Bianjie Wenti (Sino–Indian Boundary Question)*. Beijing: Renmin Chubanshe.

Renmin Ribao (People's Daily). 1993. 'Zhongguo daibiao tichu Yatai anquan jizhi wu dian zhuzhang' (Chinese Representative Proposes Five-point Proposal for Asia-Pacific Security Regime), *Renmin Ribao*, 3 February, Beijing, p. 6.

———. 1995. 'Zhong Yi bianjie huitan qude jinzhan, shuang fang xia yue juxing shouci bianfang renyuan huiwu' (Sino-Indian Border Talks Get Underway, Both Sides Will Hold Border Personnel Meeting Next Month), *Renmin Ribao*, 21 August, Beijing, p. 6.

———. 1998a. 'Waijiao bu fabiao shengming, Zhongguo zhengfu qianglie qianze Yindu hezi shiyan (Foreign Ministry Issues Statement, Chinese Government Strongly Condemned India's Nuclear Tests)', *Renmin Ribao*, 15 May, Beijing, p. 1.

———. 1998b. 'Waijiao Bu fanyanren zhichu: Zhongguo dui Yindu xin Waichang guanyu zhili gaishan Zhong Yin guanxi jianghua biaoshi huanying' (Foreign Ministry spokesman remarks: China welcomes new Indian External Minister's statements about working to improve Sino-Indian relations), Renmin Ribao, 29 December, Beijing, p. 4.

———. 1998c. 'Waijiao Bu fayanren da ji zhewen, Zhongguo zhengfu dui Yindu jinxing hezi shiyan biaoshi yanzhong guanqie' (Foreign Ministry spokesman answers reporters' questions, Chinese government expressed serious concerns over India's conducting nuclear tests), *Renmin Ribao*, 13 May, Beijing, p. 4.

——— (Commentator). 1998d. 'Chengba nanya de tumo' (Plot to achieve hegemony over South Asia), *Renmin Ribao*, 15 May, Beijing, p. 4.

——— (Commentator). 1998e. 'Lishi bu rong fouren, shishi sheng yu xiongbian' (History shall not be denied, facts speak louder than words), *Renmin Ribao*, 19 May, Beijing, p. 4.

——— (Commentator). 1998f. 'Shishi sheng yu xiongbian' (facts prevail eloquences), 19 May, Beijing, p. 4.

———. 1999a. 'Zhong Yin liang guo waichang juxing huitan' (Chinese and Indian Foreign Ministers Held Talks), *Renmin Ribao*, 15 June, Beijing, p. 1.

———. 1999b. 'Waijiao Bu fayanren fabiao pinglun, Zhongguo dui Yindu daodan shiyan biaoshi yihan he quanquie' (Foreign Ministry Spokesman Commented that China Expressed Regret and Concern Over India's Test of Ballistic Missiles), *Renmin Ribao*, 14 April, Beijing, p. 4.

———. 1999c. 'Meiguo jie renquan ganshe Zhongguo neizheng zai zao shibai' (The US Attempt to Use Human Rights Issue to Intervene China's Domestic Affairs Fails Again), *Renmin Ribao*, 24 April, Beijing, p. 1.

———. 1999d. 'Tang Jiaxuan waichang zai jiu jie quanguo Ren Da er ci huiyi juxing de jizhe zhaodaihui shang jiu guoji xingshi he Zhongguo waijiao zhengce deng da jizhe wen' (Foreign Minister Tang Jiaxuan Answer Reporters' Questions about International Situations and China's Foreign Policy at the Press Conference of the Second Session of the 9th National People's Congress), *Renmin Ribao*, 8 March, Beijing, p. 1.

Renmin Ribao (*People's Daily*). 2000a. 'Yunnan goujian xinan gonglu shuiyun guoji da tongdao' (Yunan to Construct the Great International Passage of Southwest Road and Waterborne Transport), *Renmin Ribao*, 5 June, Beijing, p. 4.

———. 2000b. 'Yunan: jianshi gouji da tongdao' (Yunan: Constructing the Great International Passage), *Renmin Ribao*, 28 August, Beijing, p. 12.

———. 2000c. 'Jiang zhuxi yu Nalayanan zongtong huitan' (Chairman Jiang Holds Discussions with President Narayanan), *Renmin Ribao*, 30 May, Beijing, p. 1.

———. 2000d. 'China Raises Five-point Proposal for Relations with India', 22 July, available online at http://english.people.com.cn/english/200007/22/eng20000722_46193.html (accessed 15 August 2013).

———. 2000e. 'Jiang Zemin huijian Mushalafu' (Jiang Zemin met Musharraf), *Renmin Ribao*, 18 January, Beijing, p. 1.

———. 2000f. 'Mei biaoshi dui Yin Ba bu pian bu yi' (The US says it take an even-handed approach to India and Pakistan), *Renmin Ribao*, 25 March, Beijing, p. 4.

———. 2001. 'Zhonggong zhongyan Guowuyuan zhaokai di su ci Xizang gongzuo zuotanhui' (The Central Committee of the Communist Party and the State Council Held the Fourth Forum on Tibet Work), *Renmin Ribao*, 30 June, Beijing, p. 1.

———. 2002a. 'Tang Jiaxuan yu BajisitanWaichang fengbie tong dianhua' (Tang Jiaxuan Held Phone Conversations with Pakistan and Indian Foreign Ministers respectively), *Renmin Ribao*, 1 January, Beijing, p. 2.

———. 2002b. 'Tang Jiaxuan yu Yindu Waichang Singh tong hua' (Tang Jiaxuan Phoned Indian Foreign Minister Xinge), *Renmin Ribao*, 25 May, Beijing, p. 4.

———. 2002c. 'Waijiaobu fayanren fabiao tanhua' (Foreign Ministry Spokesman Remarks), *Renmin Ribao*, 7 June, Beijing, p. 4.

———. 2002d. 'Yin Mian Tai shangtao jiaotong lianwang' (India, Myanmar and Thailand Discuss Transport Network), *Renmin Ribao*, 8 April, Beijing, p. 7.

———. 2002e. 'Gonggu youyi zengjin xinren kuoda hezuo' (Consolidating friendship, increasing trust and expanding cooperation), *Renmin Ribao*, 19 January, Beijing, p. 3.

———. 2002f. 'Zhu Rongji yu Yindu zongli Wajiepayi huitan' (Zhu Rongji holds talks with Indian Prime Minister Vajpayee) *Renmin Ribao*, 15 January, Beijing, p. 1.

Renmin Ribao (*People's Daily*). 2005. 'Wen Jiabao huijian guoji meiti jizhe' (Wen Jiaboa meets the reporters of international media), *Renmin Ribao*, 13 April, Beijing, p. 1.

Reus-Smit, Christian. 2001. 'Constructivism', in Scott Burhchill *et al.*, *Theories of International Relations*, pp. 209–30. Basingstoke: Palgrave.

Ross, Robert. 2009. 'China's Naval Nationalism: Sources, Prospects, and the US Response', *International Security*, 34(2): 46–81.

Rousseau, David L. 2006. *Identifying Threats and Threatening Identities: The Social Construction of Realism and Liberalism*. Stanford: Stanford University Press.

Rowland, John. 1967. *A History of Sino–Indian Relations: Hostile Co–Existence*. London: D.Van Nostrand Company Ltd.

Sandhu, Bhim. 1988. *Unresolved Conflict: China and India*. London: Sangam Books Limited.

Sen, Amartya. 2005. *The Argumentative Indian: Writings on Indian Culture, History and Identity*. London: Penguin Books.

Sen, Kaushik. 2000. 'India, China and the United States', in Kanti Bajpai and Amitabh Mattoo (eds). *The Peacock and the Dragon: India–China Relations in the 21st Century*, pp. 251–74. New Delhi: Har-Anand Publications.

Shakya, Tsering. 1999. *The Dragon in the Land of Snows: A History of Modern Tibet since 1947*. London: Pimlico.

Shao, Zhiyong. 2001. 'India's Big Power Dream', *Beijing Review*, 12 April, Beijing, pp. 9–10.

Shao, Zhiyong and Xu Xiangjun. 2000. 'Yindu Junli Pengzhang Wei Na Ban–Fan Guofan Daxue Hu Siyun Jiao Shou' (The Reason for India's Build-Up: Interview with Professor Hu Siyuan of National Defence University), *Guangming Ribao* (Guanming Daily), 15 November.

Sharma, Mukul. 2007. 'Myanmar: India Must Suspend Military Support', *The Hindu*, 6 October, available online at http://www.hindu.com/2007/10/06/stories/2007100653881300.htm (accessed 18 August 2013).

Shekhar, Vibhanshu. 2007. 'Trends in India–ASEAN Economic Relations', Article No. 2433, *Institute of Peace and Conflict Studies*, 30 November, available online at http://www.ipcs.org/article_details.php?articleNo=2433 (accessed 18 August 2013).

Shen, Junzhuan. 1987. *Zhonggong Yu Yindu Guanxi Zhengchanghu de Guocheng Yu Zhangai* (*The Process and Obstacles in the Normalisation of Sino–Indian Relations*). Taipei: National Chengchi University International Relations Institute.

Sheng, Lijun. 2000. 'Blessing in disguise for China?', *The Straits Times*, 16 July, Singapore, accessed via electronic databases LexisNexis Academic (accessed 15 August 2013).

Shukla, Saurabh. 2006. 'Return of the Dragon', *India Today*, 27 November, available online at http://indiatoday.intoday.in/story/president-of-china-visits-india/1/180183.html (accessed 18 August 2013).

———. 2008. 'Beijing Games', *India Today*, 13 June, available online at http://indiatoday.intoday.in/story/Beijing+games/1/9754.html (accessed 18 August 2013).

Sidhu, Waheguru Pal Singh and Jing–Dong Yuan. 2001. 'Resolving the Sino–Indian Border Dispute: Building Confidence Through Cooperative Monitoring', *Asian Survey*, 41(2): 364–74.

———. 2003. *China and India: Cooperation or Conflict?* New Delhi: India Research Press.

Sieff, Martin. 1998. 'Primakov Puts Russia in a Strategic Spot', *The Washington Times*, 27 December, Washington, p. A10.

Sikri, Rajiv. 2008. 'India Needs to Change its Tibet Policy', *Rediff News*, 27 March, available online at http://www.rediff.com/news/2008/mar/27guest.htm (accessed 10 August 2013).

Singer, J. David. 1958. 'Threat Perception and the Armament–Tension Dilemma', *Journal of Conflict Resolution*, 2(1): 90–105.

Singh, Bhartendu Kumar. 1999. 'Sino–Indian Ties: The 11th Round of Joint Working Group Meeting', *Institute of Peace and Conflict Studies*, no. 195, 7 June, available online at http://www.ipcs.org/article_details.php?articleNo=195 (accessed 18 August 2013).

———. 2008. 'China, India and Australian politics of "Quad"', *Institute of Peace and Conflict Studies*, 18 February, available online at http://www.ipcs.org/article_details.php?articleNo=2496 (accessed 15 August 2013).

———. 2011. 'India–China Relations: Rising Together?' in D. Suba Chandran and Jabin T. Jacob (eds), *India's Foreign Policy: Old Problems, New Challenges*, pp. 25–42. New Delhi: MacMillan Publishers.

Singh, Jasjit. 1999b. 'Pakistan's Fourth War', *Strategic Analysis*, 23(5): 685–702.

Singh, Jaswant. 2006. *A Call to Honour: In Service of Emergent India*. New Delhi: Rupa.

Singh, Manmohan. 2008. 'India and China in the 21st Century', Speech at the Chinese Academy of Social Sciences, Beijing, 15 January, available online at http://pmindia.gov.in/speech-details.php?nodeid=623 (accessed 18 August 2013).

Singh, Mahavir. 2005. *Panchsheel: Retrospect and Prospect*. Delhi: Shipra Publications.

Singh, Swaran. 1997. 'Sino–Indian CBMs: Problems and Prospects', *Strategic Analysis*, 20(4): 543–59.

———. 2000. 'Sino–South Asian Ties: Problems and Prospects', *Strategic Analysis*, 24(1): 31–49.

Singh, Swaran. 2001.'China–India: Expanding Economic Engagement," *Strategic Analysis*, 24(10): 1813–31.

Song, Dexin. 1999. 'Shi Xi Zhongguo Zhoubian Anquan Huanjing Zhong de Yindu Yinsu' (A Tentative Probe into the India Factor in China's Surrounding Security Environment), *Nanya Yanjiu Jikan*, 2: 36–42.

Song, Tianyou. 1994.'Yunnan Sheng Tong Yindu Keji Hezuo Jiaoliu de Keneng Xing' (On the Possibility of the Cooperation and Exchange between Yunnan and India), *Nanya Yanjiu Jikan*, 2: 37–41.

Sridharan, Kripa. 2005. 'Beijing's Role in SAARC Expansion Unsettles Delhi', *The Straits Times*, 23 November, Singapore, p. 29.

Stratfor. 2002.'India to Stomach US Base in Pakistan', 24 January, available online at http://www.stratfor.com/analysis/india-stomach-us-base-pakistan (accessed 10 August 2013).

Sui, Xinmin. 2007. *Zhong Yin Guanxi Yanjiu: Shehui Renzhi Shijiao* (Sino–Indian Relations: A Social Cognition Perspective). Beijing: Shijie Zhishi.

Sun, Jinzhong. 2002. 'Toushi Zhong Yin Guanxi Jiuge' ('A look at the Sino–Indian Disputes in Perspective'), *Nanya Yanjiu Jikan*, 1: 49–53.

Sun, Shihai. 1999. 'Yindu de Jueqi: Qianli Yu Zhiyu Yinsu' (India's rising: Potential and Constraint Factors'), *Dangdai Yatai*, 8: 3–14.

Suraiya, Jug. 2008. 'From Taslima to Tibet, India Proves Chicken', *The Times of India*, 21 March, New Delhi, p. 18.

Swamy, Subramanian. 2001. *India's China Perspective*. Delhi: Konark Publishers.

Synnott, Hilary. 1999. *The Causes and Consequences of South Asia's Nuclear Tests*. Oxford: Oxford University Press.

Taipei Times. 2001. 'Dalai Lama Speaks of Need to Find an Elected Successor', 29 January, available online at http://www.taipeitimes.com/News/front/archives/2001/01/29/0000071448 (accessed 13 August 2013).

Talbott, Strobe. 2004. *Engaging India: Diplomacy, Democracy, and the Bomb*. New Delhi: Penguin Books.

Tan, Chung. (ed.). 2007. *Zhong Yin Datong–Li Xiang Yu Shixian* (Chindia–Idealism and Realization). Yinchuan: Ningxia Renmin Chubanshe.

Tang, Lu. 2005.'Zhong Yin Zai Bianjie Wenti Shang Huzuo Tiaozheng' (China and India Seek Mutual Accommodation on Border Problem), *Guoji Xianqu Daobao* (*International Herald Leader*), 15 April, available online at http://news.xinhuanet.com/herald/2005-04/18/content_2844918.htm (accessed 18 August 2013).

Taylor, Jay. 1987. *The Dragon and the Wild Goose: China and India*. London: Greenwood.

The Asian Age. 2008. 'China Won't be a Problem at NSG: PM', *The Asian Age*, 8 July, New Delhi, p. 3.

The Asian Age. 2011a. 'Tibet PM Gets More Powers', 31 May, available online at http://archive.asianage.com/india/tibet-pm-gets-more-powers-797 (accessed 13 August 2013).

———. 2011b. 'US to India: Get assertive with China', 21 July, available online at http://archive.asianage.com/india/us-india-get-assertive-china-838 (accessed 15 August 2013).

The Associated Press. 2000. 'Tibetan Spiritual Leader Defects from China, Says Dalai Lama's Group', *The Associated Press*, 7 January, New Delhi.

———. 2008. 'Dalai Lama Urges Vision of Hope in Seattle Speech but Again Avoids Mention of Tibet Crisis', *The Associated Press*, 13 April, Seattle.

The Economic Times. 2002. 'Govt to Put Curbs on FDI From Neighbours', 27 September, available online at http://articles.economictimes.indiatimes.com/2002-09-25/news/27332894_1_fdi-in-sensitive-sectors-fdi-flows-fdi-policy (accessed 12 August 2013).

The Economist. 1993. 'Hands Across the Himalayas', *The Economist*, 11 September, p. 69.

———. 1996. 'All Quiet on the Eastern Front', *The Economist*, 7 December, p. 82.

The Fourteenth Dalai Lama. 1990. *Freedom in Exile: The Autobiography of the Dalai Lama of Tibet*. Kent: Hodder and Stoughton.

———. 1998. 'Strasbourg Proposal 1988', address to the Members of the European Parliament, Strasbourg, France, June 15, available online at http://www.dalailama.com/messages/tibet/strasbourg-proposal-1988 (accessed 18 August 2013).

The Human Rights Society of China. 2001. 'Meiguo Zhichi Dalai Jituan Fenlie Huodong Poxi' (Looking Into US Support for Dalai Clique's Separatist Activities), *Renmin Ribao*, 26 May, Beijing, p. 5.

The Hindu. 1998a. 'China Trying To Put India on the Defensive', *The Hindu*, 20 May, New Delhi, p. 14.

———. 1998b. 'India Ready for Talks with China: Jaswant', *The Hindu*, 25 December, New Delhi.

———. 1998c. 'BJP Leader Assails China on N-Tests', *The Hindu*, 16 May, New Delhi.

———. 1998d. 'Vajpayee-Dalai Lama Meet Angers China', *The Hindu*, 23 October, New Delhi, p. 1.

———. 1998e. 'Vajpayee Expresses Concern over Sino-Pak. Nexus', 14 June, available online at http://www.hinduonline.com (accessed 30 December 1998).

———. 1998f. 'Primakov for "Strategic Triangle" for Peace', *The Hindu*, 22 December, New Delhi, p. 1.

———. 1998g. 'China Summons Indian Diplomat Again', *The Hindu*, 9 May, New Delhi, p. 1.

The Hindu. 1998h. 'Fernandes Rules out Troop Cut along Chinese Border', *The Hindu*, 8 May, New Delhi, p. 1.

———. 1998i. 'China Sees Threat to South Asia', *The Hindu*, 15 May, New Delhi, p. 1.

———. 1998j. 'Indian Envoy to China Called for Consultations', *The Hindu*, 20 May, New Delhi, p. 1.

———. 1999a. 'Govt. Working for Consensus on CTBT: Jaswant', *The Hindu*, New Delhi, 4 January.

———. 1999b. 'Vietnam Wants India in Security Council', *The Hindu*, 30 November, New Delhi, p. 14.

———. 1999c. 'China, Not Pak, Is India's Main Enemy', *The Hindu*, 5 March, New Delhi, p. 13.

———. 1999d. 'China Opposes Minimum N-deterrence for India', *The Hindu*, 28 January, New Delhi, p. 14.

———. 1999e. 'Sino-Indian Border Talks from Today', *The Hindu*, 26 April, New Delhi, p. 14.

———. 2000a. 'Malaysia Sees India as Important Player at Global Level', *The Hindu*, 9 October, New Delhi, p. 14.

———. 2000b. 'India, Vietnam Partners in Safeguarding Sea Lanes', *The Hindu*, 15 April, New Delhi, p. 15.

———. 2000c. 'India a Factor for Stability in East Asian Region: Jaswant', *The Hindu*, 3 June, New Delhi, p. 14.

———. 2000d. 'India, China are Our Ideological Allies, Says Russia', *The Hindu*, 15 July, New Delhi, p. 14.

———. 2000e. 'India May Join "Shanghai Five"', *The Hindu*, 6 July, New Delhi, p. 13.

———. 2000f. 'China for Talks to Resolve Indo-Pak Disputes', *The Hindu*, July 25, available online at http://hindu.com/2000/07/25/stories/03250003.htm (accessed 15 August 2013).

———. 2000g. 'India, China Exchange Greetings', 1 April, available online at http://www.hindu.com/2000/04/01/stories/0101000d.htm (accessed 13 August 2013).

———. 2000h. 'India, Vietnam sign defence pact', *The Hindu*, 29 March, New Delhi, p. 13.

———. 2000i. 'Sino-Indian Ties Will Gather Momentum, Says President', *The Hindu*, 3 June, New Delhi, p. 1.

———. 2000j. 'India, China to Resume Military Ties', 30 April, available online at http://www.hindu.com/thehindu/2000/04/30/stories/0130000e.htm (accessed 11 August 2013).

———. 2000k. 'Sino-Indian Ties Look Up', 25 November, available online at http://www.hindu.com/thehindu/2000/11/25/stories/01250005.htm (accessed 11 August 2013).

The Hindu. 2000l. 'China Blames India for Deadlock in Border Talks', 11 September, available online at http://www.hindu.com/thehindu/2000/09/11/stories/03110007.htm (accessed 11 August 2013).

———. 2000m. 'No Threat from China: ITBP Chief', 26 December, available online at http://www.hindu.com/thehindu/2000/12/26/stories/02260006.htm (accessed 11 August 2013).

———. 2000n. 'India, China against Global Terrorism', 30 May, available online at http://www.hindu.com/thehindu/2000/05/30/stories/01300003.htm (accessed 11 August 2013).

———. 2001. 'Dalai Lama's Kumbh Visit Improper', *The Hindu*, 29 January, New Delhi, p. 9.

———. 2001a. 'China Supplied Missile Technology to Pak.: CIA', September 9, available online at http://www.hindu.com/thehindu/2001/09/09/stories/03090006.htm (accessed 12 August 2013).

———. 2001b. 'Agni may be inducted in Arsenal Soon: Fernandes', *The Hindu*, 19 January, New Delhi.

———. 2001c. 'China Will Improve Ties with India: Li Peng', 14 January, available online at http://www.hindu.com/2001/01/14/stories/0214000a.htm (accessed 15 August 2013).

———. 2001d. 'India, Myanmar Road Opened', *The Hindu*, 14 February, New Delhi, p.1.

———. 2001e. 'India Backs China on Human Rights', 9 April, available online at http://hindu.com/2001/04/19/stories/0119000c.htm (accessed 15 August 2013).

———. 2001f. 'PM Hopeful of Solution to Border Row with China', 16 January, available online at http://www.hindu.com/2001/01/16/stories/0116000a.htm (accessed 15 August 2013).

———. 2001g. 'No Plan for Expansion', The Hindu, 29 July, New Delhi, p. 9.

———. 2001h. 'Ties with India Not at Cost of Pak, Says Eastham', 18 April, available online at http://hindu.com/2001/04/18/stories/0118000c.htm (accessed 15 August 2013).

———. 2001i. 'Dalai Lama's Kumbh Visit Improper', The Hindu, 29 January, New Delhi, p. 9.

———. 2001j. 'Progress on LAC clarification', 30 June, available online at http://www.hindu.com/thehindu/2001/06/30/stories/01300003.htm (accessed 11 August 2013).

———. 2001k. 'India-China talks on western sector soon', 13 August, available online at http://www.hindu.com/thehindu/2001/08/13/stories/02130001.htm (accessed 11 August 2013).

The Hindu. 2001l. 'Troop Mobilisation almost Complete', 31 December, available online at http://www.hindu.com/thehindu/2001/12/31/stories/2001123100600101.htm (accessed 11 August 2013).

———. 2002. 'Spiritual Relations Binding India, Tibet, Says Dalai Lama', 9 December, available online at http://hindu.com/2002/12/09/stories/2002120901930300.htm (accessed 12 August 2013).

———. 2002a. 'We Have No Plan to Broker Indo-Pak. Peace, Says Zhu', 14 January, available online at http://www.hindu.com/2002/01/14/stories/2002011401030100.htm (accessed 14 August 2013).

———. 2002b. 'China "Even-handed" in Approach to India-Pak', 5 January, available online at http://hindu.com/2002/01/05/stories/2002010501561200.htm (accessed 18 August 2013).

———. 2002c. 'China May Share Intelligence on J&K, Northeast', 25 January, available online at http://hindu.com/2002/01/25/stories/2002012505050100.htm (accessed 15 August 2013).

———. 2002d. 'India, China Plan Push to Economic Ties', 31 March, available online at http://hindu.com/2002/03/31/stories/2002033103220100.htm (accessed 15 August 2013).

———. 2002e. 'India Seals Major Arms Deal with US', 19 April, 2002, available online at http://www.hindu.com/thehindu/2002/04/19/stories/2002041905540100.htm (accessed 15 August 2013).

———. 2002f. 'Spiritual Relations Binding India, Tibet, Says Dalai Lama', 9 December, available online at http://hindu.com/2002/12/09/stories/2002120901930300.htm (accessed 12 August 2013).

———. 2002g. 'India, China to Quicken Pace of LAC Delineation', 30 March, available online at http://www.hindu.com/thehindu/2002/03/30/stories/2002033002530100.htm (accessed 11 August 2013).

———. 2003a. 'China Stays Firm on Tibet, Sikkim', 27 June, available online at http://www.hindu.com/2003/06/27/stories/2003062703931100.htm (accessed 10 August 2013).

———. 2003b. 'Indo-US Ties Not Directed against China: Sinha', 23 November, available online at http://www.hindu.com/2003/11/23/stories/2003112306230800.htm (accessed 15 August 2013).

———. 2003c. 'China Sticks to Its Stand', 6 August, available online at http://www.hindu.com/thehindu/2003/08/06/stories/2003080604721100.htm (accessed 11 August 2013).

———. 2004a. 'India-Russia-China Triangle Has Good Prospects', 22 February, available online at http://www.hindu.com/2004/02/22/stories/2004022203210900.htm (accessed 10 August 2013).

The Hindu. 2004b. 'Ivanov Visit: Focus Likely On Security, Terrorism', 19 January, available online at http://www.hindu.com/2004/01/19/stories/2004011904941100.htm (accessed 15 August 2013).

———. 2005a. '"Guiding Principles" On Border Issue Finalised', 11 April, available online at http://www.hindu.com/2005/04/11/stories/2005041106570100.htm (accessed 11 August 2013).

———. 2005b. 'India to Join Shanghai Group as Observer', 5 June, available online at http://www.hindu.com/2005/06/05/stories/2005060506081000.htm (accessed 15 August 2013).

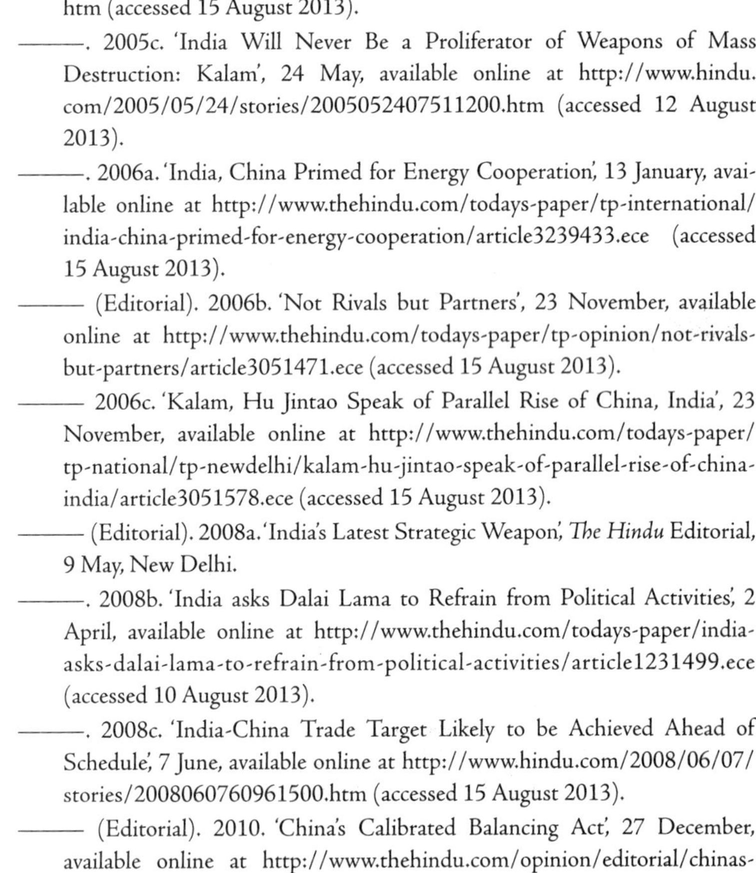

———. 2005c. 'India Will Never Be a Proliferator of Weapons of Mass Destruction: Kalam', 24 May, available online at http://www.hindu.com/2005/05/24/stories/2005052407511200.htm (accessed 12 August 2013).

———. 2006a. 'India, China Primed for Energy Cooperation', 13 January, available online at http://www.thehindu.com/todays-paper/tp-international/india-china-primed-for-energy-cooperation/article3239433.ece (accessed 15 August 2013).

——— (Editorial). 2006b. 'Not Rivals but Partners', 23 November, available online at http://www.thehindu.com/todays-paper/tp-opinion/not-rivals-but-partners/article3051471.ece (accessed 15 August 2013).

——— 2006c. 'Kalam, Hu Jintao Speak of Parallel Rise of China, India', 23 November, available online at http://www.thehindu.com/todays-paper/tp-national/tp-newdelhi/kalam-hu-jintao-speak-of-parallel-rise-of-china-india/article3051578.ece (accessed 15 August 2013).

——— (Editorial). 2008a. 'India's Latest Strategic Weapon', *The Hindu* Editorial, 9 May, New Delhi.

———. 2008b. 'India asks Dalai Lama to Refrain from Political Activities', 2 April, available online at http://www.thehindu.com/todays-paper/india-asks-dalai-lama-to-refrain-from-political-activities/article1231499.ece (accessed 10 August 2013).

———. 2008c. 'India-China Trade Target Likely to be Achieved Ahead of Schedule', 7 June, available online at http://www.hindu.com/2008/06/07/stories/2008060760961500.htm (accessed 15 August 2013).

——— (Editorial). 2010. 'China's Calibrated Balancing Act', 27 December, available online at http://www.thehindu.com/opinion/editorial/chinas-calibrated-balancing-act/article981322.ece (accessed 15 August 2013).

———. 2011a. 'No Change in India's Nuclear Doctrine: Krishna', 17 March, available online at http://www.thehindu.com/todays-paper/tp-national/no-change-in-indias-nuclear-doctrine-krishna/article1545286.ece (accessed 12 August 2013).

The Hindu. 2011b. 'India to Make the Cut for SCO; Iran May Have to Wait', 16 June, available online at http://www.thehindu.com/news/india-to-make-the-cut-for-sco-iran-may-have-to-wait/article2107530.ece (accessed 15 August 2013).

———. 2011c. 'U.S. Surprised, Happy at SAARC Observer Offer', 24 May, available online at http://www.thehindu.com/todays-paper/tp-opinion/us-surprised-happy-at-saarc-observer-offer/article2043807.ece (accessed 15 August 2013).

———. 2011d. 'India and China Can Achieve a Lot by Joining Hands: Tharoor', 14 May, available online at http://www.thehindu.com/news/cities/chennai/india-and-china-can-achieve-a-lot-by-joining-hands-tharoor/article 1697258.ece (accessed 15 August 2013).

———. 2011e. 'Gilani's China Visit to Firm Up Ties', May 11, available online at http://www.thehindu.com/todays-paper/tp-international/gilanis-china-visit-to-firm-up-ties/article2007877.ece (accessed 15 August 2013).

———. 2011f. 'India to Buy C-17 Heavy-lift Transport Aircraft from US', 7 June, available online at http://www.thehindu.com/todays-paper/tp-national/india-to-buy-c17-heavylift-transport-aircraft-from-us/article2083073.ece (accessed 15 August 2013).

———. 2012a. 'Khurshid Hits the Ground Running after Swearing-in', 28 October, available online at http://www.thehindu.com/news/national/khurshid-hits-the-ground-running-after-swearingin/article4040865.ece (accessed 10 August 2013).

———. 2012b. 'China Violated Indian Air Space At Least Thrice this Year: ITBP', 26 October, available online at http://www.thehindu.com/todays-paper/tp-national/china-violated-indian-air-space-thrice-this-year-itbp-chief/article4032996.ece (accessed 10 August 2013).

The Hindustan Times. 2008a. 'India Takes Giant Leap with Agni-III', *The Hindustan Times*, 8 May, New Delhi.

———. 2008b. 'N-Widow Opens, Deal May Be Done After All', *The Hindustan Times*, 9 July, New Delhi, p. 11.

———. 2010. 'India Hopes China Will be More Sensitive to J&K: Rao', *The Hindustan Times*, 4 December, New Delhi, p. 11.

———. 2011a. 'China Denounces Dalai Lama's "Tricks"', *The Hindustan Times*, 11 March, New Delhi, p. 19.

———. 2011b. 'Pak to Get 50 Chinese Fighters', *The Hindustan Times*, 20 May, New Delhi, p. 17.

The Indian Express. 1998a. 'Venkataraman speaks of an aborted N-test', 27 May, available online at http://www.indianexpress.com/Storyold/34309/ (accessed 12 August 2013).

The Indian Express. 1998b. 'China is No Security Threat to India: Chinese Ambassador', 15 September, available online at http://expressindia.indianexpress.com/news/ie/daily/19980915/25850454.html (accessed 12 August 2013).

———. 1998c. 'Govt Flashes China Card at the West', 14 May, available online at http://www.indianexpress.com/Storyold/32305/ (accessed 12 August 2013).

———. 1998d. 'China is enemy No 1: George', 4 May, available online at http://www.indianexpress.com/Storyold/30582/ (accessed 15 August 2013).

———. 1998e. 'Not Right to Condemn India', 16 May, available online at http://www.financialexpress.com/old/fe/daily/19980516/13655494.html (accessed 15 August 2013).

———. 1998f. 'A Coalition of Wise Guys', 25 May, available online at http://www.indianexpress.com/Storyold/33944/ (accessed 11 August 2013).

———. 1999a. 'Pak's Reply to Agni II with Shaheen', 13 April, available online at http://www.indianexpress.com/Storyold/91275/ (accessed 18 August 2013).

———. 1999b. 'India, China Sidestep Kargil, Talk Security Instead', 15 June, available online at http://www.indianexpress.com/Storyold/103772/ (accessed 11 August 2013).

———. 2000a. 'China in Waiting Game with Dalai for Control of Tibet Buddhism', 18 February, available online at http://www.indianexpress.com/Storyold/144963/ (accessed 13 August 2013).

———. 2000b. 'Confident India Gets Ready for China Talks', 24 April, available online at http://www.indianexpress.com/Storyold/151060/ (accessed 11 August 2013).

———. 2001. 'Down a Trodden Road', 10 January, available online at http://expressindia.indianexpress.com/news/ie/daily/20010110/ian10061.html (accessed 15 August 2013).

———. 2007a. 'China Draws Another Hardline on Arunachal', 7 June, available online at http://www.indianexpress.com/news/china-draws-another-hardline-on-arunachal/32925/ (accessed 11 August 2013).

———. 2007b. 'Be Ready for Adjustments on LAC: China to India', *The Indian Express*, 24 November, New Delhi, p. 3.

———. 2008a. 'China Troop Build-up, Tibet Upgrade Impact Our Security: Army Chief', 4 July, available online at http://www.indianexpress.com/news/china-troop-buildup--tibet-upgrade-impact-our-security-army-chief/331219/ (accessed 10 August 2003).

———. 2008b. 'India Overcautious on Tibet: Dalai Lama', 24 November, available online at http://www.indianexpress.com/news/india-overcautious-on-tibet-dalai-lama/389562/> (accessed 10 August 2013).

———. 2008c. 'Tip of Sikkim is Latest India–China Flashpoint', *The Indian Express*, 18 May, 2008, p. 1.

The Indian Express. 2008d. 'Strategic Helipads in Arunachal to be Upgraded', *The Indian Express*, 10 April, New Delhi, p. 9.

———. 2010. 'Antony Flags China's Rising Military Power', available online at http://www.indianexpress.com/news/antony-flags-china-s-rising-military-power/681229/ (accessed 17 August 2013).

———. 2011. 'Govt Denies, Army Downplays "Intrusion" by Chinese Troops', 11 January, available online at http://www.indianexpress.com/news/govt-denies-army-downplays--intrusion--by-chinese-troops/735912/ (accessed 11 August 2003).

The New York Times. 1975. May 19, p.1, available online at www.lexisnexis.com (accessed 18 August 2013).

———. 1998a. 'India's Letter to Clinton on Nuclear Testing', *New York Times*, May 13, A12.

———. 1998b. 'U.S. May Have Helped India Hide Its Nuclear Activity', 25 May, available online at http://www.nytimes.com/1998/05/25/world/us-may-have-helped-india-hide-its-nuclear-activity.html?pagewanted=all&src=pm (accessed 12 August 2013).

———. (Editorial). 2008. 'Beijing's Blind Spot', 26 November, available online at http://www.nytimes.com/2008/11/27/opinion/27thu2.html (accessed 18 August 2013).

The News. 2011. 'China to Take Over Operations at Gwadar: Mukhtar', 22 May, available online at http://www.thenews.com.pk/TodaysPrintDetail.aspx?ID=6163&Cat=13 (accessed 15 August 2013).

The Pioneer. 2001. 'Indian Army Gives Priority to Mapping India–China Border', *The Pioneer*, 6 September, New Delhi, p. 5.

The Times. 1981. 'Chinese Leader Tenders an Olive Branch to India', *The Times*, April 9, London, p.4.

The Times of India. 2001a. 'China's Railway Line Poses a Threat', 31 August, available online at http://articles.timesofindia.indiatimes.com/2001-08-31/chandigarh/27236315_1_railway-lhasa-tibetan-capital (accessed 10 August 2013).

———. 2001b. 'India Snubs China's Call for Restraint', 27 December, available online at http://articles.timesofindia.indiatimes.com/2001-12-26/india/27226362_1_india-snubs-saarc-pakistan (accessed 15 August 2013).

———. 2002a. 'India, China Agree on All Issues but Dalai & Tibet', 16 January, available online at http://timesofindia.indiatimes.com/india/India-China-agree-on-all-issues-but-Dalai-Tibet/articleshow/1556266279.cms? (accessed 10 August 2013).

———. 2002b. 'Jaswant Visit to Boost Sino-Indian Relations', 27 March, available online at http://timesofindia.indiatimes.com/world/Jaswant-visit-to-boost-Sino-Indian-relations/articleshow/5045557.cms (accessed 13 August 2013).

The Times of India. 2002c. 'China Threatens to Walk out on Pak Military Port Project', 8 January, available online at http://articles.timesofindia.indiatimes.com/2002-01-07/india/27141476_1_gwadar-port-saarc-summit-beijing (accessed 15 August 2013).

———. 2003. 'Official Chinese Site Says Sikkim Not Part of India', 26 June, available online at http://articles.timesofindia.indiatimes.com/2003-07-25/india/27206269_1_sikkim-issue-boundary-question-issue-in-india-china-relations (accessed 11 August 2013).

———. 2007. 'Difficulties in Sino-Indian Ties Come to Fore', 27 May, available online at http://articles.timesofindia.indiatimes.com/2007-05-27/india/27883788_1_chinese-visa-boundary-talks-india-china (accessed 11 August 2013).

——— (Editorial). 2008a. 'Chinese Checks', *The Times of India* Editorial, 10 June, New Delhi, p.18.

——— (Editorial). 2008b. 'On the Hop', *The Times of India* Editorial, 23 June, New Delhi, p. 20.

———. 2008c. 'Bigger Role for Karmapa with US Visit?' *The Times of India*, 9 April, New Delhi, p. 19.

———. 2008d. 'Now, George Says China Is "Potential Threat No. 1"', *The Times of India*, 31 March, New Delhi, p. 14.

———. 2008e. 'India to Raise Sikkim Incursion with China', *The Times of India*, 20 June, New Delhi, p. 16.

———. 2008f. 'Chinese Checks', *The Times of India* Editorial, 10 June, New Delhi, p. 18.

———. 2008g. '"Chela" Dalai Asks "Guru" India to Help Tibet', *The Times of India*, 21 November, New Delhi, p. 11.

———. 2008h. 'India and the Tibet Card', *The Times of India*, 23 November, New Delhi, p. 10.

———. 2008i. 'Army Chief's Remark on LAC Unnecessary', *The Times of India*, 7 March, New Delhi, p.15.

———. 2008j. 'Boundary Row with India Very Sensitive Issue: China', 19 June, available online at http://articles.timesofindia.indiatimes.com/2008-06-19/china/27760453_1_boundary-foreign-minister-wu-dawei-china-and-india (accessed 11 August 2013).

———. 2008k. 'Anti-Chinese Sentiment Hampering Border Talks', 19 September, available online at http://articles.timesofindia.indiatimes.com/2008-09-19/india/27892688_1_border-talks-border-issue-incursions (accessed 11 August 2013).

———. 2008l. 'Tawang is Part of India: Dalai Lama', *The Times of India*, 4 June, New Delhi, p.11.

The Times of India. 2009a. 'China Gave Uranium to Pak in 1982', *The Times of India*, 13 November, Kolkata, p. 15.

———. 2009b. 'Pak Flaunts Its All-weather Ties with China', *The Times of India*, 23 January, New Delhi, p. 9.

———. 2011a. 'With China in Mind, Agni-V Test Scheduled for December', *The Times of India*, 4 June, New Delhi.

———. 2011b. 'India, Pak added 20-30 N-warheads each in 2010: Study', *The Times of India*, 8 June, New Delhi, p. 9.

———. 2011c. 'Chinese Along LoC? Top General Sounds Warning', *The Times of India*, 6 April, New Delhi, p. 13.

———. 2011d. 'China Fear Makes India Harden Siachen Stand', *The Times of India*, 1 June, New Delhi, p. 6.

———. 2011e. 'China Agrees to Review Stapled Visas to J&K Subjects', *Times of India*, 14 April, New Delhi, p. 1.

———. 2012. 'China Violated Line of Actual Control 500 Times in Last Two Years', 17 May, available online at http://articles.timesofindia.indiatimes.com/2012-05-17/india/31748482_1_chinese-troops-sq-km-finger-area-pangong-tso (accessed 11 August 2013).

The Tribune. 2008. 'Talks with India Making Progress: China', 23 May, available onlne at http://www.tribuneindia.com/2008/20080523/world.htm (accessed 11 August 2013).

The US National Intelligence Council (NIC). 2000. *Global Trends 2015: A Dialogue About the Future with Nongovernment Experts*. Washington DC.

———. 2004. *Mapping the Global Future: Report of the National Intelligence Council's 2020 Project*. Washington DC.

Tian, Jingmei. 2006. 'Mei Yin He Neng Hezuo de Xianzhung, Yingxiang Ji Qianjing' ('US–India Nuclear Energy Cooperation: Current Situation, Impact and Prospects'), *Xiandai Guoji Guanxi*, 8: 53–6, 63.

United News of India (UNI). 2009. 'Arunachal Belongs to India, Asserts Dalai Lama', *United News of India*, 21 January, Chennai.

Van Eekelen, W.F. 1964. *Indian Foreign Policy and the Border Dispute with China*. The Hague: Martinus Nijhoff.

Vertzberger, Yaacov. 1984. *Misperceptions in Foreign Policymaking: The Sino–Indian Conflict, 1959–1962*. Boulder: Westview Press.

Walt, Stephen. 1987. *The Origins of Alliances*. Ithaca: Cornell University Press.

Waltz, Kenneth N. 1979. *Theory of International Politics*. New York: McGraw Hill.

Wang, Dehua. 1998a. 'Yindu Hui Chengwei Weilai de Chaoji Daguo Ma?' (Will India Become a Future Super Power?), *Nanya Yanjiu Jikan*, (n.s.) 1: 23–5.

Wang, Hongwei. 1998b. *Ximalayashan Qingjie: Zhong–Yin Guanxi Yanjiu (The Himalayas Sentiment: A Study of Sino–Indian Relations)*. Beijing: Zhongguo Zangxue Chubanshe.

Wang, Lixiong. 1998c. *Tian Zang: Xizang de Mingyun* (Sky Burial: The Fate of Tibet). Hong Kong: Mingjing Chubanshe.

Wang, Taiping *et al.* (eds). 1999. *Xin Zhongguo Waijiao Wushi Nian (50 Years of New China's Diplomacy)*. Beijing: Beijing Chubanshe.

Wang, Xiaodong. 1999a. '99's Duanxiang' (99's Thinkings) in Fang Ning, Wang Xiaodong and Song Qiang. *Quanqiuhua Yinying Xia de Qiangguo Zhi Lu (The Way To Be Great Power Under the Shadow of Globalization)*. Beijing: Zhongguo Shehui Kexue Chubanshe.

Wang, Yiqian. 1994. 'Zhongguo Xinan Diqu Xiang Nanya Kaifang Wenti Tantao' ('Southwest China's Opening to South Asia: An Analytical Study'), *Nanya Yanjiu Jikan*, 2: 32–6.

Wang, Yiwei. 2004. 'The Dimensions of China's Peaceful Rise', *Asia Times Online* 14 May.

———. 2007. 'Zhong Yin Gongtong Jueqi de Guoji Zhengzhi Yiyi–Cong Diyuan Zhengzhi Fanshi Dao Quanqiu "Datong" Fanshi' ('International Political Meaning of the Co-Rising of China and India: From Geo-Politics Paradigm to Global "Datong" Paradigm'), *Guoji Guancha* (International Review), 4: 10–8.

Wang, Yizhou. 1999b. 'Duojihua Bu Dengyu Fan Mei' (Multi-Polarization Does Not Equal an Anti-US Position), *Huanqiu Shibao*, 6 (Autumn): 14.

Wang, Zhongren. 1997. '"China Threat" Theory Groundless', *Beijing Review*, 14–20 July, Beijing, pp. 7–8.

Wen, Fude. 2005. '21 Shiji Yindu Jiang Chengwei Shijie Daguo' ('India: The Approaching World's Big Power in the 21st Century'), *Nanya Yanjiu* ,3: 1–8.

Wilson, Dominic and Roopa Purushothaman. 2003. *Dealing with BRICs: The Path to 2050*. Global Economics Paper No. 99, 1 October.

Winner, Andrew C. and Toshi Yoshihara. 2002. 'India and Pakistan at the Edge', *Survival* 44(3): 69–86.

Wu, Kanghe and Song Dexing. 1998. 'Lun Yindu He Zhengce de Lishi Yanbian Ji Qi Hewuhua de Wehaixing' ('On the Historical Development of India's Nuclear Policy and the Danger of its Nuclear Weaponisation'), *Shujie Jingji Yu Zhengzhi* (World Economics and Politics), 6: 25–9.

Wu, Lengxi. 1999. *Shi Nian Lun Zhan (1956–1966): Zhong Su Guanxi Huiyilu (Ten Years of Controversy (1956–1966): Memoir about Sino–Soviet Relations)*. Beijing: Zhongyang Wenxian Chubanshe.

Xia, Liping. 1997. 'The Evolution of Chinese Views Toward CBMs', in Michael Krepon (ed.). *Chinese Perspectives on Confidence–Building Measures*, pp. 15–17. Report No. 23: The Henry L. Stimson Center.

Xinhua. 1992a. 'China–India Working Group Concludes Boundary Talks', 21 February, in FBIS, *Daily Report: China*, 24 February: 19–20.

———. 1992b. 'Issues Statement', 24 May, in FBIS, *Daily Report: China*, 26 May 18–19.

———. 1993a. 'Border Talks with India Conclude; Accords Signed', 27 June1993, in Foreign Broadcast Information Service (FBIS), *Daily Report: China*, 28 June: 14.

———. 1993b. 'PRC, India Agree on Confidence–Building Steps', 28 June, in FBIS, *Daily Report: China*, 30 June: 6.

———. 1996a. '"Headway" Made in Improving Ties with India', *Xinhua* 29 November, and in FBIS, *Daily Report: China*, 3 December.

———. 1996b. 'China, India Make Progress in Border Talk', *Xinhua*, 18 October, Beijing.

———. 1998. 'India Rules Out Moratorium on Fissile Material Production', *Xinhua*, 15 December, New Delhi.

———. 2001. 'CMC Vice-Chairman Meets Pakistani Guests', *Xinhua*, 24 July, Beijing.

———. 2002a. 'Pakistan Rejects Reports of Receiving Chinese Aid in Missile Program', *Xinhua*, 2 February, Islamabad.

———. 2002b. 'Zhu Rongji zongli yu Wajiepayi zongli juxing hueitan' (Premier Zhu Rongji hold talks with Prime Minister Vajapyee), *Xinhua*, 14 January, New Delhi.

———. 2003. 'Zhuanjia jiedu Zhong-Yin guanxi yuanze he quanmian hezuo xuanyan' (Experts Interpret Sino-Indian Declaration on Principles for Relations and Comprehensive Cooperation), *Xinhua*, Beijing, 26 June.

Xinhua Agency Commentary. 1998. 'Jiujing shi shei zai gao weixie' (Who is posing threat actually?), *Renmin Ribao*, 18 May, Beijing, p. 4.

Xizang–Zhiye (The Website of Tibet). 'Yuan Yuan Liu Chang de Yin Zang Youyi' (Long Course and Remote Source of Indo–Tibetan Friendship), available online at http://xizang-zhiye.org/%E5%9C%8B%E9%9A%9B%E7%A4%BE%E6%9C%83%E7%9A%84%E9%97%9C%E6%B3%A8%E8%88%87%E8%BF%B4%E9%9F%BF/ (accessed 18 August 2013).

Yan, Xuetong. 1998. 'Zhongguo Jueqi de Guoji Anquan Huanjing' ('The International Security Environment for China's Rise') in Yan Xuetong, Wang Zaibang, Li Zhongcheng, and Hou Ruoshi, *Zhongguo Jueqi: Guoji Huanjing Pinggu* (*China Rises: An Assessment of International Environment*). Tianjin: Tianjin Renmin Chubanshe.

Yan, Xuetong. 1999. 'Guoji Huanjing Ji Waijiao Sikao' ('International Environment and China's Foreign Relations'), *Xiandai Guoji Guanxi*, 8: 7–11.

Yang, Chengxu. 2001. 'Fazhan Zhong E Yin San Guo Guan Xi de Kenengxing He Qingjing' ('Possibilities and Prospects of Developing Relations among

Russia, India and China'), *Guoji Wenti Yanjiu (Journal of International Studies)*, 6: 1–4.

Yang, Chengxu. (ed.). 2003. *Zhongguo Anquan Huanjing Toushi (Perspectives of China's Security Along its Boundaries)*. Beijing: Zhongguo Qingnian Chubanshe.

Yang, Gongsu. 1992. *Zhongguo Fandui Waiguo Qinlue Ganshe Xizang Difang Douzhen Shi (The History of China's Struggle to Oppose the Foreign Invasions and Interferences on Tibet Region)*. Beijing: Zhongguo Zangxue Chubanshe.

Yang, Pingxue. 1996. 'Leng Zhan Hou de Nanya Zhanlue Xingshi' ('South Asian Strategic Posture in Post–Cold War'), *Nanya Yanjiu Jikan*, 1: 1–3, 17.

———. 2002. 'Qian Xi Zhiyue Zhong Yin Guanxi Fazhan de Jige Zhuyao Yinsu' ('A Trial Analysis of Factors Limiting Development of Sino–Indian Relations'), *Nanya Yanjiu Jikan*, 1: 38–41.

Ye, Zhengjia. 1999. 'Zhong Yin Jianjiao 50 Zhou Nian – Jingyan, Jiaoxun, Ji Qianjing' ('Sino–Indian Relations in the Past 50 Years: Experiences, Lessons and Prospects'), *Nanya Yanjiu (Southeast Asian Studies)*, 1: 3–10.

Ye, Zicheng *et al.* (eds). 1997. *Diyuan Zhengzhi Yu Zhongguo Waijiao (Geopolitics and Chinese Diplomacy)*. Beijing: Beijing Chubanshe.

Yin, Xinan. 2003. 'Lengzhanhou Zhong Yin E Sanbian Hezuo Chutan' ('A Trial Discussion of Trilateral Relationship Among China, India and Russia After Cold War'), *Nanya Yanjiu Jikan*, 1: 50–6.

———. 2007. 'Chindia: Sin Shiji "Zhong Yin Datong" Yundong Jianxi' (Chindia: Sino–Indian Great Harmony Movement in the New Century), *Nanya Yanjiu* , 4: 80–5.

Yu, Huachuan. 2004. 'Zhong E Yin Sanbian Hezuoyu Zhongguo de Xuanze' ('Sino–Russo–Indian Trilateral Cooperation and China's Choice'), *Guoji Luntan (International Forum)*, 6 (2): 40–5.

Yu, Tian. 1992. 'Sichuan Han Nanya Guojia de Maoyi Qianjing' ('A Prospect for the Trade between Sichuan of China and South Asian Countries'), *Nanya Yanjiu Jikan*, 3: 25–31.

Yuan, Di. 1998. 'Yindu He Xuanze Yu Duai Hua "Zhanlue Siwei"' ('India's Nuclear Option and "Strategic Thinking" on China',) *Nanya Yanjiu Jikan*, 3: 1–4.

———. 2001. 'Zhongguo Dui Nanya Anquan de Yingxiang Ji Qi Zhiyue Yinsu—Yi Yin Ba Kajier Chongtu Weili' ('China's Influence on Security of South Asia and Factors Restricting China's Influence—A Study of the Case of Kargil Conflict between India and Pakistan'), *Nanya Yanjiu Jikan*, 3: 8–14.

Zakaria, Fareed. 2006. 'Nixon to China, Bush to India', *Newsweek*, 27 February, available online at http://www.thedailybeast.com/newsweek/2006/02/26/nixon-to-china-bush-to-india.html (accessed 18 August 2013).

Zhan, Shiliang. 1999. 'Fazhanzhong Guojia Yu Guoji Xin Zhixu' ('Developing Countries and New International Order'), *Renmin Ribao*, 25 December, Beijing, p. 3.

Zhang, Lixia *et al.* 2005. 'Zhoubian Guojia Bu Mangcong, Mei Baowei Zhongguo de Tumou Jiang Luokong Huan Qiu Shi Bao' (Neighbouring Countries Do Not Follow Blindly, the US Plot to Encircle China Comes to no Avail), *Huanqiu Shibao*, 23 March, Beijing, p. 7.

Zhang, Ming. 1999. *China's Changing Nuclear Posture: Reactions to the South Asian Nuclear Tests*. Washington, DC: Carnegie Endowment for International Peace.

Zhang, Minqiu. 2000a. 'Zhong-Yin Guanxi de Gaishan Han Jinyibu Fazhan de Zhang'ai' ('The Obstacles to Improvement and Further Development of Sino–Indian Relations'), *Guoji Zhengzhi Yanjiu* (Studies of International Politics), 1: 27–36.

———. 2004. *Zhongyin Guanxi Yanjiu (1947–2003)(Sino–Indian Relations: 1947–2003)*. Beijing: Peking University Press.

Zhang, Wenmu. 1998. 'Yindu de Diyuan Zhanlue yu Zhongguo Xizang Wenti' (India's Geo–Strategy and China's Tibetan Question'), *Zhanlue Yu Guanli*, 5: 105–9.

Zhang, Yan. 2008. 'A Perspective on India and China–India Ties', *The Hindu*, 1 July, available online at http://www.hindu.com/2008/07/01/stories/2008070152211100.htm (accessed 15 August 2013).

Zhang, Zhirong. 2000b. 'Zhong Yin Guanxi de Huigu Yu Fansi—Yang Gongsu Dashi Fantan Lu' ('The Retrospection and Reconsideration of the Sino–Indian Relations—An Interview with Ambassador Yang Gongsu'), *Dangdai Yatai*, 8: 17–25.

Zhao, Zhangyun. 2001. 'Bu Fu Zeren de Lundiao' (Irresponsible Statements), *Renmin Ribao*, 7 June, Beijing, p. 3.

Zhao, Bole. 2003. *Dangdai Nanya Guoji Guanxi* (*Contemporary International Relations in South Asia*). Beijing: Zhongguo Shehui Kexue Chubanshe.

Zhao, Gancheng. 2006. 'Guoji Tixi Junheng Yu Zhongyin Gongtong Jueqi' (Equilibrium in International System and Co-Emergence of India and China), *Xiandai Guoji Guanxi*, 7: 3–9.

Zhao, Gancheng. 2007a. 'Yindu Dong Xiang Zhengce de Fazhan Ji Yiyi' (India's Look-East Policy: Development and Significance), *Dangdai Yatai*, 8: 10–16, 64.

Zhao, Hong. 2007b. 'Zhongguo Shijiao Zhong de Yindu Yu Dongmeng Guanxi' ('India's Changing Relations with ASEAN in China's Perspectives'), *Nanyang Wenti Yanjiu* (Southeast Asian Affairs), 1: 27–34.

Zhao, Weiwen. 2000. *Yin Zhong Guanxi Feng Yun Lu* (A Record of the Changes in India–China Relations). Beijing: Shishi Chubanshe.

Zheng, Bijian. 2005. 'China's "Peaceful Rise" to Great–Power Status', *Foreign Affairs*, 84 (5): 18–24.

Zheng, Yongnian. 1998. *Zhongguo Minzu Zhuyi de Fuxing: Minzu Guojia he Chu Qu?* (*The Revival of Chinese Nationalism: Where will the Nation–State Go?*). Hong Kong: Sanlian Shudian.

Zhongguo Shibao (*China Times*). 1999. 'Zhonggong Yindu mimi tanpan bianjie wenti' (China and India Held Secret Talks over Border Problem), *Zhongguo Shibao*, 1 December, Taipei, p. 14

———. 2000. 'Yi haijun jiyu Nanhai Beijing gaodu guanzhu', (Indian Navy Covets after South China Sea, Beijing on High Alert), *Zhongguo Shibao*, 20 September, Taipei, p. 14.

Official Documents

A Shared Vision for the 21st Century of the People's Republic of China and the Republic of India, 14 January 2008.

Agreement between the Government of the People's Republic of China and the Government of the Republic of India on the Maintenance of Peace and Tranquility along the Line of Actual Control in the China-India Border Areas, 7 September 1993.

Agreement Between the Government of the People's Republic of China and the Government of the Republic of India on Confidence Building Measures in the Military Field Along the Line of Actual Control in the China–India Border Areas, 29 November 1996.

Agreement on Political Parameters and Guiding Principles for the Settlement of the China–India Boundary Question, 11 April 2005.

China–India Joint Declaration, New Delhi, 21 November 2006.

Declaration on Principles for Relations and Comprehensive Cooperation Between the People's Republic of China and Republic of India, Beijing, 23 June 2003.

———. 1998a. *China's National Defense*. Beijing, July 1998.

Information Office of the State Council of the People's Republic of China (SCIO). 1992. *Tibet—Its Ownership and Human Rights Situation*. Beijing, September, available online at http://www.china.org.cn/e-white/tibet/ (accessed 10 August 2013).

———. 1998b. *New Progress in Human Rights in the Tibet Autonomous Region*. Beijing, February 1998.

———. 2000a. *China's National Defense in 2000*. Beijing, October 2000.

———. 2000b. *The Development of Tibetan Culture*. Beijing, June, 2000.

———. 2001. *Tibet's March toward Modernization*. Beijing, November 2001.

Information Office of the State Council of the People's Republic of China (SCIO). 2002. 'East Turkistan's Terrorist Forces Cannot Get Away with Impunity', Beijing Review, 21 January 2002: 149, 22–3.

———. 2003. *Ecological Improvement and Environmental Protection in Tibet.* Beijing.

———. 2004. *Regional Ethnic Autonomy in Tibet*, Beijing.

———. 2006. *China's National Defense in 2006*, 29 December.

———. 2008. *Protection and Development of Tibetan Culture*, September.

———. 2011. *Sixty Years Since Peaceful Liberation of Tibet.* Beijing, July.

———. 2005. *China's Endeavors for Arms Control, Disarmament and Non-Proliferation.* Beijing, September 2005.

Joint Statement of the People's Republic of China and the Republic of India, New Delhi, 11 April, 2005.

Ministry of Defence, Government of India, *Annual Report 2006–2007.*

Ministry of External Affairs, Government of India (MEA), *Annual Report (1 January 2003–31 March 2004).*

Ministry of External Affairs, Government of India, "Summary of Press Briefing by the Official Spokesperson," 22 June, 2001, available online at http://meadev.nic.in/news/20010622.htm (accessed 15 July 2001).

Shanghai Convention on Combating Terrorism, Separatism and Extremism, 15 June 2001.

Sino–Indian Joint Communiqué. New Delhi, 16 December1991.

Sino–Indian Joint Press Communiqué. Beijing, 23 December, available online at http://www.fmprc.gov.cn/eng/wjdt/2649/t15800.htm (accessed 10 August 2013).

The Government of Tibet in Exile, *Tibet: Proving Truth from Facts*, July, available online at http://tibet.net/wp-content/uploads/2011/07/Tibet ProvingTruthFromTheFacts.pdf (accessed 1 August 2013).

Index

About the Author

Tien-sze Fang is a faculty member, Center for General Education and Institute of Sociology, National Tsing Hua University, Taiwan. He holds a PhD in International Relations from the London School of Economics and Political Sciences, UK, and got his Bachelor's and Master's degrees in Diplomacy from the National Cheng-chi University, Taiwan.

He was Officer at the Department of East Asian and Pacific Affairs, Ministry of Foreign Affairs, Taiwan, between 1996–98. He also worked as Assistant Research Fellow at the Prospect Foundation, Taiwan (2004–5), and Assistant Director and Acting Director at the Science and Technology Division, Taipei Economic and Cultural Center in New Delhi, from 2005 to 2011. His research has appeared in several refereed journals, book chapters, conference papers, and newspaper commentaries. His recent research interests include the rise of India, China–India relations, soft-power diplomacy and international relations theories. He can be reached at fang@mx.nthu.edu.tw.